Social Work Practice
in Health Care

Fields of Practice Series

Francis J. Turner and Herbert S. Strean, Editors

Social Work Practice in Health Care

An Ecological Perspective

Carel Bailey Germain

THE FREE PRESS
A Division of Macmillan, Inc.
NEW YORK
Collier Macmillan Publishers
LONDON

The Free Press
A Division of Macmillan, Inc.
866 Third Avenue, New York, N.Y. 10022

Collier Macmillan Canada, Inc.

Printed in the United States of America

printing number

  2 3 4 5 6 7 8 9 10

Library of Congress Cataloging in Publication Data

Germain, Carel B.
    Social work practice in health care.

    (Fields of practice series)
    Includes bibliographical references and index.
    1. Medical social work—United States. I. Title.
II. Series. [DNLM: 1. Social work. 2. Delivery of
health care. 3. Sociology, Medical. W 322 G372s]
HV687.5.U5G47 1984   362.1′0425′0973   83–48757
ISBN 0-02-911660-0

to
W.P.G.

Contents

Service to the Community
Politically Oriented Activity
Research Opportunities

Foreword

In 1978 The Free Press published the first of a series of books each of which addresses a particular theoretical approach of significance in the helping professions. Once this series was well underway it became evident that a second series was needed, one that differentially examines practice from the dimension of specific fields of practice.

Every profession has to face the complex question of specialization versus generalization. In this regard it has to come to terms with issues related to training and practice, and to make decisions about the relative emphasis given to those matters that are common to all areas of the profession's various fields of practice and those that are specific to each area.

There are of course dangers in emphasizing either extreme. If the generic is overemphasized there is a risk that important aspects of practice will be dealt with at a level of abstraction that bears little immediate relevance to what the worker actually does. If the emphasis is on the particular there is the danger of fragmentation and neglect of the need to search for commonalties and interconnections. Obviously, a balance between these two extremes is desirable.

Many of the human services, and social work in particular, have tended to overemphasize the generic to the detriment of the specific needs of clients with highly specialized needs. The majority of social work literature over the past three decades has focused either on modalities of practice as a single entity or on a specific theoretical basis of practice. This is not to say that there are not practitioners who are highly skilled in working effectively with specialized groups of clients. What is lacking is an organized compilation of the particular practice components of each of these specialized areas of practice in a way that is readily accessible to other practitioners in these areas.

Certainly within the periodical literature of social work there is a rich array of individual articles addressing specific components of practice involving work with particular client target groups. But such articles are scattered and not written from a common perspective and thus are of varying utility to practitioners.

It is the purpose of this new series to move in the direction of tapping this rich wealth of practice wisdom in a way that makes it readily available on a broad basis. To this end a series of specific fields of practice has been identified and known experts in each field have been asked to write about practice in their specialty from a common framework.

The goal of each book is to address not only the therapeutic aspects of practice in these fields but also the range of sociological, policy, administration, and research areas so as to present the reader with an overview of the specific field of practice as well as the specifics about therapy. In addition to helping the individual worker to learn more about a specific field of practice, the series as a whole, it is hoped, will provide an opportunity to make comparisons among fields of practice and thus facilitate the ongoing expansion of general knowledge.

Certainly there is growing awareness of the need for addressing the specific training and practice needs of each field of practice. Many schools of social work now arrange their curricula along the line of fields of practice. The NASW has utilized the notion of fields of practice to relate systematically to how some social workers are employed and to prescribe the roles most appropriate for them.

The fields selected for coverage in this series may or may not represent clearly defined areas of specialization in social work. Rather they are identifiable human needs or problem populations or even settings for which a discrete and identifiable cluster of attitudes, skills, and knowledge is thought to be needed in order to intervene effectively.

We are extremely pleased to welcome Dr. Carel Germain's book to our Fields of Practice series. Internationally respected as a leading figure in social work education, Germain has now adapted her ecological approach to practice to health care settings. Creatively, lucidly, and systematically, she focuses on the interactive and transactive processes among the client, his or her personal environment, the worker, and the health care system.

Social Work Practice in Health Care offers unique insights into the social and psychological dynamics of the client in a medical setting and the range of interventions available to help him or her. In addition, Germain sensitively examines the social worker's responsibilities and his or her interactions with other health professionals. Germain's ecological perspective contributes to the multidisciplinary holistic medicine movement in providing an important alternative to the disease-oriented approach to health care.

This book will be of immense value to practitioners, students, administrators, and educators.

FRANCIS J. TURNER
HERBERT S. STREAN

Preface

At last count there were approximately 43,000 social workers practicing in the field of health care, or about 20 percent of the total number of social workers. Of these, 11,800 or 5 percent were in medical settings, and the balance or 15 percent in mental health. Social work departments were in place in 58 percent of the reporting hospitals (*Health Resources Statistics*, 1976–1977, p. 247). It is likely that the figures have grown since then. The government no longer collects such statistics, but the National Association of Social Workers estimates that 15.4 percent of its 95,000 members practice in medical-health care agencies, the third largest group of members after mental health (27.8 percent) and children's and youth services (15.9 percent) (Johnson, 1983). If this figure were combined with that of nonmember social workers (unknown), the percent of all social workers in health settings would probably exceed the 1976 1977 figure. Medical social work, as the field was once called, is one of the oldest specializations in the profession. In the mid-1880s the first settlement house and the first charity organization society, usually considered the progenitors of modern social work, were founded. Only twenty years later, in 1905, medical social work came into existence in the outpatient department of the Massachusetts General Hospital.

In contrast to the charity organization and settlement house movements, however, medical social work was not actually begun by a social worker or by someone who would at a later point call herself a social worker. It was originated by a socially minded physician at Massachusetts General, Dr. Richard Cabot (Bartlett, 1975). A member of the board of the Boston Children's Aid as well, Cabot was acquainted with how the social work staff there studied the needs of children. He observed that they designed their help to fit those needs and used the community resources then available. Out of concern about the seeming inability of his clinic patients to carry out treatment regimens because of social problems pressing upon them, Cabot invited social workers to work with him in the clinic. He believed they could help patients with individual and family problems, either the result of illness or preexistent, that were interfering with effective treatment.

For two years Dr. Cabot directed the service himself, but in 1907 he engaged Ida Cannon as a staff member. Several months later she became head worker, and for thirty-seven years she continued to direct the expanding department of social service within the hospital. Ida Cannon had trained as a nurse and served as a visiting nurse with the Associated Charities in St. Paul. Her experience there with social workers and their clients, together with the impression made upon her when she heard a speech given by Jane Addams of Hull House, stimulated her interest in becoming a social worker. In 1906 her brother, Walter B. Cannon, the famous Harvard physiologist, invited her to Cambridge so that she might attend the newly opened Boston School for Social Workers (later the Simmons College School of Social Work). While in school she volunteered at Dr. Cabot's clinic on Saturdays.

The program and services that Cabot and Cannon developed were successful, and the idea of social work in the hospital soon spread. Cannon, and the many skilled social workers associated with her over the years, contributed to the development of practice theory, in general, and were particularly responsible for the development of the field of practice known as medical social work. By 1918 the American Association of Hospital Social Workers was established. Soon the young schools of social work were introducing specialized courses in medical social work, while some schools later developed a second-year concentration in medical social work. With curriculum changes in the 1950s, however, such specializations were discontinued. The amount of medical-social content in schools' curricula steadily declined despite the growing numbers of social workers practicing in medical settings. But in the final decades of the twentieth century interest in specialization has again come to the fore.

Many schools have designed specialized sequences of health care courses that include practice methods, policy issues, program development, service delivery, and research for those preparing for social work careers in health care. It is for such students, and social workers already in the health care fields as practitioners, administrators, and educators, that this book was written. It is hoped that other social workers may find it pertinent to their interest in the influence of health, illness, disability, and the health care system on the lives of the individuals, families, groups, and communities they serve.

The functions, roles, and tasks of the social worker in contemporary health care, while they rest on the foundation that Cannon and others built, are expanded far beyond the earlier conceptions. The growing complexities of the health care system; the pressures, constraints, and opportunities provided by the health care organization; the proliferation of biomedical knowledge and technology and the ethical dilemmas they generate; and the development and refinement of social work theory, knowledge, and skills have all combined to make of social work in health care a demanding, sometimes frustrating, but always rewarding professional practice. Because the interplay of these many factors significantly influences social work practice in health care, this book is divided into two parts.

Part I (Chapters 1 through 4) examines the context of contemporary practice in health care, while Part II (Chapters 5 through 9) considers the practice itself. Chapter 1 presents the major policy issues and the structures and programs created in response to them. Together they constitute what is meant by "Health Care System." The nature of that system as context influences every aspect of social work practice and must be understood by the practitioner.

Chapter 2 describes health care organizations and aspects of their environments that are pertinent to effective social work practice within them. The organization shapes and influences such practice by the operations of its philosophy, purpose, structures, and procedures. As context, it provides both opportunities for service and constraints upon service.

Chapter 3 explores dimensions of the patient role and the nature of the illness or disability experience as it is affected by personal, environmental, and cultural features, and their contextual implications for social worker practice.

In Chapter 4 specialized theory, and basic processes common to all social work practice but reshaped by the theory, are considered as the professional context of health care social work. An adaptational model of stress and coping in situations of illness and disability is presented. The model is then applied to some fundamental processes of social work for use in health care practice.

Part II is directed to practice itself. Chapters 5 through 7 analyze principles, skills, and techniques in practice with individuals, families, and patient and relative groups in health care settings.

In Chapter 5 the focus is on social work practice in the initial phase, and in chapter 6 it is on practice in the ongoing phase. Chapter 7 focuses on social work in the ending phase. Chapter 8 examines collaborative practice.

Chapter 9 considers another level of practice that is concerned with organizational innovation and change. An Epilogue attempts to draw together the threads of present and future opportunities for social work in health care. Throughout these practice chapters, as well as in Part I, examples have been chosen to illustrate the influence on practice of differences in illnesses and disabilities, gender, age, culture, environments, and types of settings. Where specific types of settings have not been included it is assumed that principles and skills can be usefully generalized to practice in those settings.

CAREL B. GERMAIN

Acknowledgments

This book draws on the author's own practice and consulting experiences in health care settings, and on those of colleagues and friends in the United States and Canada who were exceptionally gracious and generous in sharing them for inclusion in the book, either as illustrations or as clarification of practice issues. They include Margaret Altman, Cynthia Banfield-Weir, René Bergeron, Rita Beck Black, Carolyn Boynton, Jon Bradley, Ruth Breslin, Betty Brodsky, Leo Bulgar, Susan Chaleff, Scott Clark, Herman Curiel, Amy Dorin, Claudia Fedarko, Regina Furlong, Joan Glaser, Julie Glover, Elyse Goldberg, Dennis Haubrich, Jan Jess, Deborah Laine, Mary Beth Langton, Eileen Delaney Leo, Nancy Lindquist, Carolyn Longo, James McCreath, Judy McKay, Nancy Nation, Martha Pope, Penny Schwartz, Helen Sheehan, Barbara Sherman, Sheila Small, Ann Sherwood, Rochelle Somer, Carol Swenson, Eleanor Ward, and Jeanne Wess.

I am especially grateful to Judith A. B. Lee and Jo Taylor Marshall, who not only shared rich practice materials but lent me their vision and wisdom and provided warm encouragement; and to Alex Gitterman, Tom Heald, Tim Ackerson, Kenneth Smith, Josephine Vignone Turner, and Barbara Davis Clark for their interest, support, and practice examples; and to Laura Wolff of The Free Press and the Series Editors, Herbert Strean and Francis J. Turner, for their patience and practical help.

C.B.G.

PART ONE

THE CONTEXT OF SOCIAL WORK PRACTICE IN HEALTH CARE

CHAPTER 1

The Health Care System as Context for Social Work Practice

THE HEALTH CARE SYSTEM in general and the health organization in particular are part of the context that helps shape the structure and content of social work services, programs, and practices in health care. Both are themselves influenced by economic, political, historical, and social forces in their environments. Knowledgeable awareness of both, and of their operations, is critical to effective social work practice. This chapter will examine the health care system.

Issues and Programmatic Responses

POLICY ISSUES

The health care system in the United States comprises a vast, complex array of structures, programs, and services under public and private auspices. The system is technically capable of providing a high level of care but is beset by serious problems of access, quality, equity, and costs (Lewis, Fein, and Mechanic, 1976). Access issues refer to the demographic, geographic, economic, and cultural factors governing the availability of quality care to all segments of the population. Such system interventions as Medicaid, Medicare, Health Maintenance Organizations (HMOs), and primary care programs are designed to deal with access problems.

Quality issues include problems in measuring and monitoring the

3

outcomes of services; the effects on patients, families, and staffs of dehumanizing physical and social environments created by some health care organizations; professional education, practices, and behaviors and their negative consequences for patients and families; and the moral and ethical dilemmas posed by technological advances in biomedicine. System interventions to address quality issues include Professional Standards Review Organizations (PSROs) and utilization review committees; problem-oriented recording; ombudsmen and patient service representatives; statutory protection of patients' rights; studies of patient satisfaction; supports and incentives for education and practice in primary care programs; and new emphases on the psychosocial aspects of illness in medical, nursing, and even dental education.

Equity issues refer to problems in the distribution of health care services to children, youth, women, and elderly, the rural and urban poor, and those suffering from particular illnesses or disabilities. They also refer to regional differences in diagnostic, treatment, and rehabilitation services affecting all residents of a region. Matters of equity arise from problems in access, quality, and cost control. System interventions to deal with equity issues include the use of physician extenders such as nurse practitioners and physician assistants; Health Systems Agencies (HSAs) in which consumer participation is mandated; urban and rural primary care programs; and the encouragement of family practice residency programs.

Cost issues refer to physicians' services, hospital services, third-party reimbursement policies, technological developments, and unnecessary diagnostic and treatment procedures, including surgery and hospitalization. A further cost issue is the inappropriate use of medical services by those suffering from psychological stress and/or social problems. System interventions include HSAs; HMOs; primary care programs; home health care; utilization review; and health education, promotion, and primary preventive programs.

Access, quality, equity, and cost issues are clearly interdependent, making them very difficult to resolve. Increasing access, for example, is likely to increase costs, and so on. Since the 1960s the federal government has played a dominant role in shaping the health care system through its efforts to resolve issues of access, quality, equity, and cost by the system interventions mentioned. The issues arose as consequences of the free market approach to medical care. So it is ironic that even the successful interventions are being terminated or their financial support cut back by the present Administration in favor of a return to market mechanisms.

A philosophy of deregulation and minimal "interference" by government in the affairs of its people—as well as a concern for escalating health care costs—underlie this reversal of national policy. The health care system now consumes 9.6 percent of the gross national product. The cost of medical care increased 12.5 percent in 1981, the largest increase ever (*New York Times*, January 25, 1982). The escalation of health care costs is a matter of deep concern to everyone. But some observers believe that a return to a private market in health care is likely to *shift* the burden of costs rather than reduce them. The burden will be shifted to the most medically needy: the poor, the elderly, and the chronically ill. Young and Saltman (1981) of the Harvard School of Public Health suggest:

> In the long run, by dismantling rather than reforming the regulatory struc-
> tures in our health care system, the Administration's program may result in
> higher costs for less adequate health care for all of us.
>   The answer to the problem of maintaining adequate access and quality at
> reasonable cost doesn't lie in some pernicious form of competition, but in
> devising forms of regulation that can better meet the divergent requirements
> of patients, providers, and payers alike. Rather than putting consumers at
> greater risk, we ought to develop more effective regulatory means to address
> the realities of the health-care marketplace.

Others believe that a combination of regulation, competition (incentives to providers), voluntary self-regulation, and innovation is the best answer to cost containment. In this view, regulation alone is ineffective and costly, and competition alone can leave gaps in coverage and benefits. Because of the distinctive character of the health care market, "government regulation and self-regulation must be equilibrating forces" (McNerney, 1980, p. 1090).

The federal government has long provided health services directly to members of the armed services and Coast Guard, veterans, merchant seamen, federal prisoners, and Native Americans. Its huge support of biomedical research since World War II led to increasingly higher levels of scientific and technological care, and hence to growing specialization in medicine and other health care professions. But increasingly since the mid-1960s, the federal government has intervened directly into the system of health care itself by developing new structures and services. What follows is an overview of several of those interventions and some of their impact on access, equity, cost, and quality.

ACCESS AND EQUITY

In the mid-1960s the federal government set out to alleviate problems of access and equity through changes in the Social Security Act to provide federal reimbursement of medical costs of the poor (Medicaid), and creating the still larger program of federal health insurance for the elderly (Medicare). Ironically, Medicaid increased access for some low-income people but decreased equity by creating a two-class system of health care. Unlike Medicare, which is a uniform federal program that fully reimburses hospital costs for patients over sixty-five, Medicaid comprises fifty different programs, with each state deciding eligibility and reimbursement levels. Because these levels are unrealistically low, many physicians refuse to treat Medicaid patients, who must then resort to "Medicaid Mills" where care is likely to be mediocre or even dangerous, or to emergency rooms where continuity and coordination of care is impossible. Medicaid has also increased costs by shifting them to private patients and insurers and by inviting provider fraud.

Medicare, however, has been faulted because it spends a disproportionate amount of health care dollars—$26.8 billion in 1978—on 11 percent of the population when another equally needy group—children under nineteen years of age, who constitute 31 percent of the population—receives far less, that is $3.8 billion in 1978 (*New York Times*, December 3, 1980). Medicare is also criticized for not covering the cost of long-term care frequently needed by the elderly. Besides, both Medicaid and Medicare are oriented toward illness rather than prevention and health promotion, and their operations favor hospitalization over ambulatory care.

Despite such criticisms, both programs have undoubtedly increased access to needed health care for the poor. In 1981 Dr. Karen Davis of the Johns Hopkins University School of Hygiene and Public Health said, "There have been major declines in infant and maternal mortality, in death rates from influenza, pneumonia, diabetes, in those causes of death that historically have been higher among the poor" (*New York Times*, July 12, 1981). Earlier she had attributed these declines to improved access to medical care:

> In 1964, two years before Federal Medicare and Medicaid programs began to pay health care bills of the poor and the aged, Americans visited physicians 3.8 times a year on the average, but the figure for the poor was 4.7. By 1978, visits to doctors among the poor had climbed to an average 6.2 times a year, compared to five times annually for other Americans. . . . In 1964, for example, one out of three poor children had not seen a doctor in the previous two years. Ten years later, the figure was one out of five. [*New York Times*, December 3, 1980]

Increased access, reflected in the rise in the number of visits, seems to have paid off in declining death rates. However, the situation is more complex, because about 10 percent of the U.S. population lack any form of insurance coverage. First, incomes of the working poor, while close to the poverty line, exceed the Medicaid ceiling. They lack other insurance and cannot pay for needed care, so their health problems intensify, often to the point of permanent damage. Second, with the high rate of unemployment, millions more are now losing their work-connected health insurance. It is estimated that 91 percent of all laid-off people lose their health benefits. With reduced income, many unemployed workers find they cannot maintain their health insurance and are doing without needed care at the very time when the stress of unemployment aggravates or even causes health problems (*Wall Street Journal*, April 6, 1982, pp. 1, 20).

Despite the progress achieved through Medicaid and Medicare, scandalous differences in the mortality and morbidity rates continue to exist between minorities and whites. Not only does the U.S. rank twelfth among forty countries in infant mortality, but the morality rate for nonwhite children is 70 percent greater than for white children (Lazarus et al., 1977):

> After infancy, contrasts in mortality remain. Death rates for minority children are two-thirds again as high in the 1–4 and in the 4–14 age groups. Among 40 countries, the U.S. ranks 19th in the proportion of children who can be expected to survive to age 15. [p. 86]

While the infant mortality rate (the number of children who die before the first year) has been declining in recent years (12.5 per 1,000 live births in 1980), the discrepancy between white and and nonwhite (21.7) infants is still shocking. There are probably many reasons for these statistics, but foremost among them is poverty. Inadequate maternal and child nutrition and low birth weight, which occurs mostly among infants born to teenage mothers (whose income is apt to be low and who are less likely to receive prenatal care, especially the unmarried), are contributing factors. Among children past infancy, other conditions associated with poverty—lead paint, child abuse and neglect, dilapidated and vermin-infested housing, accidents, and poor nutrition—are contributing factors.

Among minority adults, the morbidity rates of stress-related illnesses such as hypertension and heart disease is considerably higher than for white persons. This is true of blacks, Hispanics, and Asian and Pacific peoples (Weaver, 1979). Death rates for these groups from the three major causes of death for ages twenty-five through sixty-four far exceed those of whites (*Healthy People*, 1979). These conditions, heart disease, cancer, and stroke account for 75 percent of all deaths in this country. In the case of Native Americans, the situation is worse still. Only 5 percent of the population live beyond sixty-five years.

> The incidence rates for leading notifiable diseases for Indians are astronomical in all categories with amoebic and bacillary dysentery, gonorrhea, hepatitis, measles, mumps, syphilis, and tuberculosis heading the list. . . . Meaningful and quality health care is not available to Indian people because it is not planned for them. How can it be that the preservation of the life of a people is either overlooked or left out of the budget? Is it you? Is it I? How is that decision really made? [Blanchard, 1976]

Geographic factors in access refer to proximity and such concerns as the availability and expense of transportation and child care, costs of taking time off from work or from other pressing demands, and the availability of services in the inner city. In rural areas, shortages of trained personnel compound the problems of distance, remoteness, and isolation. Emergency services are less available; public health services and comprehensive health care services are not readily accessible. Poverty aggravates these problems, so that infant mortality rates and age-adjusted death rates are higher in many rural areas than in urban areas. Poor nutrition, lack of prenatal care, lower levels of education, inadequate housing, high rates of occupational accidents and disease (as in mining areas, for example), and a high percentage of older persons in the population all contribute to the prevalence and severity of chronic illness and disability among the rural poor.

Federal efforts to reduce such barriers to access in both urban and rural areas have included educational incentives for physicians to practice in unserved or underserved areas. Success has been limited, as many leave such areas after fulfilling their obligated term. The creation of neighborhood health centers in urban and rural areas has been more successful. These were established through a Comprehensive Health Services program in the Office of Economic Opportunity in 1966 and were later transferred to the Bureau of Community Health Services of HEW, now the Department of Health and Human Services (DHHS).

The emphasis of these centers is on primary health care, including "preventive health services, diagnostic services, treatment, family planning, in-home care of the chronically ill and other home health services, rehabilitative services, dental care, and mental-health services" (Lewis, Fein, and Mechanic, 1976, p. 191). Other programs supported by the Bureau of Community Health Services include Appalachian Demonstration Health Projects, Genetic Diseases Programs, Hemophilia Diagnostic and Treatment Centers, Maternal and Child Health Programs, Migrant Health Projects, Sickle Cell Screening and Education Clinic Program, and Sudden Infant Death Syndrome Program. In 1978, 455 centers were serving 2.5 million persons, most of whom were young, poor, and members of minority groups. About half were women (*Bureau of Community Health Services and Programs*, 1978).

Even in neighborhood-based health services, however, there are often cultural barriers affecting utilization. Dr. Henrik Blum of the School of Public Health, University of California, suggests:

> These primary service centers close to people should be kept small to minimize bureaucratic tendencies and should service no more than 10,000 persons. People indigenous to various segments or subcultures served would be drawn into employment at the unit. In all but sparsely populated areas there would be many such units from which to choose. In this way almost everyone would

find one center with workers with compatible culture, language, health beliefs, and practices. *Curanderos,* medicine men, transcendental meditators, and so on can be well-absorbed into centers with appropriate clientele. [Blum, 1976, p. 109]

At this writing, however, cutbacks in federal support of the centers make any implementation of these ideas a forlorn hope.

COSTS

Increasing access and equity increases costs. It has been easy to blame escalating costs on this factor alone, particularly with reference to Medicaid and Medicare. But the issue of cost is more complex. For example, many observers consider the rapid growth of private health insurance to be the primary contributor to excessive costs. When Medicaid and Medicare were introduced in 1965 and 1966, respectively, almost 141 million people had private health insurance. By 1980 the number had risen to almost 193 million (and 50 million people were covered by Medicaid and Medicare) (*New York Times,* March 30, 1982). Private health insurance invites expensive treatment, including hospitalization and high-cost technology, and fails to induce cost-consciousness in the patient or the physician. The supplier (physician) exerts the demand since the consumer (patient) does not know what he needs, and the insurers provide a blank check to cover the cost. Demands increase and costs rise, and reimbursement is made "after the fact."

In 1973 Congress responded to rapidly increasing costs by legislation to support the establishment and expansion of HMOs. An alternative to third-party insurance coverage, HMOs provide direct medical service on the basis of a prearranged fee. Service is provided by a group of health professionals in a central facility or by independent practitioners in a variety of locations. Both types serve voluntarily enrolled populations for comprehensive care. Since the organization's income is limited to its membership fees, a strong incentive exists to reduce the number and length of hospital stays and to keep patients well through preventive care and health education.

Studies have shown that HMOs do hold down costs, largely because of lower rates of hospitalization (Luft, 1978), and with no adverse effect on quality of care. Surveys reveal a high level of patient satisfaction. This form of health care is spreading rapidly, supported by the law requiring that any company with more than twenty-five employees must offer an HMO plan as an alternative to conventional health insurance. They are popular with employers because fees are less than insurance rates, and employee absence is reduced because of less hospitalization. By 1981 there were about 240 HMOs with more than 10 million members, and two hundred more were under development. Originally it was hoped that about 10 percent of the population would be enrolled before the end of the 1980s. But the Reagan Administration ended federal support through grants in September 1981 and will end the loan provisions by the end of 1983, on the grounds that HMOs, having proved their worth, are now attractive arenas for private investment by banks, corporations, hospitals, physicians, and insurance companies. This raises questions about the effects on cost, quality, access, and equity exerted by the profit-making interests of investors.

There is evidence that health care is already undergoing transformation owing to the presence of the medical-industrial complex (Relman, 1980). Proprietary hospitals and nursing homes, diagnostic laboratories, home care and emergency-room services, dialysis centers, and a variety of other services owned by physicians, management firms, and corporate investors produced a gross income of $35 to $40 billion in 1979. Such structures, while apparently more efficient than the nonprofit sector, create problems of overuse and fragmentation of services, overemphasis on technology and "cream-skimming" (eliminating inefficient and unprofitable services regardless of medical and social need; exclusion of uninsured patients, welfare patients, and those with complex and chronic illnesses; and dispensing with expensive residency and educational programs). According to Dr. Relman, this "cream-skimming" leaves the expensive but needed remainder to nonprofit hospitals. He also suggests there is a conflict of interest posed for physicians by their ownership, or service on boards of directors, of proprietary facilities.

Returning to HMOs, it is noteworthy that they have not really increased access and equity, because few from the elderly and low-income populations have been enrolled. At this writing, however, the Administration is considering the use of vouchers for the Medicaid and Medicare populations, which will then permit them to select HMO enrollment if they wish.

As another means of cost containment, the Congress created Health Systems Agencies (HSAs) in 1974. These bodies were designed to undertake rational health planning and coordination on a regional basis through assessment of need for hospital expenditures of $150,000 or more and the elimination of duplicate equipment and services. All states were required to have certificate-of-need programs in place by 1980. HSA legislation also mandated majority participation in health planning by a defined set of consumers. The HSA program is to be dismantled by the Reagan Administration on the grounds that it has been ineffective in achieving cost control. Observers note that this may or may not have been an accurate assessment since HSAs were not in existence long enough to prove their effectiveness. Five years into the program, however, HSAs were demonstrating some effectiveness:

- Prevented expansions: Health-planning groups in recent years have blocked new hospital construction in such hospital-surfeited areas as Honolulu, Atlanta, Dayton, San Francisco and Baltimore.
- Less-costly facilities: While holding down expensive expansion of regular hospitals, planners in Rochester, N.Y., promoted walk-in clinics and home care; planners in the Virginia suburbs of Washington approved more nursing homes.
- Shared services: At planners' insistence, many hospitals are consolidating services ranging from laundries to costly new medical equipment. Five Milwaukee hospitals have shared a $500,000 body-scanning machine since July. [*Wall Street Journal*, May 5, 1977]

However, the Health Research Group of Ralph Nader's consumer lobby asserted that HSAs had failed to prevent surpluses in hospital beds. It contended that 100,000 unneeded hospital beds across the country were costing $2 billion to maintain, and that HSAs were ineffective in controlling this major element in high hospital costs.

In any case, the termination of HSAs is in keeping with the Administration's interest in deregulating the health care system in favor of free-market forces.

Still another factor in escalating costs is expensive technology. Observers in and outside organized medicine assert that technological achievements have had little impact on the general health of the nation but have increased the cost of care. Most of the decline in mortality and morbidity rates is attributed not to medical care but to the control of the infectious diseases achieved early in the century and by improved standards of living, education, nutrition, and sanitation (Cassel, 1976). The major medical problems in the closing decades of the twentieth century, such as cancer, heart disease, and stroke, have so far resisted medical control. This is not surprising in the face of evidence that behavioral, environmental, and life-style factors appear to play a significant etiological role in these conditions. Yet modern medicine is characterized by what Dr. Anne Somers (1979) has called the "technological imperative." The technological imperative reflects a misplaced emphasis on acute care when the nation's greatest need is care of the chronically ill and disabled. The federal government has addressed these issues by providing support to primary care programs.

Primary health care is defined as the "first contact" provision of ambulatory services by a variety of health care disciplines; it is designed to be comprehensive, coordinated, and continuous. As the first point of entry into the health care system, it serves as the link to secondary health care for conditions requiring specialized diagnostic and treatment services and to tertiary care for diagnosis and treatment of unusual and complicated conditions (as provided in a medical center or regional facility).

The hope for primary care is not only that costs will be reduced by preventive care and elimination of expensive hospitalization and un-needed specialized care, but that it will be characterized by quality because care will no longer be fragmented. Oriented to the patient's environment, primary care is family-centered and seeks to integrate the physical, emotional, and social aspects of health and illness in a team approach to health care. These aspects makes the participation of the social worker especially valued and valuable.

Another federal effort to contain costs and also to increase access in rural and inner-city areas is its support to physician extender programs (physician assistants, nurse practitioners, child-health associates, family-planning specialists, and primary care associates). Nurse practitioners, in particular, are trained to make psychosocial assessments, including assessments of family relationships and home, school, and work environments, in primary and acute care settings—a potential source of territorial conflict with health care social workers.

Still another cost factor identified by many observers is behavioral—the life-styles and personal habits of an affluent society, known or believed to be risk factors in certain illnesses and injuries. These include smoking and lung diseases, alcoholism and liver disease, substance abuse and fetal damage, stress and hypertension, obesity and heart disease, reckless driving and auto accidents, availability of handguns and homicide or gunshot wounds, and negligence or lack of knowledge and home accidents and poisonings (Knowles, 1977). The federal government has attempted to modify this cost factor through health promotion and health education activities of the Office of the Surgeon General, the National Institutes of Health (NIH), and the National Institutes on Alcohol Abuse and Alcoholism, Drug Abuse, and Mental Health (ADAMHA), as well as through training support. A 1982 report calls for a reordering of research interests to foster prevention and promote health.

Despite the logic of a preventive approach and official interest in it, changes in behavior affecting health are hard to achieve. Americans find it difficult to maintain diets, refrain from smoking and illicit drugs, follow exercise programs, and observe effective medication regimens. Some critics are disturbed by the value dilemmas and paternalism in imposing health values on the uninterested or in depriving individuals and groups of the right to make their own decisions about habits and behaviors once they have the needed information about all factors involved. Still others, however, are disturbed by the fact that such persons, when they do become seriously ill as a consequence of personal habits and behaviors, impose the high cost of their care on the rest of the population.

From another perspective, the approach does blame the victim, ab-solving the media and other elements of the culture that invite and support disease-inducing behaviors. Blaming the individual for her or his health problems also draws attention away from powerful social determinants of illness and disability such as poverty, unemployment, discrimination, technological pollution, and an organization of the health care system that does not yet provide access to primary health care for all. In announcing the Reagan Administration's approach to health care, HHS Secretary Richard S. Schweiker (1981) said:

> "The future of health care under the Reagan Administration can be described in two words: competition and prevention. Restoring competition to the health industry and preventing disease before it strikes will be two themes central to our policies.... We must convince people how to take control of their own health, how to adopt habits that can make trips to the doctor less frequent." He added that the new direction would include an effort toward "health promotion, health prevention and disease prevention."

Clearly, these three emphases are important components in improving the nation's health and reducing costs, but they may be futile in the context of cutbacks in social programs, environmental protection, and protection of workers' health and safety. A healthy society is a humane society that is concerned with the physical, social, and emotional health and wellbeing of all its members.

Cost containment is likely to be an ongoing problem, but the shifts to primary care and to prepaid group practice are promising directions. Also, the Administration's proposals for prospective payments to hospitals for the care of Medicare patients appear to give hospitals an incentive to operate more efficiently, since they will be permitted to retain any savings in cost below the reimbursement level. Fixed amounts for particular diagnoses will be paid in advance and will replace present cost controls of hospital rooms, routine nursing services, and ancillary services such as X-rays and laboratory work, now in effect until 1986.* Although questions arise about how prospective reimbursement can be designed to protect hospitals and patients while saving the government money, insurance companies are advocating that such a scheme should be applied to all patients to replace "blank check" financing. Likely consequences for social work services are not yet clear.

Under consideration at this writing are proposed increases for Medicare premiums and deductibles based on income. Political and practical problems will arise in imposing a means test on the elderly, and such a proposal is likely to face stiff opposition. At this writing DHHS also pro-

---

*Since this was written, the federal government has instituted predetermined rates for all hospitals treating elderly and disabled patients under the Medicare program, effective October 1, 1983. All cases will be classified according to a system of 467 diagnosis-related groups (DRGs). Fixed amounts will be paid for all cases in the same category regardless of length of stay.

poses to eliminate standards for social services in hospitals choosing to participate in Medicaid and Medicare programs. While the Social Security Act does not require hospitals to provide social work services to their patients, HEW regulations have always specified the standards hospitals must meet if they do have a social work department. Removing them threatens the continued participation of professional social workers in hospital services to Medicaid and Medicare patients. The proposed plan to deregulate the nursing home industry would have a similar effect.

QUALITY

In 1972 Congress amended the Social Security Act to establish PSROs to review physicians' care of Medicaid and Medicare patients. The aim of the Act was to limit unnecessary diagnostic procedures and surgery and excessive hospital stays, thus contributing to cost control. But it also embodied concepts of peer review, quality assurance, and accountability, thereby contributing to quality care through evaluation of outcomes, written standards, norms, and criteria. Emphasis was placed on maintaining skill and upgrading knowledge through continuing education. In general, physicians have been opposed to the program on the grounds that it interferes with professional judgment. Critics outside of medicine have claimed that the cost of the program outweighs benefits.

While utilization review makes modest contributions to cost containment, assuring quality is far more complex. Eli Ginzberg, the Columbia University health economist, underscores the complexity in his analysis of the interplay among physician, patient, community, and health organization in issues of quality, as well as the relationship between quality and matters of cost and equity (1977, pp. 80–98). As of this writing the Reagan Administration is planning to abolish or greatly modify the PSRO program in line with its interest in deregulation. On balance, this may be a wise decision.

It is noteworthy, however, that social work as one of the nonmedical health care professions anticipating PSRO involvement, has moved effectively to clarify its own measures for accountability, quality assurance, and peer review. In many instances this preparation has led to new and more effective procedures with respect to case finding and discharge planning; new skills and knowledge building through staff development; new interest in accountability, especially to clients, and evaluation of service outcomes; and greater clarity about social work functions, roles, and tasks.

Summary

This chapter has reviewed some of the federal controls and programs introduced since the 1960s to deal with the issues of access, quality, cost, and equity. These issues arose earlier out of the operations of the health care market. The characteristics of that market had themselves changed because of the development of medical technology and medical specialization, the spread of private insurance, the shift from acute to chronic illness, growing demands by consumers, and other factors. Clearly, there are no easy remedies to the health care system's ills of fragmentation, escalating costs, and other effects of piecemeal regulatory processes on the difficult problems of access, quality, and equity. For many years health planners placed their confidence in national health insurance proposals, but the likelihood of achieving either national health insurance or a national service system is remote, at least for the 1980s.

Social workers will continue to practice in a context of uncertainty regarding health care policies, structures, and programs. Given the unquestioned need for cost containment, social work's own commitment to increased access, quality, and equity in health care suggests certain directions for its own services. These include:

1. Ongoing work on achieving quality assurance in social work services
2. Acquisition and refinement of skills in policy analysis, political advocacy, and organizational innovation
3. Ongoing development of functions related to cost control and to quality such as discharge planning, case finding and screening, and research (especially into service effectiveness, contributions to cost containment, and patient satisfaction)
4. Continuing experimentation with a marketing approach in sustaining and expanding social work services (Rosenberg and Weissman, 1981) directed to consumer needs and consumer satisfaction, and developing new opportunities for service
5. Continued refinement of social work skills in outreach, linkage to the community, coordination of services, and case management functions

CHAPTER 2

The Health Care Organization as Context for Social Work Practice

LIKE THE HEALTH CARE SYSTEM, the health care organization is part of the context of social work practice in health care. In one sense it mediates the effects of the wider health care system as they bear on practice. But more important, it exerts its own special imperatives that influence the behaviors of clients and staff. Health care organizations are complex social structures, although the degree of complexity will vary between a large university medical center, for example, and a neighborhood-based family planning clinic. Whatever the degree of complexity, the social worker must understand fully how the organization works so that she or he may function more effectively within it. This chapter first presents a general description of health organizations and then describes some of the external pressures impinging on them in addition to the impact of the health care system.*

Proliferation and Reduction

The variety of health organizations in which social workers now practice has expanded rapidly since the 1960s. Recently developed structures in-

*Chapter 9 will provide a more specific analysis of organizational processes as a base for practice principles used by the social worker to increase organizational responsiveness to the individuals, families, groups, and communities using or needing the organization's services.

clude neighborhood health centers, HMOs and other primary care facilities, centers for the victims of rape and family violence, family planning clinics, home health agencies, occupational health facilities, hospices, abortion clinics, adolescent walk-in health centers, free-standing outpatient surgeries, and genetic counseling services. They also include such planning bodies as ethnic health councils, women's health planning groups, and regional health systems agencies (HSAs). Within hospitals there are now new specialized services such as burn units; intensive care units, including coronary care units and neonatal intensive care units; child abuse units; and pain clinics.

These and other new structures for the provision of health care join traditional organizations such as acute and chronic care hospitals, skilled nursing facilities and nursing homes, rehabilitation facilities, outpatient clinics, state and local departments of health, and disease-related foundations and organizations such as those concerned with multiple sclerosis, cancer, heart disease, cerebral palsy, cystic fibrosis, lung disease, and renal disease. The complexity is increased because these varied structures exist under varying fiscal and administrative auspices. There are public tax-supported facilities at local, state, and federal levels; not-for-profit facilities; proprietary for-profit facilities; and quasi-public facilities operated under private voluntary auspices but supported, in part, by public funds. In addition, labor unions have joined private industry and fraternal lodges as contractual providers of health services to employees or members. Social workers practice in most, if not all, the traditional and new structures and also in private group practices of physicians.

In contrast to the proliferation of health agencies providing programs and services, the variety or number of health care organizations in some localities has diminished. Because of the declining birthrate, for example, some hospitals have eliminated obstetrical services; usually one hospital in the area agrees to handle all maternal and newborn care for that area. When HSAs engaged in efforts to centralize care in this way, the public often protested. In its attempt to close maternity services at thirteen hospitals around Pittsburgh, the HSA received a flood of letters opposing the plan. One woman wrote, "It is unbelievable you would even think of closing the obstetrics unit at St. Francis Hospital. Three generations of my family have been born there" (*Wall Street Journal*, May 5, 1977).

Such hospital-based services may decline further (even without the presence of HSAs) with the resurgence of midwives and the growing interest of expectant parents in birth at home. Some hospitals have met this interest by providing Alternative Birthing Centers designed to "feel like home" for the parents, their families, and the infant. It is noteworthy that at the other end of the life course, fatally ill patients and their families, in growing numbers, are requesting that the terminal stage take place at home. In response, free-standing hospices have been established to provide home care for the dying as well as a homelike setting away from home for those who need or prefer such an alternative. Hospice areas, separated from acute care areas, have been established in many hospitals, and many home health agencies are providing hospice home care to the dying.

Some services, programs, and institutions disappear not so much in response to consumer interests and health needs as in consequence of economic and political forces. The closing down of some public hospitals in disadvantaged urban areas appears to reflect issues of political power and powerlessness. And health organizations sometimes experience the withdrawal of financial support by an individual private donor for personal or economic reasons, and the futures of patients and staff involved in the supported service are threatened. The changing interests of federal and state granting bodies often shape the development of new programs and the phasing out of others in the health organization.

The Organization and the Professions

A critical feature of health care organizations is the variety of occupations and professions on which they depend in order to carry out their mission, dominated for the most part by the powerful profession of medicine. The history of social work in health care is a history of struggle to achieve professional identity, competence, and autonomy (self-directedness) in such a complex setting, while developing effective services to patients, families, groups, and communities. The struggle in some settings has been marked by lack of recognition from the medical profession and by some rivalry with other health professions, notably nursing. In other settings, however, social workers are valued not only for their services to patients and families but also as interdisciplinary team members, researchers, community liaison, and teachers of medical students and residents in social work areas of expertise bearing on health and illness. In new kinds of settings geared to comprehensive care and prevention, such as primary care facilities; family planning clinics; community based services to women, adolescents, or the elderly; and rehabilitation facilities, social workers tend to have more influence, and their contributions are more valued than in settings in which the physician's special expertise preempts all others because of acute illness. Partly this is because social workers are generally recognized as having valuable knowledge and linkage skills with respect to community resources needed in primary and nonacute settings, and their focus on person-in-environment is seen by other health care staff as pertinent to those settings.

However, in hospital-based child abuse units and in facilities for the developmentally disabled, the social worker's role is usually valued, regardless of medical dominance, perhaps because social workers traditionally have been the primary profession in child welfare services for the abused and the handicapped child. And even in acute care settings such as pediatric units, where work with the family has come to be recognized as critical to recovery (or to organizational needs, as in the discharge planning function), greater value is accorded to social work services.

Another organizational feature affecting the nature of social work functions and roles is the need for interprofessional collaboration and consultation, which has given rise to health care teams. Team practice has characterized health organizations for a long time. As the benefits of ministering to the "whole person," functioning in various social and physical environments, have come to be more clearly recognized, however, the use of team practice has increased, as has interest in team structure and development. The approach assumes that coordination of the several disciplines leads to more effective care. It further assumes that no single health care profession alone can meet the biopsychosocial needs generated by illness and disability or can manage the complex of biopsychosocial and cultural forces involved in health maintenance and prevention. As health occupations proliferate, the complexities of team practice are amplified. The functions, value systems, and practices of each occupation and profession have to be understood by the others for effective integration in diagnosis, treatment, or health maintenance. The emphasis on team practice and on newer forms of interdisciplinary teams requires the social worker's attention to the issues generated and to principles and skills needed for effective team practice. These will be the subject of Chapter 8.

The resources of time and space are important in all organizations, but especially so in health care. The physical space of the organization itself, its arrangement, design, and even location, are important influences on illness behaviors and coping behaviors. The importance of primary care, for example, rests on its accessibility. Neighborhood health centers may have a greater impact on the health and illness of particular populations than the outpatient services of a renowned medical complex situated outside the neighborhood. Often the distance from client to health facility is as much social as geographic.

Inside the facility, matters of "ward geography" and the "anthropology of space" come to the fore, as the needs of patients and families for both privacy and interaction with other patients and families are either ignored or accommodated by providing both kinds of arrangements. Varieties of colors and textures, movable furniture, and opportunities for impressing one's personality on one's living quarters have important consequences for patients' sense of competence, level of self-esteem, and sense of dignity and self-directedness. Such considerations may be of greater importance in long-term facilities than in acute care.

Issues of organizational space and time have an impact on social work practice. They are resources in short supply, and their availability to social work departments and individual social workers may be limited. For the hospital-based practitioner, the continuous presence of the patient in the workplace increases flexibility by diversifying the practitioner's options regarding time. Depending on need, the patient may be seen several times a day for a few minutes each time or at longer intervals for longer sessions. The availability of the worker in the patient's space, however, may also increase the demandingness of the setting on the worker. The very demandingness of the setting may interfere with the worker's responsiveness to families' needs. For example, time may make it difficult or even impossible to make home visits to families who, for whatever reason, are unable to come to the worker's space in the worker's work time.

Hospital and institutional patients are usually more readily accessible than outpatients for group services, provided group sessions are arranged at times when patients are not scheduled for diagnostic and treatment procedures. Time, like space, is in short supply in health facilities, and competition for it is keen. Sometimes the social worker is at a competitive disadvantage, because, unlike other health professionals, she or he in most instances is unavailable outside of working hours, usually 8:00 to 5:00, five days a week, excluding weekends. Other health professionals and the patients (and their relatives in some instances) are continuously present together in their shared space. This is a particularly acute problem in emergency rooms, where the heaviest burden of patient and family psychosocial needs is felt during night and weekend times, when social workers in many facilities are not available. This limitation is changing, however, as more social workers are providing round-the-clock services in emergency rooms.

In those health organizations that provide community outreach and health education and promotion activities, the worker's space often expands to include neighborhoods and dwellings of the population to be served. In such instances the matters of organizational space and time may become more similar to those in other fields of social work practice. In all health care settings, however, patients' biological, social, psychological, and cultural orientations to time and space—together with the facility's spatial arrangements and the tempo, rhythms, and timing of its activites—bear heavily on coping tasks and resources. They need to be taken into account by the social worker (Germain, 1976; 1978).

Pressures on the Organization

In addition to internal structures and processes alluded to in this section and others to be analyzed in Chapter 10, external sources of pressure also influence the operations of the health care organization (and influence the health care system as well), thereby affecting social work practice. Pressures coming from spheres outside the organization include public attitudes, the development of patient rights, the growth of information systems and technological advances that have led to ethical dilemmas, and professional standard-setting bodies. They affect organizational functioning and hence help to shape social work practice in the organization.

All professions are experiencing public criticism on matters of effectiveness, ethics, and costs. The decline of public trust in the professions, especially the role of expert, became more apparent in the 1960s and accelerated over the 1970s (Burnham, 1982). It was attended by growing disenchantment with other social institutions and a general cynicism toward establishment features of American life. Complaints about professional competence, motivations, and the depersonalization of the relationship between client and professional mounted; so too did public demands for increased participation on the part of those served and increased control over matters previously considered to lie within the realm of professional privilege. The elderly, ethnic and racial groups, students, women, and consumer groups turned to litigation to redress grievances against a variety of professions through malpractice suits and class actions (Yarmolinsky, 1978).

These changed and changing attitudes affect public expectations and perceptions of health organizations and the professionals who staff them. A striking example is (1) the protests by women that male physicians view many of their physical complaints as psychogenic, and that some perform unnecessary surgery on women patients, combined with (2) the demand by women for control over their own bodies and responsibility for their own health care, including birthing. As a consequence:

> Since 1969 [women] have formed at least a thousand women's health organizations, twenty-five alternative women's clinics and an uncountable number of small "self-help" physiology groups. These groups exist in almost every major city and in many rural areas. All of them make up the sprawling, vibrant Women's Health Movement.

The health organizations publicize problems in the delivery of woman's health care, educate themselves and other women about their bodies and guide consumers in finding the services they need. They run "Know Your Body" courses, explaining female anatomy and physiology in laywoman's terms. Some groups publish newsletters and health booklets, hold conferences, speak-outs and demonstrations. Others work politically to change the medical system into one which emphasizes preventive health services, eliminates profit-making in the healing of the sick, and shares decision-making with patients and health workers. [Corea, 1977, pp. 254–55]

Another example is the Hispanic Health Council of Hartford, Connecticut, originally founded in the early 1970s to gather data on health care issues facing Hispanics (mostly Puerto Ricans) in the Hartford area. The research function continues. For example, the council has studied sterilization among Puerto Rican women in Hartford and is currently conducting a research and service project with emergency rooms and police precincts, focusing on Puerto Ricans in crisis. But, on the basis of its research findings on access, quality, and equity, the council now also develops curriculums for health care providers and students, including those in medicine, social work, allied health, and nursing. It also engages in individual advocacy and political advocacy in matters of health care and joins with other groups concerned with housing, employment, and income maintenance in advocating on behalf of Hispanics. Community health education is provided to Puerto Rican teenagers, elderly, and parents of young children; neighborhood networks and support systems are developed for child care and transportation services in the obtaining of health care. The council has also gained beginning acceptance as consultants in the social and cultural patterned responses of Puerto Ricans to diagnostic and treatment procedures. The council is supported by federal research funding and private foundations (Gonzales-Borrero, 1982).

Patient Rights

The matter of patient rights is closely related to matters of equity and quality of care, as well as to issues of availability of options in health care services. The concern for patient rights arises from the inequality of power, status, knowledge, and understanding between the health professional and the patient in such areas as surgery, treatment, autopsy, participation in research and professional education, and donation of tissues and organs. In such areas, truly informed consent and freedom from overt or subtle coercion are essential (Mechanic, 1979). This principle raises questions for many social workers about the ethicality, for example, of not telling a patient or family member that a practitioner is a social work student.

Ethical problems are especially acute in government programs for the poor, where patients are additionally vulnerable because of stigmatized statuses such as AFDC mother, alcoholic, teenage multiple abortion patient, or aged person and because of class-based social distance, value differences, and language barriers. Another example is the homosexual patient whose right to equitable care is violated.

[A] lesbian who made her sexuality clear to the doctor, on admission for abdominal pain, was told she must have VD. She tried to explain to him how unlikely this was—lesbians are known to have one of the lowest VD rates of any group in society—but the doctor was so committed to his stereotype of homosexuals that he wouldn't listen. After much time, pain, and expense, it was finally discovered that she had a serious kidney ailment. [Brossart, 1979, p. 51]

The gay or lesbian patient and partner may be subject to staff gossip, neglect, punitive attitudes, and stereotypical assumptions. Here, "staff" refers to all health personnel, including social workers. The practitioner must develop self-awareness of her or his attitudes and values and must have knowledge about sexuality in general and homosexuality in particular. These requisites for protection of patient rights can be acquired through staff development programs to raise staff consciousness within the health organization and its social work department.

Indeed, it is possible that health organizations may themselves discriminate against homosexual professionals applying for a staff appointment. An "employee's sexual orientation may be more frequently assumed (on the basis of rumor, hearsay, or characteristics of their associates) than actually known (by public record or self-declaration)" (Berger and Kelly, 1981). It should be noted, however, that the research of the authors quoted here did not find evidence of discrimination in hiring practices at the initial level of screening in *social agencies.*

Rights of the handicapped have been established by the social action of the disabled themselves and by federal legislation. These rights include accessible physical environments and least restrictive psychosocial environments for the highest degree of independent living possible. Lifchez (1979) has conceptualized the environment of the disabled as comprising (1) the intimate environment that includes the disabled person and her bed or wheelchair or her interaction with an attendant; (2) the dwelling environment including the residence, school or work place, and areas for social, political, or recreational activities; and (3) the community environment including its physical accessibility and the services and supports provided to the handicapped.

Social workers in home health agencies, rehabilitation services, facilities for the developmentally disabled, hospital departments of physical medicine, and ambulatory services all are in strong positions from which to advocate on behalf of the handicapped for the above-noted rights regarding independent living and the right to easy access to equitable quality health care.

Adolescents are an underserved group in health care whose rights have not been legislated. They are "all but invisible in terms of health care services, research, or education focused on the prevention of disease. Yet it is during this key transitional period that so many habits—both health-enhancing and health-compromising—are developed and carried into adulthood" (Hamburg and Brown, 1978, p. 1). There are notable exceptions to this service gap, few as they are, and one is The Door—a Center of Alternatives, and its Adolescent Health Center in New York City. Established in the early 1970s with federal, state, and city funds, the Health Center provides free medical and gynecological services, family planning and sex counseling services, an early childrearing program, and nutrition counseling to inner city youth. Those served are young people, between twelve and twenty-one, who are unlikely or unable to seek help from traditional health and mental health facilities. The emphasis is on holistic health care, focused on the young person's total life situation, carried out by interdisciplinary primary health teams on which social workers serve.*

There are, of course, ethical dilemmas for social workers serving adolescent clients. One of the foremost in health care is the issue of parental consent for contraceptive services and abortion. What seemed to be a clear-cut right to access for needed services in reproductive control without parental consent, recently achieved, is again, at the time of this writing, being threatened by legislative or judicial action affecting publicly financed services. It is feared by many that securing parental consent will deter many teenagers from using contraceptive counseling and services, thereby leading to an increase in unwanted births to young women. Those in favor of parental consent point to the rights and responsibilities of parents for the health care of their minor children. This ethical issue bears heavily on the practice of the many social workers in abortion clinics, family planning services, and prenatal and obstetrical units.

Truthful information as the basis for patient choice or patient consent is another dimension of patients' rights in both medical and social aspects of health care. An unusual example of the former is a policy developed at the burn center, Los Angeles County–University of

---

*The Door, an integrated service agency, also provides psychiatric services; social services; legal, education, and vocation counseling services; drug education and prevention services; a learning center; vocation training; creative and rehabilitation workshops; a recreation and physical education program; a Country and Wilderness Program; and an Eastern Alternatives and Martial Arts program. This information was secured from annual reports, visits to the agency, and communication with social work staff, 1972–80.

Southern California Medical Center. When burns are of a severity that no previous patient has survived, and while patients are still lucid and mentally competent, during the first few hours after the injury, they are informed about their condition and asked if they wish "to choose between a full therapeutic regimen or ordinary care, reassured that with either choice, the burn team will provide the constant presence of human caring and full use of its professional skills" (Imbus and Zawacki, 1977, p. 308).

Two sisters, 68 and 70 years of age, and their husbands were searching for a schizophrenic daughter who had disappeared after her discharge from a psychiatric hospital. While their car waited for a stoplight, a nearby construction machine hit a gasoline line. The spraying gas exploded, leveling a city block and igniting the car.

The sisters arrived in our burn center two hours later. The younger sister had 91 per cent full-thickness, 92 per cent total-body burn, with moderate smoke inhalation; the older had 94.5 per cent full-thickness, 95.5 per cent total-body burn, with severe smoke inhalation. The burn team agreed that survival was unprecedented in both cases. Both women were alert and interviewed separately.

The younger sister asked about death directly, looking intently into the physician's eyes. When he answered, she replied matter-of-factly, "Well, I never dreamed that life should end like this, but since we all have to go sometime, I'd like to go quietly and comfortably. I don't know what to do about my daughter..."

After she was made comfortable, the nurse obtained a description of the missing daughter and possible whereabouts. The social workers alerted the police to look for her, and telephoned relatives, informing them of the accident as gently as could be conveyed by telephone. The husbands were located at another burn unit. An attempt was made to arrange a final spousal conversation, but both husbands were intubated. [p. 309]

The older sister doubted that her injuries were severe because she was not in severe pain, and the injury to nerve endings was explained to her. She was offered complete therapy, and refused but continued to deny she was dying.

The sisters' beds were placed next to each other so that they could see and touch each other easily. They discussed funeral arrangements and then joked, in the next breath, about the damage done to their hair. The hospital chaplain prayed with them. By active listening, he was able to convey to the older that her husband was not to blame for the accident as she had thought. "It's good to go out not cursing him after all our years together," she said. The younger sister died several hours later after her sister lapsed into a coma; the older died the next day. The daughter was not located. [p. 309]

In the case of those patients who deny the seriousness of their condition, the denial is interpreted as a wish to live, and full thereapeutic efforts are provided. In the case of those who truly hear the facts that no patient of similar age and size of burn has ever survived and then elect to avoid heroic measures receive ordinary medical measures and sufficient amounts of medication for the control of pain. Both types of patients, as well as those who actively choose heroic measures, may change their minds, and their decision is reviewed with them daily (Imbus and Zawacki, 1977).

Some of the ethical and humane issues in the provision of information to terminally ill patients will be discussed in Chapter 8.

Information affects patients' rights in many ways. For example, patients have long been denied access to their medical records, but this prohibition has begun to yield to court decisions, efforts to pass "direct access" laws, consumer demand, and the conviction among some physicians that access to information by the patient leads to improved health care. In at least twelve states patients have a legal right to see their hospital records. Patients in VA hospitals have had the right of access since the passage of the Federal Privacy Act in 1974. But proposed federal legislation to extend the right to patients in all hospitals failed passage in Congress in 1980.

In health organizations where social work entries are made directly into the patient's chart, the right to access should have an equally beneficent effect on social work clients. In health care settings where social workers maintain their own records, and in states where direct-access laws are not in place, social work departments are moving rapidly to make their records accessible to patients, now also required under the revised NASW Code of Ethics.

Another aspect of information bearing on patient rights is confidentiality. Social workers subscribe to the principle of confidentiality and protection of the client's privacy as a matter of ethics and based on professional values. The revised NASW Code of Ethics includes the following provisions:

1. The social worker should share with others confidences revealed by clients, without their consent, only for compelling professional reasons.
2. The social worker should inform clients fully about the limits of confidentiality in a given situation, the purposes for which information is obtained, and how it may be used.
3. The social worker should afford clients reasonable access to any official social work records concerning them.
4. When providing clients with access to records, the social worker should take due care to protect the confidences of others contained in those records.
5. The social worker should obtain informed consent of clients before taping, recording, or permitting third party observation of their activities. ["NASW Code of Ethics," 1980]

Situations inevitably arise for the social worker in health care settings, in which information must be shared without consent of the client. "Compelling professional reasons" might include preventing child abuse, preventing the spread of disease, and the diagnostic and treatment imperatives of other team members. In such cases ethical behavior demands that the client be aware that the information is being shared and why, thereby maintaining some protection of his or her right to participation in, and maintaining mutality of, decisions (Fanning, 1976).

The issues of patient choice and decision-making, informed consent, and ethical behaviors of health professionals, including social workers, are central to equitable and quality care in all health organizations. Mechanic (1979) suggests three organizational means for minimizing inequality between professionals and patients: effective grievance procedures, ombudsmen, and extrainstitutional pressures (p. 118). *Grievance procedures* should include involvement of consumers or their representatives and should also provide for staff initiative in addressing problems and abuses. The role of *ombudsman* (sometimes also called patient representative) is that of an advocate. But it creates ambiguity for the person as an employee of the organization whose practices she is expected to monitor. Nevertheless, such a person can help with problems of communication between patients and health professionals as an alternative to inflexible rules and regulations in those situations, at least, where a social worker is not involved. Many health organizations have drawn up statements of rights, which they distribute to patients. Such *extrainstitutional pressures* decrease inequality by providing clear expectations regarding surgical consent, research participation, organ donation, autopsy permission, and the like. They provide "criteria by which outside groups can document failure in institutional operations" (p. 120).

The same issues of client choice and decision-making, informed consent, and ethical behavior are also central to social workers' individual practices and the social work department's policies and programs.

> The medical social worker confronts a host of ethical conflicts because, in the health care setting, the goal, role, purpose, and even the client are often unclear. Social workers must resolve value dilemmas as they attempt to deliver services and meet their various obligations. If they are to make ethical choices, they must also grasp the intricacies of the particular milieu. [Ross, 1982, p. 96]

Ross suggests that dilemmas arise from the institution's purpose, the social work role, relationships with colleagues, relationships with clients, and the nonmedical nature of social work practice. Conflicts that arise between the needs or wishes of the family and those of the patient often require an ethical choice by the social worker.

Concern for patient rights has led to increased interest in the satisfaction of clients of social work services. Some social work departments participate in the health organization's patient questionnaire; others design their own instruments, which generally elicit data more pertinent to the department in taking any needed corrective action.

Dilemmas Posed by Technology

Advances in biomedical technology have not only contributed to costs, as described in Chapter 1, but they have also created harsh moral dilemmas for patients, families, and health care professionals, including social workers. Resuscitation of terminally ill patients, renal dialysis, coronary-artery surgery, *in vitro* fertilization, organ transplants, fetal monitoring, and fetal surgery lead to conflicts of moral, ethical, and sometimes religious values. When resources are scarce, questions arise about who is to be served and about the relative value of spending huge financial and staff resources on the care of a few rather than spending them on less advanced but less expensive interventions on behalf of far greater numbers. For example, in 1981 a young woman, ten days postdelivery, was admitted to Columbia–Presbyterian Hospital, New York City, suffering from an unusual blood disorder. The cost of the needed (and rare) drug came to $261,800, and the total hospital bill was $333,858, including 225 laboratory tests. The patient was covered by Medicaid. In line with 1981 Medicaid rates, the hospital was paid a total of $12,600 in the case of this patient, while the hospital assumed the balance.

> And now the complex methods by which the bill was paid are going to raise hospital bills for thousands of other patients and their health-insurance carriers.
>   What is the alternative? To let a patient die? "We knew we were getting into big money, but we had no choice," says Dr. Frederick Rapoport, the hematologist . . . who arranged the superexpensive medications given the woman. . . . "We couldn't let [the cost] influence our decisions on what had to be done." (*Wall Street Journal*, December 10, 1981).

Another kind of dilemma occurs every day in neonatal intensive care units. "'Withholding care from all newborns weighing 1000 grams [about 2.2 pounds] or less to avert the exceptional costs of the severely abnormal survivors would take the lives of many potentially normal babies,' said Dr. Peter Budetti of the University of California at San Francisco, who, with colleagues, conducted a study for the Federal Office of Technology Assessment" (*New York Times*, March 30, 1982).

But because modern technology is now able to keep alive severely affected newborns who would have died not long ago, parents and their physicians face difficult decisions concerning heroic measures. These decisions are made not on the basis of system cost but most often on the basis of the future quality of life for the child, or in some instances on the quality of life and financial and emotional costs for the parents and siblings. In the case of survival where there is profound physical and/or mental handicap, parents may initiate or be guided by others to a second round of decision-making with respect to home care or institutional care. All these decisions are accompanied by grief, guilt, fear, anger, and sometimes the attribution of blame to others, especially the spouse. If the cause is genetic, the parents may seek or be referred to genetic counseling. Again, emotional responses are apt to be deep and extensive. In all these areas of decision, social workers in neonatal intensive care units, Ob-Gyn services, pediatric units, genetic counseling services, institutions for the physically handicapped and developmentally disabled, and other pertinent settings have an important function in providing emotional support to the parents and other family members as they make decisions and in mobilizing social supports.

> Sometimes the families are so distraught or so frightened that they will not or cannot say what they want done. Doctors may decide, then, not to operate on infants with major birth defects or they may decide to withhold antibiotics from senile patients who develop respiratory infections. [*Science,* August 31, 1979]

In recent years the decision-making process with respect to incompetent patients, including the senile and the comatose as well as newborn, has been referred to the courts. This use of two-party adversarial litigation, in the judgment of some, "reflects the failure of the policy process to recognize fully the public and multifaceted character of modern scientific and technological development" (Jasanoff and Nelkin, 1981). Others are concerned that treatment decisions should remain with physicians, with the participation of family members, and perhaps with the concurrence of several disinterested physicians documented in the medical record. The latter would help dispel concerns about the private, almost clandestine, nature of the decision-making process (Jasanoff and Nelkin, 1981; *Science,* August 31, 1979).

As of this writing only four states (Minnesota, North Carolina, Alabama, and New York) and some individual hospitals have developed guidelines for withholding emergency resuscitation from a terminally ill hospital patient undergoing cardiac or respiratory arrest. Such guidelines have no legal authority, but they have been developed out of a concern for possible criminal and civil consequences. "The issue of withholding cardiopulmonary resuscitation from the dying is ethically, medically, and legally distinct from the issue of withdrawing life-support measures once given" (*New York Times,* September 19, 1982).

The Saikewicz decision handed down by the Supreme Judicial Court of Massachusetts in November 1977 was frequently interpreted as requiring the court's permission if doctors were to issue "do not resuscitate" orders for dying patients. For example, it was reported by an attorney at Boston University School of Medicine that "a terminally ill woman was subjected to cardiac defibrillation 70 times in a 24-hour period before she finally died" (*Science*, August 31, 1979).

Environmental Pollution

Other kinds of technological developments have created pressures that bear heavily on health and disease, the health care system, and health care organizations. These include nuclear and toxic wastes in our communities and the presence of carcinogens and other pollutants in industry and in our food, water, and air. All of these affect the health not only of those now living but of coming generations. Many bioscientists and citizen groups worry about the long-term consequences of weakening environmental protection, diminishing the enforcement potential of the Occupational Safety and Health Administration (OSHA), and deregulating industry in matters of health and safety.

The extent of death, injury, and chronic disease and disability generated by the workplace makes it one of the most dangerous of environments. Indeed, a book on the topic is entitled, *Work Is Dangerous for Your Health* (Stellman and Daum, 1973). The rates of accidents due to fire, explosion, electrocution, unsafe machinery, falls, moving and lifting equipment, and so on, are still high. OSHA estimates that in the past thirty years more U.S. workers have been killed in the workplace than in any modern war. Each year 16,000 workers die in industrial accidents, and one out of ten is injured.

Safety hazards, however, are far easier to control than health hazards, because the latter are more difficult to recognize and their consequences may not appear for many years. One hundred thousand die from occupational disease and 390,000 more suffer work-related illness or disability.

In 1973 the National Institute of Occupational Safety and Health (NIOSH) listed 12,000 toxic materials. Just one, asbestos as an exemplar, can give an indication of the extent of the problem. Asbestos is used in many occupations and is a significant cause of cancer, asbestosis, and a variety of other illnesses.

Irving J. Selikoff, Chief of Environmental Medicine at Mount Sinai Hospital in New York, estimates that about 27.5 million workers were exposed to asbestos from 1940 to 1980. That estimate does not include their families, who may have breathed the fibers the workers brought home on their clothes, nor people living near industries that used asbestos. Neither does it include people exposed to asbestos products. It is estimated that six million schoolchildren, for instance, attended schools where asbestos building material is in various stages of crumbling.

Dr. Selikoff said medical evidence suggested that exposure to asbestos resulted in 8,000 to 10,000 cancer deaths a year above the normal cancer rate in the population. [*New York Times*, September 5, 1982]

Besides fibers and harmful dusts, metals, chemicals, and radiation, such other stressors as excessive noise, heat or cold, and temporal demands such as rotating shifts can, over time, lead to disease.* Health hazards to employees may be present not just in mines, textile mills, and industrial plants but in dentists' offices, hospital operating rooms, and some other professional and clerical settings.

Despite the extent of occupational mortality and morbidity, few educational programs of any of the health professions, including social work, have a place for occupational health and disease in their curricula. Therefore, many illnesses coming to the attention of personnel in health care settings are never diagnosed as occupational in origin. The appalling statistics are probably only the tip of the iceberg.

Few health care organizations provide programs and services directed to the diagnosis of occupational disease and to action dealing with the potential effects on other workers beyond therapy for the afflicted. Notable exceptions appear here and there in occupational health clinics in medical centers. In these settings, new roles are being developed for the social worker on the team as skilled gatherer of pertinent occupational history and workplace data, Workers' Compensation Advocate (Shanker, 1983), and collaborator with labor organizations, lawyers, and government officials.

Since many patients are still unaware of a possible connection between their illness or disability and the workplace, the social worker in *all* health organizations must have knowledge of occupational hazards and should review work histories with all clients (for present stress factors in any illness—preexistent or consequential—as well as for factors in the kinds of illnesses being discussed here). All health care social workers

> . . . can join forces with those who are fighting for enactment and strict enforcement of health and safety legislation. They can demand that every candidate for public office take a stand on the issue of job health and safety.
>
> They can call their governor and write their Congressman [sic]. They can picket an unsafe factory alongside the workers. They can protest company

*Findings from a study conducted by the Stanford Research Institute International and sponsored by NIOSH "confirm studies of European shift workers that demonstrate a significantly greater difficulty in adapting to work schedules experienced by all other categories of shift worker than by day shift workers. Rotating shift workers, who not only work at unconventional hours but who move from shift to shift, clearly encounter the most difficulty in adjusting their biological rhythms and patterns to their work schedules. Shift work may well pose a distinct health hazard for certain rotating shift workers." Twelve hundred nurses and a similar number of food processors constituted the study sample (Tasto et al., 1978, p. iii).

practices at a shareholders' meeting. They can make speeches and write letters to the editor. . . . Those who work in public health can insist that job health become a major ingredient of every public health program, and that workers and their unions be involved to the maximum. . . . All of us know that the goal of a safe and healthy work place will not be won overnight. . . . But what is essential is that we begin now—because time is not on our side. [A. Miller, 1976, pp. 94–95].

Demographic Factors

Demographic aspects are a potent source of external pressures affecting health care organizations and social work practice. The proportion of aged persons in the population is steadily increasing, accounting in part for the prevalence of chronic disease over acute illness. And,

> . . . the largest growth now is in the group over 75 years of age, which is projected to make up 5 per cent of the population by 1990 as compared with the present proportion of 3.7 per cent. The hospital-admission rate for patients 75 and over is 54 per cent higher than the rate for those between 65 and 74. . . . The needs of the aged for longer term care of chronic and mental illness, support services, and special care for the terminally ill are well known. Less widely recognized are the requirements for high-technology services: organ repair and replacement, rehabilitation aids, surgery, and irradiation and chemotherapy for neoplasms. The growth in the elderly population foretells greater demand for a greater variety of services. [McNerny, 1980, p. 1089]

Decreasing birthrates have already been cited as leading to centralization of obstetrical services. However, the alarming increase in teenage parenthood, bringing teenagers and their babies into a growing category of health and social risk, suggests a growing need for ready access to more health care programs offering innovative, quality services to mothers and infants, especially among the poor. While state and local health departments have developed such programs and expanded the more traditional maternal and infant services, these have suffered major cutbacks in federal funding.

Migration patterns also affect health care organizations. The numbers of refugee populations and undocumented Mexican immigrants require carefully planned health services that will be congruent with cultural patterns and will take account of the difficulties experienced by these populations in using the biomedically oriented health services of Western society.

Standard-setting Bodies

A final external factor impinging on the health care organization and the activity of its professional practitioners is professional regulatory institutions. These include the Joint Commission on Accreditation of Hospitals (JCAH); the specialty boards of medicine, surgery, and so forth; licensing bodies of the health professions, including social work (in some states); codes of professional ethics; and membership organizations such as the National Association of Social Workers (NASW). These bodies, and their interaction, influence the nature of programs and forms of practice as, for example, in NASW's efforts to develop licensure and vendorship for social workers. NASW has also negotiated with the JCAH for increased participation of social workers in commission activities, including strengthening the standards for hospital social services. It has also prepared and published *Standards for Social Workers in Health Care Settings* and *Standards for Social Work in Public Health Settings* and is developing standards for social work in nephrology and developmental disabilities. This work was accomplished jointly by the NASW Health Quality Standards Committee and the Society for Hospital Social Work Directors of the American Hospital Association. The society is also working to increase the interest of the graduate schools of social work in meeting the pressing need for specialized curricula for social work in health care. NASW chapters and the national office mobilize membership support for legislative advocacy and coalition-building on matters of health policy and organizational structures.

Summary

Several structural and functional aspects of health care organizations, and external pressures impinging on them, have been examined in this chapter. The interplay among these factors affects the availability of social work positions, the status of the social worker vis-à-vis the other health professionals, and the nature of social work functions, roles, and tasks in health care. And they influence the actual practices, services, and programs of social work.

But the description of the practice context is incomplete without the inclusion of a third—and for social workers the foremost—component: the role of the patient and the dimensions of patienthood. For social workers, the term "clients" is more appropriate, not only on philosophical and professional grounds but because it embraces family members, communities, or special populations to whom the health care social worker may also provide services. However, the term patient is relevant to the next chapter, which considers, in particular, the person who is suffering from illness, injury, or disability; and the role of patient is a significant contextual component of social work practice.

CHAPTER 3

Illness and the Sick Role as Context for Social Work Practice

Health, Disease, Illness, and Sickness

"HEALTH," DIFFICULT TO DEFINE, in biomedical terms has been considered freedom from disease. Yet a person may harbor disease without having symptoms or, conversely, may feel unwell without having a discoverable disease. The biomedical definition of health as the absence of disease tends also to focus on disorder rather than on the promotion of wellness. It also inhibits the view of the patient as a total person in a total environment by overlooking the personal and environmental dimensions in health and illness. In the 1940s the World Health Organization defined health as a state of complete physical, mental, and social wellbeing—a definition criticized as an unattainable ideal for individuals or societies. Ahmed, Kolker, and Coelho (1979) define health as "*a multidimensional process* involving the well-being of the whole person in the context of his environment" (p. 9; Italics in original). This is a more useful definition for the social worker, because it takes into account personal and cultural variations in how health and illness are defined and experienced.

"Disease" is explained in the biomedical model as deviations from the norm of measurable biochemical variables (Engel, 1977). "Illness" refers to the subjective state of being unwell, of experiencing distress or pain. Just as organic malfunctioning or disease may not be accompanied by subjective discomfort, "illness" can be experienced in the absence of disease. Whereas disease is a biological concept, illness is a sociopsychological one, and it includes the cultural meaning of the discomfort or

34

pain to the patient and her family. Kleinman (1979, p. 58) suggests that in situations where only "disease" is treated, care will be less satisfactory to the patient and less clinically effective than in situations where both "disease" and "illness' are treated together. Problems of illness and problems of disease are complementary, and both require intervention for effective care. The work of Mechanic over the last two decades (1961; 1966; 1970; 1972) clarifies this notion of illness. His concept of illness behaviors refers to how an individual experiences and defines symptoms, illness, and disability; attributes meaning to them; and takes action with respect to them. An important aspect is the nature and quality of symptoms and their impact on capacity and functioning. But the meaning attributed to symptoms is also affected by their interplay with cultural patterns, life difficulties, age, sex, peer pressures, the social and geographic accessibility of the health care facility, and its social arrangements (Mechanic, 1976a, pp. 161–176; 1976b).

"Sickness," in contrast to "disease" and "illness," is a social concept. It refers to a social label applied by others and accepted by the individual (Ahmed et al., 1979, p. 11). It is often assumed to reflect "disease" or "illness" but may actually be unrelated to either one. Some conditions previously labeled sinful and requiring religious intervention, or criminal and requiring punitive intervention, are now regarded as sick and requiring intervention by health care professionals. Fox (1977) declares that society is becoming medicalized as more and more behaviors that deviate from social norms are defined as "sickness." Examples are child abuse, alcoholism and drug abuse, obesity, and some behaviors now labeled mental illness. Other conditions, previously defined as "sickness" are slowly being demedicalized. These include certain sexual behaviors and, to some extent, birthing and dying.

The illness role is deviant, but it differs from other deviance roles, such as sinner or criminal, in that the patient presumably enters it through no fault of his own. As Parsons and Fox (1952) pointed out, the illness role permits the patient to default on his obligations and responsibilities and to become dependent on the ministrations of others—as long as he does everything possible to recover, including seeking and following medical advice. Symptoms may be ambiguous, however, and individuals differ in their evaluations of the costs and benefits of the illness role. Accepting the social identity of "ill person" therefore involves a process of negotiation between the individual, his social network, and the physician. If there is consensus, the social identity of "ill person" is clear, and treatment can begin. However, because there are differences among cultures in how illness is conceptualized, and often differences in conceptualizations between the individual and her family, or between them and the physician, consensus may be difficult to reach. In such instances, treatment will be adversely affected (Kleinman, 1979, p. 58).

Becoming a Patient

Suchman (1965) hypothesized five stages that a person may pass through of perceiving himself to be ill: (1) the symptom experience; (2) assumption of the sick role; (3) medical care contact; (4) dependent-patient role; and (5) the stage either of recovery or rehabilitation. In the first stage the individual feels unwell or weak and incapacitated for fulfilling his responsibilities, or experiences changes in appearance, and so forth. He must make a decision based on his interpretation of the meaning of the symptoms or discomfort. "Some symptoms, such as a fractured leg, are so clear-cut and disabling that they allow very few socially acceptable attributions (or only one). Other symptoms are amenable to alternative meanings: myocardial pain may be perceived as indigestion; a severe headache as a manifestation of stress; and lack of energy may be defined as either a physical or psychological problem" (Mechanic, 1970, p. 164). The person may experience anxiety about the meaning of the symptoms, he may deny their significance and delay seeking treatment, or he may resort to folk medicine or self-treatment.

The second stage may be more clearly understood within the conception of illness behavior rather than as sick role assumption, which tends to come later in the formulations previously described. If the person has acknowledged the likelihood of illness, then he may enter a stage of seeking advice or information from family or friends about the meaning of the symptoms and what to do about them. His network or lay referral structure is also a source of provisional permission to relinquish responsibilities and to be cared for. In our society, however, it is only the physician who has "official" authority to declare a person ill and excused from responsibility (Ahmed et al., 1979, p. 11). At this stage there is again a decision to be made about denying the illness or continuing with lay treatment or self-treatment, and/or seeking medical advice. If medical care is sought, the person enters the third stage, medical care contact. In the consultation with the physician the individual receives or is denied legitimation of the sick role. If the role is authorized and accepted, the patient and physician negotiate the treatment to be followed. If the physician does not authorize the sick role or if the person is dissatisfied with the proposed treatment, he may seek the advice of another physician or return to lay remedies and self-treatment.

If the person and physician agree, however, the individual enters the dependent-patient stage (actually the illness role as it was defined earlier) and becomes a patient. In doing so, he transfers control of his condition to the physician and other health professionals. Nevertheless, he still may terminate the treatment at any time, or he may so enjoy the secondary gains of the role that he does not fulfill his responsibility to try to recover. Or, in some instances, he may resist the dependent-patient role and attempt to retain or regain control over his condition to a point that interferes with successful treatment. This behavior may result in his being labeled a problem patient with potentially negative consequences. However, assuming an active role by disregarding older norms for the patient role is becoming more prevalent as other societal processes such as consumerism exert their influence.

Where treatment proceeds successfully, the patient next enters the final stage of recovery in which he relinquishes the patient role and resumes his usual responsibilities. In some instances, however, the patient may not recover because of the nature of the illness or disability and must assume, instead, the role of chronic invalid or of rehabilitee. All three outcomes, but especially the latter two, may be fraught with difficulties. Resuming usual familial and work roles may be difficult because of interim events and processes occurring in the family, at the work site, or in the perceptions, conceptions, and actions of the former patient. In rehabilitation or in chronic invalidism, vastly more is at stake, including a new self-concept; inability to carry out one's usual and valued familial, work, and community roles; changes in physical and other capacities; physical and psychic pain; and, in some instances, having to adapt to institutionalization.

Figure 3–1 (p. 38) shows the five stages of the illness experience and potential outcomes for each stage. It is clear from the diagram that denial of illness or rejection of care can occur at any stage and may lead to the individual's exit from the system.

This model of illness experience is a generalization. In any episode of illness, not every stage may be involved. The patient suffering a heart attack, for example, may proceed immediately from the symptom experience stage to the medical care stage. A person living alone who experiences any symptoms she regards as serious may not go through the second stage. In office practice it frequently happens that the medical care stage itself results in immediate recovery (for example, through illness-specific medication), so that the dependent-patient or sick role stage is skipped. There are temporal variations as well. Duration of the first stage depends, in part, on the severity of the symptoms and how they are interpreted. The duration of the third and fourth stages will vary from case to case. Social work has most often made its contributions to health care during the fourth and fifth stages of the illness experience. In the fourth stage, for example, the patient and family may face many unanticipated and disquieting consequences of the illness. In the final stage, both patient and family may experience various kinds of "reentry" problems, even in recovery, but especially where the patient is inducted into the new and terrifying roles of chronic invalid or disabled

FIGURE 3-1. The Stages of Illness Experience

	I Symptom Experience	II Assumption of the Sick Role	III Medical Care Contact	IV Dependent-Patient Role	V Recovery and Rehabilitation
Decision	Something is wrong	Relinquish normal roles	Seek professional advice	Accept professional treatment	Relinquish sick role
Behaviors	Application of folk medicine, self-medication	Request provisional validation for sick role from members of lay referral system—continue lay remedies	Seek authoritative legitimation for sick role—negotiate treatment procedures	Undergo treatment procedures for illness—follow regimen	Resume normal roles
Outcomes	Denial (flight into health) → Delay → Acceptance	Denial → Acceptance	Denial / Shopping → Confirmation	Rejection / Secondary gain → Acceptance	Refusal (chronic sick role) / Malingerer → Acceptance

Source: Rodney M. Coe, *Sociology of Medicine*, 2d ed. (New York: McGraw-Hill, Inc., 1978), p. 116. Used with permission.

rehabilitee. Both the individual and the family are likely to have needs stemming from chronic illness or rehabilitation that will require the services of the social worker.

In some neighborhood-based health organizations such as primary care facilities, centers for victims of rape and family violence, family planning services, and emergency rooms of some hospitals, staff social workers may also help with the tasks of the first three stages. This activity is likely to increase as social workers become more involved in health promotion, primary prevention, and early case-finding at the community level. Indeed, all social workers in all fields of practice have opportunities to help individuals, families, and groups with appropriate decision-making in matters of health and illness during the first three stages by considering with them the available alternatives, dealing with access problems, clarifying misperceptions, and influencing social network and organizational responsiveness.

Conflicting Explanatory Models of Illness:
The Influence of Culture

Kleinman, Eisenberg, and Good (1978), in examining the influence of culture in illness behavior, postulate the existence of three domains of health care: popular or lay care; folk care; and scientific health care. The domain of popular or lay care includes self-treatment, family care, and the advice of network figures such as friends, neighbors, druggists, and work mates. While some ethnic groups might rely on herbs, amulets, and rituals, white middle-class persons rely on aspirin, sun lamps, over-the-counter sleeping aids, "tonics," digestive aids, vitamins, and the latest diet fad—however inappropriate they may be to a biomedical explanation of symptoms or illness.

The domain of folk care includes spiritists, shamans, and other healers outside the licensed professional organizations. It is estimated that 70 to 90 percent of all illness is treated in these two domains (Kleinman et al., 1978, p. 251). This is not necessarily undesirable since most users find relief from illness and occasionally even from disease through such care (Delgado, 1979). Moreover, if even a small percentage of those now receiving care in the two realms of lay care and folk care were, instead, to appeal to the professional domain, the health care system would be overwhelmed.

Even more significant for the social worker, however, is Kleinman and associates' (1978) suggestion that each domain has its own explanatory model of illness, including explanations of cause, onset, course of sickness, and treatment goals. The explanatory models of the lay and folk realms are usually far different from that of the biomedical realm of scientific health care. When the patient holds a different explanatory model from that of the professional practitioner, communication about illness and disease is apt to be distorted, clinical management adversely affected, and patient satisfaction diminished. Here are two case examples provided in the study cited:

A 26-year-old Guatemalan woman who had resided in the U.S. for 10 years and who was being treated for severe regional enteritis with intravenous hyperalimentation and restriction of all oral intake had become angry, withdrawn, and uncooperative. She believed her problem to be caused by the witchcraft of her fiancé's sister. She also believed that because she was no longer receiving food by mouth, and especially because she could no longer regulate her hot/cold balance of nutrients [for an explanation of this concept, see Harwood, 1971], the basis of the traditional folk medical system she grew up in, she had been written off by her doctors as unlikely to live. Her behavior followed directly from this mistaken belief. She was unable to talk about her ideas because of fear of ridicule, and her doctors were totally unaware of this problem, except as manifested in her difficult behavior. [Kleinman et al., 1978, p. 254]

A 56-year-old Italian-American former railroad conductor, recovering from an acute myocardial infarction in the coronary care unit of the Massachusetts General Hospital, had been evaluated in the same facility 2 years before for chest pain. At that time his cardiologist gave him a full explanation of the etiology, pathophysiology, and course of atherosclerotic cardiovascular disease. During the more recent hospitalization the patient reported a rather different model of his problem. He had never told his cardiologist about this model, even though it was his chief belief about his illness and had been since the time of his last admission. In his view and that of his family, there are two major heart diseases: angina pectoris and coronary thrombosis. The former is mild and self-limited. He believed that the former and the latter are *mutually exclusive,* so that to suffer from the milder one is to have the good fortune not to have to worry about experiencing the more severe and dangerous one. He thus justified his almost complete failure to comply with his medical regimen on logical grounds, understood and supported by his family, who had shared his denial of serious illness. [Kleinman et al., 1978, p. 255; Italics in the original]

Such discrepancies between the patient's and the physician's explanatory models, which lead to poor or inadequate care, have implications for the social worker. In many health care organizations, she may be the only professional who is aware of and concerned about the cultural and social factors in illness behavior. Kleinman and colleagues believe that the patient's explanatory model must be elicited and understood, the biomedical model explained in lay terms (by the physician), and the two models openly compared for the patient and practitioner to identify discrepancies, clarify value conflicts, and plan appropriate patient education. Needed information includes what the patient thinks caused the illness, why it started when it did, what the illness does, how severe it is, what kind of treatment it needs and what kinds of results are hoped for, what kinds of problems it has caused, and what is most feared about the illness. The authors assert that such information ''should be recorded in the patient's record as *illness problems* alongside the list of *disease problems. Illness interventions,* primarily psychosocial in nature, should be formulated and applied along with *disease interventions''* (p. 257). [Italics in the original.] Sometimes, it is advisable also to elicit the family's explanatory model because it may conflict with the patient's as well as with the physician's. The suggested questions need to be framed, of course, in language suitable to the individual patient and family.

In many health care organizations, however, service arrangements are based on the biomedical model, and treatment is directed to disease. The patient's and family's explanatory models, which remain unknown, may interfere with that treatment, and their pressing concerns about the illness as experienced may be overlooked. Perhaps in all cases, but certainly in those involving management problems, the social worker has an opportunity to make an important contribution to effective care by securing information about the patient's model and communicating it to the physician or the health care team. In the following case the social worker may have missed just such an opportunity:

Anita Garcia, an unmarried Mexican-American woman, age sixty-four, suffers from degenerative joint disease and possible angina. She is being treated at a neighborhood health center where she has been seen for six years for these complaints and for others in which an organic base was not found. In the course of treatment she became dependent on *Dalmane* prescribed for sleeplessness some four years earlier. Present efforts by the physician to withdraw the drug have caused the patient to become very angry, manipulative, and difficult to manage. She was referred to the psychiatrist (Anglo), whose diagnosis was "Dalmane-dependent; personality disorder," and he referred her to the social worker (also Anglo) for therapy. The patient's response to the referral was that "talking" would do no good, and without the drug her leg would become paralyzed, she would have a heart attack, and so forth. Nevertheless, she did agree to see the social worker for one time.

The worker learned that the patient was brought to the U.S. at age twelve, after living with her grandparents in Mexico from babyhood when her parents emigrated to the United States. She had never married, and her only sibling, a younger brother, said to be a policeman, died at age twenty-seven of "poisoning." She worked as a music teacher, taking care of her parents until their deaths. When the patient was forty, her mother died of a heart attack (age at death not given), and when she was fifty-three her father died after a long illness (his age and cause of death not given). She now lives alone in the house that had been owned by her parents, and she receives Supplementary Security Income (SSI) and food stamps.

The patient blamed her health problems on having had to work so hard taking care of her parents that "my physical nerves were weakened." About nursing her father during his final illness, she said, "I worked so hard that I got paralyzed in one leg, and I couldn't take care of him any longer. So the two of us were paralyzed, and someone else had to take care of us. But I sacrificed my life for my father, and I feel good about it." In the social worker's assessment, the patient is described as responding to stress (source and nature not specified) by somatic complaints and coercing others into taking care of her. The patient's extensive, manipulative demands for time and attention were said to be due to her repressed anger toward her parents for having had to nurse them through their illnesses.

Even leaving aside such questions as the possible iatrogenic (physician-caused) nature of the drug dependency and the patient's possible fear of dying of a heart attack like her mother and at her mother's age, the assessment has limited use in planning intervention, because cultural elements were not considered. The speculation about repressed anger toward the parents might be valid, but it does overlook the nature of generational and familial relationships among Mexican-Americans and the value placed on caring for elderly family members. Beyond this, however, it might have been helpful in managing the patient's concerns and her resistance to medical advice, had understanding been sought of her own explanatory model of her illnesses. Some hint of the importance of her model lies in the idea of working so hard that her physical nerves were weakened, causing one leg to become paralyzed.

Psychological and Social Factors in the Patient Role

Illness and the responses to it are shaped not only by cultural factors but by psychological and social-structural factors as well. What some people regard as problems in living, others may experience as illness. Ms. Garcia may have felt socially and emotionally isolated and needing the attention of others to validate her very existence. One-half of ambulatory patients seek help with vague or generalized physical complaints for which no somatic base can be found. Such efforts to assume the sick role represent a means of coping with stressful problems in living; they represent a search for social support and reassurance, sanction for the relinquishment of role responsibilities, or, perhaps, financial and other gains (Mechanic, 1977).

Hospital emergency services are geared to caring for the immediate needs of patients suffering from accidents and acute episodes of illness. But such services are also populated by large numbers of persons who staff feel are using the services inappropriately for nonmedical concerns. Some observers even suggest that the urban hospital's emergency room has taken over the functions of a family agency or other social services during the late evening and weekend hours, when such agencies are closed. It may also be that for many persons it is easier to seek help with a problem they have defined medically instead of sociopsychologically.

Sometimes, also, the medicalizing of problems in living may be the result of emotionally or culturally determined inability to distinguish between the psychological and the physical origins of a particular symptom. For example, languor, loss of appetite, and sleeplessness may be regarded by the patient as signs of somatic illness, with no thought of the possibility of a depressive origin. (Certainly, an investigation of possible organic factors must be made before a diagnosis is reached.) Too often, when no somatic base is found, such persons are dismissed as malingerers or worse, when their psychic pain is real. In HMOs and other prepaid plans for health care, and even in some emergency rooms and outpatient clinics, physicians' workloads and income arrangements may not allow for the time required to understand and deal with a patient's problem in living that is masked by a somatic complaint.

The social worker's function and role in such settings may be crucial in meeting the patient's real needs. An added bonus is the consequent reduction in cost for the organization by saving the physician's time for those situations that require their medical expertise—thereby adding to the value of social work in the perception of administration. There is some evidence, however that many patients do not perceive the social worker on the team in these settings as a potential helper for them; they regard her as a special person for special problems, which they do not believe they have. Instead, they prefer the nurse as someone who is willing to visit their homes and give knowledgeable attention to what ails them. This suggests the necessity for social work practitioners, and the profession, to clarify social work functions and roles in certain ambulatory settings and to educate patients and other team members. Research to secure data on the savings in physicians' time and costs engendered by social work services to the patient population being described will provide a base for seeking support and expansion of social work services.

At the other extreme from this patient population are those who fail to respond appropriately to serious symptoms and even painful illness. Instead, they deny the existence of illness as a way of coping with the anxiety the symptoms arouse. They are apt to enter the health care system so late that treatment is more difficult, and positive outcomes may be jeopardized. For example:

Mrs. Meyer, age fifty-two, white, Jewish, youthful in appearance, was brought to the emergency room of a large Chicago hospital by her sixty-year-old husband. She had fainted at home, and her husband feared she was dying. Although she said she had no health problems now or in the past, she was found to be suffering from diabetic ketoacidosis, peripheral vascular disease, and gangrenous toes of the right foot. The toes were amputated, the foot debrided, and skin grafts from the thigh were made to the amputation site. Mrs. Meyer was started on insulin, but when the nursing staff tried to teach her how to test her urine and other procedures, they discovered she was unable to see well enough for the tasks of self-maintenance. Throughout the fourteen weeks of hospitalization the patient minimized her illness, denied any stress arising from the treatment or the hospitalization, and denied the possibility of a serious eye condition. She maintained an almost euphoric mood, inappropriate to the circumstances. Walking was extremely difficult for her, and the physician ordered orthopedic shoes. When the shoe fitter came, both Mr. and Mrs. Meyer adamantly rejected the shoes because they were too ugly and, in their judgment, were not custom-made.

Mrs. Meyer had not worked in many years but had been an entertainer in her youth. Her husband had at one time been a successful free-lance journalist. Their present financial situation was precarious, as Mr. Meyer's dwindling royalties were their only income. They had no children and said they had no need for friends, as their chief interest was in caring for sick and injured pigeons that visited their window sills. Mr. Meyer was seemingly as unconcerned as his wife about her disease and its poor prognosis and about his own health, although he looked even sicker than his wife. Both consistently refused to talk with the social worker, saying they had no problems, and Mrs. Meyer consistently protested she would be well in a day or so. As discharge approached, the worker renewed her efforts to engage them in planning for their financial and housing needs and posthospital treatment arrangements. Both refused to discuss the possibility of SSI, and Mrs. Meyer declared she would be able to walk to the hospital for outpatient visits from her apartment some blocks away.

On the day before discharge the worker stopped in for one more attempt and found Mr. Meyer standing outside the room. Together they went inside, where Mrs. Meyer was crying bitterly. On seeing her husband, she lashed out at him, saying he had never been a good husband, that he had run away from everything and could never face the truth. Mr. Meyer tried to make light of all this with his customary jocularity. When the worker commented that Mrs. Meyer was upset about many things, the defense gave way. She recalled her mother's serious diabetic condition and, for the first time, expressed her worries about her condition and her fear of returning home. Mr. Meyer began to indicate that he felt guilty at not seeking help for her sooner. She responded to this by saying she had acted "foolishly" in hoping the gangrene would just go away. Both talked of Mr. Meyer's depression and his irritability, which had lost them their friends. The worker's offer of a home visit on the day following discharge, in order to help them with planning, was accepted.

The worker did visit and maintained contact with the Meyers. Subsequently arrangements were made for Mr. Meyer's successful application for SSI and food stamps. He was examined at the clinic, and found to be suffering also from diabetes. Both he and Mrs. Meyer then joined a diabetic group at the hospital, and Mr. Meyer later accepted a referral for outpatient psychiatric treatment for his depression.

In this instance the personal and social meanings attributed to the symptoms, the disease, and their consequences were undoubtedly influenced by the interplay of each spouse's thoughts, feelings, and perceptions; genetic-constitutional factors; their past experiences and sense of pride and independence; their own marital interaction; and their differing capacities and coping styles. Perhaps a different approach on the worker's part might have engaged them earlier. But her seemingly simple dropping by continually and offering help and, most of all, her visit on the last day helped avert a potential posthospital disaster. But with the social worker's help Mrs. Meyer began to accept the reality of her chronic illness and moved into the tasks of coping with it. Mr. Meyer gradually accepted the role of patient and successfully negotiated the health care system for sanction and treatment. Worker and clients together improved the environment through financial entitlements, transportation services, group affiliations, and the initiation of a search for better housing.

Patienthood

Most of what has been hypothesized, observed, and reported in the literature about the patient's perception of patienthood refers to the hospitalized patient. This probably reflects the greater impact on the hospital patient of a total-institution type of social structure than the impact on the ambulatory patient of the structure of an office practice or other outpatient service. The illness role, patienthood, is not merely a response to illness. It is a formal social role involving reciprocal expectations, perceptions, and relations with a variety of health care professionals. It must therefore be understood also within the role network or social structure of the organization itself. Hence, some of the aspects identified in relation to the hospital patient will have a bearing on the ambulatory patient as well, but to a lesser degree. And other aspects will not apply at all.

A patient entering a hospital for hemorrhoid surgery writes, "The hospital to which I reported is a large, university institution of the type that health-policy planners would like to take apart and reassemble for purposes of 'cost-containment,' improved community service, rationalization of departments and all the other organizational ills that are said to have accumulated in our health-care system without anyone's having paid much attention.

"The admissions maze through which I was routed could have profited from a study by a first-year student in traffic management, but it was reassuring to find that each person with whom I dealt at one or another counter or window was obsessively concerned with ascertaining that I was, indeed, the individual identified on the sheaf of papers that followed me about. . . .

"Finally, I was led to a room where I donated a container of urine, was relieved of four vials of blood, and was x-rayed, front and side. Since I had gone through an identical process of fluid collection and photography just a few days earlier, in the course of my annual examination, it occurred to me that the drainage and x-ray exposure need not have been duplicated. But then I thought of the managerial and organizational prowess that would be required for transferring that juice and film from one place to the other. It probably could be done, I figured, with no more than one error per 500,000 transfers, with some saving in health care's grab on the GNP. It occurred to me, however, that the one error would probably accrue to the legal profession's cut of the GNP, and that the overall savings would be washed out. I chose not to advise the technician that the data he had just collected from me were already available a mere three blocks away. . . .

"Installed in my room, I now encountered the experience of being 'clinical material' in a teaching institution. It seemed altogether proper that the surgeon would come by for 'a look.' Not long afterward, a green-robed gentleman, identifying himself as the surgeon's assistant, also came by for a look. Then someone whose identity I didn't quite catch presented himself to take a look. This trio was followed by a nurse who wanted to know my name, age, weight and reason for my presence. The nurse was followed by another nurse, who collected the same information. She, in turn, was followed by a group, of perhaps 10, led by another green-rober, who introduced himself as Doctor someone-or-other; he, too, wished to organize a look, not only for himself, but also for the swarm he led. They looked, exchanged comments and filed out. Whereupon, a young man, also green-robed, showed up and said he wished to have a look.

"At this point, I explained that whatever there was to look at had been exhaustively examined, and that I doubted that there was any need for further scrutiny. He explained that he was a third-year medical student and seemed to suggest that the curriculum required him to have a look. Rather than go into the records as an impediment to medical education, I obliged. The student concluded that part of his studies by recording my name, age, weight and the reason for my presence. . . ." [Greenberg, 1977]*

*Reprinted, by permission of *The New England Journal of Medicine,* 296 (February 3, 1977): 291–292.

And so on through surgery, recovery, and discharge. In a light-hearted way, the writer is recording the dehumanizing processes involved in patienthood that make of the human being a mere object. Such discomforts of patienthood may be considered a fair exchange for the benefits of recovery or of having one's condition meliorated. But many observers have raised a question about how much depersonalization is necessary for treatment. Freidson (1970) suggests that while some practices are the result of bureaucratic problems in service provision and some are related to staff convenience, the most hurtful depersonalizing procedures are those which stem from professional orientations. These are the practices that undermine patients' and family members' hard-won capacities for competence and effectiveness, human relatedness, self-regulation, and the sense of personal identity and dignity.

The central issue for Freidson is the withholding of information from the patient and family. The patient is frequently regarded not as a responsible adult, but as a child who lacks knowledge for understanding the esoteric realm of medicine and who, weakened by illness, cannot handle information vital to her or his continued functioning as an adult. Without information, however, the patient cannot evaluate what is being done to her, why she feels as she does, what to expect next, how long the wait is likely to be, and whether changes she observes in her care and medication are errors or by order. Without information not only is she incompetent in judging the competence of her role partners, but she cannot be fully competent even in carrying out the responsibilities of the patient role. Instead of informed cooperation as a competent adult, she is expected to conform to orders on the basis of faith. Nonconformity labels her as a problem patient. In a way, eliciting the patient's explanatory model and sharing the physician's model, as urged by Kleinman et al. (1978), bear on the issue of information to support the patient's competent participation in the scientific treatment carried out by the physician.

Although the concept of patient rights includes the provision of information, the issue is complicated. On the one hand it is understandable that physicians are chary of giving information that may increase anxiety, lead to depression, and destroy hope. On the other, research findings suggest that patients who are given information about painful diagnostic procedures handle the procedures in a more cooperative way that benefits them and the physician (Johnson and Leventhal, 1974). Patients who are supplied with a description of their surgery and told what to expect afterward are able to leave the hospital on the average of 2 1/2 days earlier than patients having the same operation but without the informational preparation (Egbert et al., 1964). Presumably, the positive feature of information is the lessening of anxiety about the unknown. Efforts to replicate these findings, however, have produced ambiguous results.

Besides, social workers know from experience that some patients do not wish information because of fear of its implications or because they prefer to let matters rest in the hands of the "expert." Some respond to information with more anxiety, not less. Thus the social worker, by assessing the coping capacities of patient and family, can suggest to the physician or the team when information is needed or is likely to be helpful and when it is not.

In addition to his or her concern for the patient's ability to handle and act on information, the busy physician's withholding of information is sometimes the result of not having time to present it, answer the questions it engenders, and deal with the feelings it arouses. Here, too, the social worker may collaborate with the physician by helping the patient and family deal with their feelings about the information, repeating it to them from time to time until it is completely "heard" and assimilated, and helping them consider ways to act constructively on the information. At other times communicating the patient's fears and confusions to the physician—often more easily shared with the social worker than with the awesome physician—results in the physician's immediate willingness to give the needed information or to clarify for the patient whatever has caused the confusion. In these and 'other ways social workers may mediate between patients and other health care professionals in order that patients and families will have the information needed for competent coping with the stress of the illness.

When patients enter the hospital they leave behind family, friends, and valued activities. They enter a new and confusing world of strangers on whom they must depend and to whom they may have to submit for a variety of arrangements and interactions concerning bodily functions normally conducted in complete privacy. Patients also confront diagnostic and treatment activities of a frightening and/or painful nature. The visitation of unintroduced "green-robed" figures who come for a look or to palpate, purge, poke, inject, or question—but not to communicate—leave the patient feeling like an object and without a sense of human relatedness. The lack of privacy is a loss of dignity. The absence of opportunities for social interaction and the consequent loss of relatedness compound the problem. Hours of visiting and routinized regulations about numbers of visitors and length of stay and so on may interfere with the patient's remaining in touch with significant members of his intimate social network who can be important sources of coping strength. In some facilities patients' children or grandchildren below a certain age are not permitted to visit. And since patients come and go, and staff assignments may shift in time or space, there is for the patient a bewildering loss of relatedness to others. This may be particularly upsetting as the patient faces frightening or painful procedures.

Issues of privacy, on the one hand, and opportunity for social interaction, on the other, are tied also to the patient's sense of autonomy or self-directedness, because these issues are related to the capacity for regulating the self–other boundary (Altman, 1975; Schuster, 1976). Altman suggests that people use a variety of spatial, verbal, and nonverbal behaviors to achieve a desired level of privacy. If these behaviors result in more privacy than is desired (not enough social interaction), then the person experiences an unpleasant state of social isolation. If the behaviors result in less privacy than is desired (too much interaction), the person experiences an unpleasant state of crowding or what, in the case of the hospital patient, might be called intrusiveness. Thus individuals, families, and groups normally control their access to others by interpersonal boundary-maintaining processes. Where the physical and social environment of the health care organization interferes with this process, and especially where the interference is not required by the treatment process itself, then the patient loses a sense of adult autonomy or self-regulation.

Schuster (1976), in her study of hospitalized white, middle-class patients, found that the loss of control over the distancing of one's self from others is often aroused by being asked for personal and seemingly irrelevant information, for example, or by being examined by persons other than one's own physician. She identified four major variables influencing the patient's ability to control the interpersonal boundary process: decreased mobility, impairment of consciousness, relaxation of the boundary vis-à-vis other patients, and perception of role (certain territorialities, that is, areas out of bounds to patients; assaults on the personal boundary by injections, sampling of body specimens, and other intrusive procedures; or staff behaviors beyond the legitimate access provided by role, as when a nurse comments unfavorably on the welfare status of a patient). Schuster suggests that while hospitalization inevitably must affect the patient's control over his needs for privacy and for interaction, staff awareness of the problem may help them to reduce unnecessary violation of the patient's control. The task involves striking a balance between protecting the patient's privacy as much as possible and meeting the patient's need for emotional support from staff. Schuster found that patients were unable "to discuss concerns and worries because 'no one was there to listen' or 'they're all in such a hurry.'" Again, the social worker is often in a position to be there to listen and to collaborate with team members in the dual task involved in the patient's control of his interpersonal boundary.

Upon entering the hospital, the patient leaves not only his family but his familiar surroundings and cherished objects, is confined to a small physical space on which he can make no personal imprint, and is clothed in hospital garb without individuality. His personal identity is reduced often to an identification bracelet bearing a number. He may even become known by the number of his room: "364 wants to be turned over" or, worse yet, "The gastric resection in 201 needs a change of dressing." The noise level and the sounds, smells, and sights to which the patient is exposed in his physical setting may be frightening, stressful, or merely annoying. In any case, they are dehumanizing if they are controllable but are not controlled.

Temporal arrangements in hospitals can undermine autonomy (self-directedness), and if they do they are dehumanizing. Long waits in ambulatory services, especially in dismal, dingy settings, can be dehumanizing. Restrictive visiting hours, long and often unexplained waits for what was previously described to the patient as an important procedure, or being awakened for an apparently trivial reason may violate personal biological rhythms and/or cultural orientations to time, and thus undermine autonomy unnecessarily.

Lack of opportunities to participate in decisions about diagnostic procedures, treatment regimens and other matters affecting one's destiny—however modest the participation might be in light of the patient's condition—undermines the capacity for self-regulation and so is dehumanizing. Even the lack of decision-making power in seemingly minor matters such as selecting the color of one's linens, the time for lights out, or having the position of one's bed shifted to take advantage of a window's view, diminishes the capacity for self-regulation and for effective control over one's environment. It is dehumanizing.

Fortunately, these and other practices are disappearing from many ambulatory and hospital settings. But they remain in others and are especially prevalent in the care of the minority poor (Egbert and Rothman, 1977); women; the elderly, especially those in nursing homes; and children, especially those in institutions for the developmentally disabled or the physically handicapped. Wherever such practices exist they damage the patient's (and often the family members') capacities for relatedness, competence, identity, and self-directedness. Moreover, these aspects of patienthood are superimposed on the anxiety, pain, discomfort, and fears connected to the illness or disability. They are also superimposed on the stress felt in other areas of the patient's life, which either antedated the illness or resulted from it. Instead of being eased by professional and organizational practices and procedures, the adaptive burdens on the patient and family may be increased. Dehumanizing practices adversely affect the patient's ability to fulfill the responsibility of the sick role, that is, to manage the stress of the treatment, keep immobilizing negative feelings under control, and bend all efforts toward recovery from illness or effective management of disability.

A practice implication for the social worker is that opportunities must be provided, in every episode of service, for maintaining relatedness, self-directedness, self-esteem, and the sense of competence to the degree permitted by the patient's condition and the family's capacities. In addition, these issues are also significant foci for the social worker's attention in team practice, staffing and clinical rounds, consultation, collaboration, and so on (Germain, 1977). These practice implications will be taken up in later chapters.

There is some evidence that the norms of patienthood as perceived by both patient and staff may actually be dysfunctional and may make their own contribution to the patient's stress. A study of hospital patients' perceptions of the patient role (Tagliarozzo and Mauksch, 1972) found that patients consistently felt that physicians and nurses expected their cooperation as well as their trust and confidence in their physicians. Patients believed they should accommodate their demands to the needs of sicker patients and to the pressures on physicians and nurses. They saw themselves as subject to rewards and punishments, assuming that essential services could be withheld unless they made themselves acceptable to their caretakers.

The researchers suggest that the calmness of the so-called good patient may actually hide anxieties and fears of which the staff are unaware. Open questioning and assertiveness are met with criticism and possible retaliation, so that the patient becomes more passive and conforming out of self-interest. But by engendering feelings of helplessness, staff may make the actual coping with the stress of illness more difficult. The expression of emotional needs is considered outside the dimensions of the "good patient" role, and patients' efforts to conform by suppressing the need for emotional support and more personalized care can be alienating. Here, too, the social worker can play a critical part in treatment as that team member whose own role functions include the encouragement of self-expression, provision of concern, and emotional support. Suchman's (1965) stage of dependent-patient, described earlier, is the stage in the illness experience when the patient transfers control of his condition to the physician. In many instances the patient may consider that this includes his emotional condition, but the physician and nurse may not share this perception of their role responsibility. While the transfer of emotional needs is not legitimized in the norms of the patient role, those needs may become dominant, especially in matters of compliance with medical orders and recovery. However, the provision of emotional support *is* institutionalized in the social worker's role (not by excluding support from other staff members where it is proffered, but by complementing it) so that she can provide what others may be constrained from providing by norms or other restrictions.

It is likely that some of the norms of the sick role will fade in the face of changing norms in general and the growth of consumerism, concern for patient rights, and public demands for greater control of professionals' practices. Indeed, research (Lorber, 1975) indicates that patients now differ in the extent to which they observe the norms of trust, cooperation, uncomplainingness, and undemandingness. Lorber found few differences in attitudes toward the norms of the sick role between men and women. But age and education were a strong influence: younger and better educated patients expressed less conforming attitudes than older, poorly educated patients.

Nevertheless, even in this study medical and nursing staff tended to regard as problem patients those who violated the norms. Ease of management was the basic criterion for the label "good patient"; patients who occupied the time and attention of staff when it was believed unwarranted by their illness earned the label "problem patient." How problem patients are treated depends on the severity of their condition, but potential consequences are the administration of sedative or narcotic drugs, premature discharge, neglect, and referral to a psychiatrist. The implication of such findings is that the social worker can be particularly helpful to patients and staff in problems of patient management arising from the stress imposed by the patient role. A decade ago, however, Berkman and Rehr (1972) found that social work intervention came most frequently in the final stage of recovery/chronic illness/rehabilitation and was largely for the purpose of discharge planning. Even the referrals that were made during the dependent-patient (sick role) stage were largely for posthospital planning. The authors concluded that the profession had communicated to patients, families, and staff its capacity for providing this critical health care function. But it was less successful in communicating its ability to help patients and families with the stress of assuming the patient role, illness behaviors, and the impact of illness on the social roles of the patient and family members.

Berkman and Rehr suggested that hospital social workers find ways to influence referrers to make referrals earlier in the hospital stay and, further, that they take responsibility for their own case-finding/screening procedures. Until they do so, they will be dependent on others to define the range of social work functions and to determine the need for social work service. In a more recent study, Rehr, Berkman, and Rosenberg (1980) offer such a screening procedure "for the early identification of patients and members of their families who face social and emotional stress related to the patients' illness" (p. 403). Figure 3–2 shows the form developed for "high social risk screening." "High social risk refers to an alteration in the life of a patient or family that is caused by social or physical stress." The objective is to identify high-risk patients at or even before admission for adequate planning, for less extensive but more effective service. In their experience with the procedure, the authors found that high risk screening has a quantitative impact on and improves the quality of social work services. Therefore staff deployment and skills development become very important. Workers must relate to patients at

FIGURE 3-2.   High Social Risk Screening Form
High Social Risk Screening Form A

Category I.   Automatic Review by Social Work Assistant—High Social Risk:
_____ 1. Over 70 years, living alone, eye surgery projected.
_____ 2. Institutional transfer into the hospital.

Category II.   Social Worker Review—High Social Risk:
_____ 1. Eighty years old or over.
_____ 2. Seventy years old or over, living alone.
_____ 3. Emergency admission, except appendicitis, hernias, pneumonias.
_____ 4. Severity of illness is life threatening—metastatic or terminal cancer and blood dyscrasias; all admissions to intensive care units and cancer and radiotherapy services.
_____ 5. Severity of illness is causing physical dysfunctioning—organic and/or mental brain syndrome, encephalopathies; syringomyelia; cardiovascular accident and stroke; aphasia; pathological fractures; carcinoma of the colon, rectum, pancreas, brain, or masses leading to ostomies; any limb surgery leading to amputation because of diabetes, gangrene, or circulatory diseases; carcinoma of the throat, vocal chord, larynx, tongue, or airway obstructions leading to ectomies; renal diseases leading to dialysis and/or transplant; multiple fractures; eye disorders, such as glaucoma and retinal detachment, which are sight threatening.
_____ 6. Chronic diseases—lupus, Hodgkins, myasthenia gravis, ulcerative colitis, multiple sclerosis, cerebral palsy, hemophilia, sickle cell, muscular dystrophy, rheumatoid arthritis, liver diseases.

Research Assistant _____ *Date* _____
Patient's Admission Date _____ *Worker Assigned Review* _____
Patient's Name _____

Source: H. Rehr, B. Berkman, and G. Rosenberg, "Screening for High Social Risk: Principles and Problems." Copyright 1980, National Association of Social Workers, Inc. Reprinted, with permission, from *Social Work*, Vol. 25, No. 5 (September 1980), p. 405, Figure 1.

the very beginning of the dependent-patient stage, or entrance into the sick role, when anxiety is high, implications of the hospitalization are not yet known, and diagnosis may not yet be available. This means that the social worker must be knowledgeable, competent, and secure in her professional identity.

The improved quality of service often improves the social worker's relationship with the physician. The service makes possible for his patient a more comprehensive and individualized program of social-health care, eases the transition into the difficult dependent-patient stage, helps the patient and family deal with the stress of the illness and the hospitalization, and provides more careful planning for discharge or transfer to the roles of chronic invalid or rehabilitee. Here is an example of social work service provided at admission:

Mr. Romano, age forty-five, married seven years to a woman thirteen years younger, was admitted to the coronary care unit following a myocardial infarction with angina. He and his wife have no children. They live in a small apartment in the building where Mr. Romano works as an elevator operator. He had little formal education and ran away to join the Marines at sixteen. He has worked as bartender, bouncer, and bodyguard. His marriage was a satisfying one, and he spoke affectionately of his wife as a "good woman" who was able to handle manly tasks such as bartending. The couple seemed to have no friends, although they mentioned several well-known entertainment figures as friends who live in the apartment building and for whom Mr. Romano occasionally works as chauffeur. He did, indeed, receive get-well gifts from at least two of these individuals during his hospital stay.

The social worker in the coronary care unit involved herself with Mr. and Mrs. Romano from the beginning and throughout the hospital stay—not only because of his serious medical condition but because of his inability to follow medical advice and the effect of his disruptive behaviors on the staff. He spoke in a crude and rough fashion and was angry and abusive toward staff. He referred to the doctors, loudly, as "those bananas" and addressed female staff members in sexually-tinged ways they found offensive. He complained about his lack of mobility, boasted of having smoked a cigarette during his heart attack, and said he would continue to smoke, drink, and eat heartily. He described himself as a "hard-living animal" to whom nothing could happen. He refused to follow medical orders and complained loudly and graphically about the "tortures" of his confinement.

When he was free from pain, he was moved to the general floor. He was soon returned to the CCU for monitoring because of severe pain following upon inappropriate activities. This happened three more times. He blamed his recurrent pains on poor hospital care. The worker confronted him with the likely consequences of his continued interference with medical procedures, using the suggestion that since he was used to being an effective and valued bodyguard to others, he could now undertake to guard his own body. This had some effect, and Mr. Romano was finally able to say he would really adhere to medical instructions as he couldn't take any more pain. He said he couldn't stand taking orders instead of giving them and wished he could have his wife wheel him along the corridor so he could direct her steering. Because the passivity of hospitalization and loss of control were so threatening, the worker secured approval for the wheelchair, and Mrs. Romano was permitted to wheel her husband about for a short time each day. Throughout his stay in the CCU a relationship of trust was established with the worker, and a good deal of Mr. Romano's anger was drained off. By the time he moved to the general floor the doctors were referring to the possibility of cardiac surgery, which again stirred Mr. Romano's anger. He said he would rather die on the street than be "cut open on the table." Although staff reiterated it was only a possibility, the patient continued to speak of it, in agitated and angry ways, as a definite plan. The worker conferred with the doctor, who agreed to clarify the facts for the patient.

In the same way Mrs. Romano often displaced her fright and anxiety by speaking angrily of the doctors' failure to telephone her when her husband's condition worsened or of inconsistencies in their information. The worker arranged for a joint meeting of the doctor, Mrs. Romano, and herself so that she could encourage Mrs. Romano to express her feelings and could support her need to know answers to the concerns troubling her. When Mr. Romano was suffering pain and anxiety he tended to direct anger at his wife as well as at staff. This was upsetting to her, especially because of her own anxiety about his condition. The worker provided supportive services to her and helped her understand that the behavior stemmed from the serious heart condition and his feelings about it and not from their relationship.

As discharge neared the Romanos were seen together for planning. Since they lived in a five-story walkup, it was medically advisable that the patient not return to these quarters immediately. Many alternatives were explored (staying with relatives, moving, a temporary convalescent facility, and so on), but none was acceptable to the couple. The physicians then agreed Mr. Romano could return home if he walked the steps slowly and stayed upstairs as much as possible. The worker remained in contact after discharge. Mr. Romano complained he was bored, had not gone outside for walks, felt fatigued, and hated his bland diet. The worker conferred with the doctor, who agreed to talk with Mr. Romano and his wife about the need for exercise and diet. As time went by, Mr. Romano cooperated well with his regimen. His defensive posture of being an "indestructible animal" relaxed, and he talked of how such unpredictable events as a heart attack could strike anyone. He became cheerful about his diet and spoke of how he couldn't tell the difference between cholesterol-free eggs and regular eggs. He wondered if a suction device could be invented to rid the arteries of fatty material clogging them. Service was discontinued when it was agreed with the family that both were coping satisfactorily with the demands of Mr. Romano's chronic illness.

Mr. Romano had defied all the norms of the patient role. He was complaining, demanding, and uncooperative, and he voiced his lack of trust and confidence in his physicians. His behavior was disturbing to the staff, who were bewildered and resentful. The social worker mediated between them and the patient to prevent potentially undesirable consequences. She interpreted to staff the patient's behavior as stemming from the underlying fears, while confronting him steadily and supportively with the dangers to his wellbeing posed by his behavior. She was able to tolerate his negative outbursts by understanding their source, to encourage his expression of his fears and perceptions, and to communicate her personal concern and emotional support. Slowly the patient responded by relaxing the dysfunctional denial and coping with his anxiety in a more realistic way. This stimulated his motivation to learn more about his illness and to deal more appropriately with it. Fortunately, he had the love and support of his wife and was untroubled by financial problems. But an additional and most important factor was the worker's availability in the coronary care unit from the day of Mr. Romano's admission. The assumption of the social work department in that hospital was that all patients on that unit are at serious social risk because of the nature of their life-threatening illness. The worker determines with each patient and family the need for specific social work services. Considered a valued member of the treatment team, she maintains open communication with physicians and nurses, aided by her physical presence and office space on the unit.

Summary

This chapter has described the stages of the sick role and implications for entry points for social work service. It has considered the influences of culture, particularly with reference to patients' and families' explanatory models of illness, with a suggested role for the social worker in helping to reduce conflict between the models held by the patient/family and that held by the physician and the treatment team. Psychological and social influences on the meanings attributed to the illness or disability, and their consequences, were also considered. Finally, some dimensions and norms of patienthood were examined with particular reference to how the social worker might mediate some of their negative consequences.

These first three chapters have presented three sets of interacting forces that the social worker needs to understand: the health system, the health care organization, and the patient role. The next chapter examines a fourth contextual element, the professional framework of basic social work concepts, along with processes that shape social work practice in health care.

CHAPTER 4

The Professional Frame of Reference as Context for Practice

A RECENT AMERICAN TRAVELER to China wrote regarding the contrasts between Western and Eastern medicine:

> If you are a Westerner, your doctor asks what is wrong with you. You show him the swollen finger, he examines it, feels, x-rays it, asks you about its history. He focuses on it, and on you, looking for cause and eventually cure. In times past in China, when you showed the doctor your swollen finger, he would ask, "Who was in the room when it first began to hurt?" "What is your relationship with your in-laws?" "Is there any new building being constructed in your neighborhood?" "Have you had any severe storms, floods, or earthquakes in your area?" It is obvious to the doctor that something has disturbed your relationship with your environment. A cure to what ails you will be found when your proper relationship to your environment is restored. [T. Marshall, 1979]

This little allegory reflects a theme of this chapter, that is, the complex interplay among genetic, somatic, psychological, and environmental factors in health, illness, and disability. For social work practice in health care the theme is best expressed as an adaptational or ecological perspective. The theme will be explored in this chapter, first through a description of three ecological concepts specifically pertinent to practice in health care, and second through the analysis of basic social work processes common to all practice approaches and here adapted for specialized use in health care.

An Adaptational Model

Something akin to the ecological view reflected in the allegory is appearing in Western medicine and health care. A prominent medical spokesman advances a biopsychosocial model likely to be more useful in this era of (1) increased chronic illness as people live longer; (2) growing need for prevention and health promotion as health care costs in human and financial resources escalate; and (3) concern for the quality of life as the goal of a caring society (Engel, 1977).

René Dubos, the internationally respected microbiologist, asserts that health and disease are the outcomes of a complex interaction involving an assault (microbial, chemical, physiological, or psychic), the state of the human organism and its response, and the past and present environments of the individual. This is a shift away from the traditional biomedical model of medicine to an adaptational model based upon the equilibrating forces between individual and environment, or the two ecological systems of outer and inner environments (Dubos, 1978, 1965, 1959). It relates to the interests of many social workers, physicians, allied health professionals, and social scientists—particularly, but not only, in interdisciplinary approaches to health promotion and the problems of disease, illness, and disability.

An ecological perspective in social work practice has been described elsewhere (Germain, 1979; Germain and Gitterman, 1980). The focus here will be on three core concepts that are especially pertinent to social work practice in health care: adaptedness, stress, and coping. The perspective views human development and functioning—including health and illness—as outcomes of continuous exchanges between the individual and the social environment, the physical setting, and the cultural context. The exchanges have the properties of circular feedback loops rather than those of one-directional, linear chains of cause and effect. Circular feedback loops refer to transactional processes in which internal and external "messages" about the outcomes of the processes feed back to the individual and shape the continuing processes. For example, efforts to cope with the stress of illness or disability feed back to influence the individual's perception of the stressful demands and the effectiveness of the coping activities, serving to guide continued efforts to deal with the stress.

ADAPTEDNESS

When exchanges go well, a state of adaptedness, or person–environment fit, is said to exist between the individual's rights, needs, goals, and capacities *and* the qualities of the environment. People's genetic potentialities for health and social functioning are released, and environments retain or even increase their capacity to support health, development, and adaptive functioning. People use an almost limitless variety of physiological, cognitive, emotional, social, and cultural processes (adaptations) to reach toward adaptedness. These may involve (1) active changes in the self to meet environmental demands such as those imposed by a disability, or to seize environmental opportunities such as vocational rehabilitation; (2) active changes of the environment so it will conform to human needs, goals, or rights, such as modifying a dwelling to accommodate the requirements posed by the disability; and (3) migrating to a new environment, as when a handicapped person moves to a setting permitting more independent living.

Adaptation is continuous because environments continually change and people's needs and goals also change. People must adapt to all changes they or the environment have induced. Moreover, the degree of adaptedness, or person–environment fit, is a transactional phenomenon, an outcome of reciprocal exchanges between the individual and the environment which change them both over time. Adaptedness therefore expresses a particular kind of person–environment relationship; it is not an attribute of either the individual or the environment alone. An example of adaptedness maintained by a patient and spouse despite catastrophic illness is seen in the case of Mrs. Dempsey:

Mrs. Dempsey, age seventy, has had diabetes for many years. Her eyesight failed two years ago, and her kidneys failed last year. She was placed on renal dialysis at a hospital center about 30 miles from her rural village. She is brought to the hospital three times a week by a transportation service for the handicapped. She is very weak and cannot move without assistance. She has serious bladder and bowel complications, which her husband treats with enemas and catheterization. The visiting nurse and homemaker come three times a week. Mr. Dempsey, a devoted, intelligent, and hardworking man, receives a retirement pension, and the couple also receive Social Security. They have two daughters, one of whom lives next door, and Mrs. Dempsey has nine siblings, nephews, and grandchildren who are all close to her.

The couple live in a summer cottage, where Mrs. Dempsey grew up and where the couple raised their children. It was prepared for retirement living, and they both love it. Mrs. Dempsey entertains herself with Talking Books, visits from relatives, and the company of her husband. She sits all day in the picture window because, though blind, she says she has the view of the pond in her mind's eye, and she continues to draw pleasure and strength from it. She requires total care, and this is well provided by her husband, the nurse, and the homemaker. They know the social worker is available should they need her services, but so far they have not. Clearly, Mr. and Mrs. Dempsey, by drawing on personal and environmental resources, have been able to maintain an adaptive person(s)–environment relationship in the face of grave illness, disability, and advancing age.

STRESS

In contrast to adaptedness, stress represents a poor person–environment fit, that is, a distressing person–environment relationship. Stress arises when the individual makes a conscious or unconscious appraisal of discrepancy between a demand (stressor) and his or her personal and environmental resources for meeting the demand, where it is important to do so (Lazarus and Launier, 1978). Lazarus and his colleagues distinguish between harm or loss and threat, and between threat and challenge (Coyne and Lazarus, 1980). Harm or loss refer to past or present damage such as serious illness, injury, or disability. Threat refers to the anticipation of inevitable or threatened harm or loss in the future. These may alternate in matters of illness and disability as patient and family struggle with the present demands and with plans to handle future demands or sequelae of the illness. Such concerns may, of course, appear together.

The distinction between stress and challenge lies in the stress-related negative feelings such as anxiety, depression, guilt, despair, lowered self-esteem, and the sense of being in jeopardy as against the positive feelings of zest and anticipated mastery and growth associated with challenge, even though challenges are stressful. It is true that some persons do experience illness as a challenge, but it is not deliberately sought (except, perhaps, among a relatively few patients whose motivations might then be considered problematic). The critical element is the appraisal of an imbalance between a painful demand and the personal and environmental resources for dealing with it. *Primary appraisal* is involved in evaluating the significance of demands posed by the illness, while *secondary appraisal* is involved in assessing internal and external resources for coping with these demands (Coyne and Lazarus, 1980). Primary appraisal includes the search for meaning and social attribution as conceptualized by Mechanic (1977). The search for meaning refers to the person's efforts to understand and define the experience of serious illness, of what has happened to him or her, and its implications. Only when meaning is established will it be possible to devise strategies for coping with it. One must understand something of the threatening situation in order to deal with it effectively.

Social attribution refers to the patient's ideas about the cause of her or his condition. Cause may be ascribed to internal factors such as willfulness, sinfulness, or negligence; to external factors such as the negligence of others, forces of fate, or the "evil eye"; or to existential factors as expressed in the resigned, "That's life" (Mechanic, 1977). Lipowski (1970) suggests that people may interpret illness as a challenge to be mastered, an enemy either to be fought or to be met with helpless surrender, a punishment that is experienced as just or unjust and as an opportunity for redemption or not, a weakness that reveals failure and loss of control, a welcome relief from role demands or internal conflicts, a strategy for manipulating others, an irreparable loss or damage, or a valued opportunity for growth. Individual interpretations of illness may also reflect cultural features, as described in Chapter 3. The environment also plays a role in social attribution as family, friends, employer, health care staff, and others define and react to the patient's situation. They may overprotect, stigmatize, or exclude the patient from roles she or he can still carry out (Mechanic, 1977). All these forms of social attribution have positive or negative implications for coping options and strategies.

Secondary appraisal refers to judgments regarding internal and external coping resources, options, and constraints. In situations of illness and disability, secondary appraisal is influenced by the stage of the illness, previous experiences, beliefs about the self and the environment (culturally and psychologically based), the availability of resources, and the processes of meaning and social attribution in primary appraisal.

Both primary appraisal ("Am I OK or in trouble?") and secondary appraisal ("What can I do about it?") shift in response to feedback processes. They also shift in response to changing demands as the illness proceeds through stages and as changes take place in internal and external conditions. Such shifts represent reappraisals.

One source of feedback is considered by Mechanic (1977) to lie in *social comparison*. This is a process by which patients (and presumably family members) evaluate their coping behaviors by comparing them to others in a comparable situation. The process takes place informally as patients and relatives share rooms or floors in inpatient facilities or waiting rooms and offices in ambulatory settings. In informal ways they gain some prognostic information and clarify ambiguities in what they have been told by their physicians. Social comparison also occurs in a planned way through the formal provision of group services. A beneficial aspect of patient groups and family groups is that members experience relief from knowing that others have shared the same kinds of feelings and that some members may already have coped successfully with stress. A successfully rehabilitated cardiac patient, for example, becomes a role model who inspires others with courage to confront the coping tasks.

As a consequence of an appraisal that the demand exceeds coping resources, the individual experiences the subjective state of emotional stress. The subjective experience then evokes physiological and psychological responses or coping efforts. These will be considered later in the chapter.

As an upset in adaptedness, stress—like adaptedness itself—expresses a particular person–environment relationship. Whether as stressor or as subjective state, stress is not lodged in either the individual or the environment alone but is the outcome of their exchanges. But stress is also a perceptual phenomenon. What is experienced as stressful will depend on the interplay among (1) personal and cultural factors, (2) the nature of the demand, and (3) environmental features—all of which must be understood by the social worker if help in dealing with the stress is to be effective.

Personal factors include physical, cognitive, and sensory-perceptual capacities; language facility; and personality (including, for example, the sense of identity and level of self-esteem, the sense of competence or effectiveness in one's environment and as defined by one's culture, connectedness to other people, and the capacity for self-directedness). These are outcomes of past and present exchanges between genetic potentialities and environments. Sometimes environments may not have nurtured these capacities, or the eroding effects of frequent or chronic stress may have worn them down. Personal factors also include the life experience and particular life stage of the individual and its characteristic tasks as they affect the stressful demand of the illness or are affected by the illness or disability. And the individual's cultural background of norms, values, and knowledge and belief systems affect the perception of the demand and capability for dealing with it.

Environmental factors have a powerful influence on the experience of stress and efforts to deal with it. The availability of environmental resources such as accessible quality health care, adequate income, safe housing, formal services, natural or informal support systems, the nature of the law and statutory entitlements, and so on, affect the appraisal of capability to deal with the demand and hence the perception of stress.

What is stressful for one person might not be so for another; how one person responds to a given demand might be very different from how another responds to the same demand. Cox (1978) in his perceptual model of stress suggests that there may be a discrepancy between the *actual* demand and the *perceived* demand, or between the *actual* capability and the *perceived* capability. This is a useful distinction for the social worker, because perceived demands and capabilities are often quite different from actual ones. Any one of these four variables may be overestimated or underestimated, and the social worker can help bring the perceived and actual into realistic alignment. Some of the common actual or preceived demands generated by serious illness, disability, and the patient role are shown in Table 4–1.

Different illnesses and different disabilities (stressors) pose different coping tasks and have different consequences. Some of these differences will be noted in later chapters. Chronic illness, in particular, also has predictable and unpredictable stages, each with its own set of harms or losses that vary with the kind of chronic disease. One example, the stages and coping requirements of cancer, is shown in Table 4–2 (p. 64).

TABLE 4-1.   Common Actual or Perceived Demands Generated by Serious Illness, Disability, and the Patient Role

1. Separation from family, friends, pets, and treasured belongings
2. A new environment pervaded by unpleasant and frightening sights, sounds, and smells, and peopled by strangers whose legitimate care-taking tasks can be intrusive; frightening subenvironments such as intensive care units, emergency rooms, surgeries and recovery rooms, and delivery rooms; bleak and dingy out-patient facilities often characterized by dehumanizing waits for attention and depersonalized services
3. Possible loss of statuses and roles in family, work, and social networks, creating or recreating problems of dependence/independence, activity/passivity, and threatening identity and self-esteem, competence, and self-directedness
4. Threats to future plans and valued activities
5. Depletion of resources for financial, housing, child-care, and other practical needs
6. Painful and distressing symptoms, and difficult diagnostic and treatment procedures
7. Threats to the self-concept and relatedness to others (including sexual problems resulting from the illness or disability) posed by loss of body parts or loss of function, or changes in appearance
8. Unpleasant feelings of anxiety, depression, guilt, rage, shame, despair, and so on, which, when intense, can interfere with recovery
9. Threats to survival, anxiety about death in the case of serious illness, or about an uncertain future in the case of chronic disease or disability
10. The interaction of any of these with preexistent stress

SOURCE: Adapted from Hamburg et al., 1953; Hamburg and Adams, 1967; Hamburg, Adams, and Brodie, 1976; Moos and Tsu, 1977; and Germain, 1977.

A parallel set of demands in any serious illness or disability is faced by family members. For the family, as for the patient, the impact of the demands is mediated by the nature and stage of the illness and by age, sex, culture, past experience, personality, and environmental resources. Like the patients, not every family in every setting will experience all of these demands or will experience any of them in the same way. But for each family some or all of these represent harms and/or losses that must be accommodated or mastered. For the patient the need to cope with such awesome demands is experienced just at the time when biological and emotional resources are depleted by pain, fear, and loss of physical vigor. For the family—depending on whether the patient is a child, a spouse, or a parent—emotional resources, financial resources, and the energy for dealing with the everyday management of family life may all be depleted by fear and the realities of the patient's condition.

TABLE 4-2.   Stages of Cancer and Associated Coping Requirements

ILLNESS STAGE	COPING REQUIREMENT
Discovery of cancer	Appraise the significance of the discovery and initiate appropriate treatment
Primary treatment	Recognize and deal with the realities, regulate the emotional reactions, and integrate the experience with the rest of one's life
Damage to one's body from the cancer and/or treatment	Mourn the loss, replace or compensate where possible and maximize other potentials in order to maintain self-esteem and sense of intactness
Maintaining continuity	Understand and communicate one's changed attitudes toward time, mortality, work, relatedness, and their priorities, in order to reach a new person–environment fit
Possibility of recurrence and progression of the disease	Put the fear out of one's mind most of the time while continuing medical follow-up, and taking realities into account in long-range planning
Persistent or recurrent disease[a]	Exercise choice where possible, and accept helplessness and dependence when necessary without excessive regression or resorting to magical solutions
Terminal illness[a]	Prepare to leave family and friends, provide for loved ones, and learn to use medical assistance and internal resources to minimize pain and retain as much self-directedness as possible

[a] Many patients, fortunately, will escape these stages, but the first five must be dealt with by all cancer patients.
SOURCE: Adapted from Mages and Mendelsohn, 1977.

Serious illness, then, represents perceived demands that may exceed perceived resources for handling them, and so is a source of stress. The stress of illness, in turn, may lead to stress in other realms of life, especially in family, work, and community roles, thereby interfering with recovery or with management of disability. Conversely, stress in those realms predating the illness may continue, adversely affecting recovery or management and increasing the stress of the illness. These feedback processes are well known to social workers in health care. But another feedback loop needs to be taken into account as well. Beginning with precursors in psychosomatic research and in the early work on stress by Selye (1946, 1956) and carried forward in contemporary research, the idea that illness is etiologically linked with prolonged stress has steadily gained ground.

One example of contemporary research is the study of stressful life events that require a change in the individual's way of life and their connection to the onset of illness (Dohrenwend and Dohrenwend, 1974). The approach, generally a checklist of life events (Holmes and Masuda, 1974; Rahe, 1974), has been criticized because it fails to (1) differentiate events according to age, socioeconomic, and ethnic variables; (2) distinguish between positive and negative events, and events that are or are not controllable by the individual; and (3) consider the presence or absence of social support systems as protection against the impact of high life-change scores (Rabkin and Struening, 1976; Cassel, 1976).

Nevertheless, there is increasing sophistication in life-change studies, with findings that are pertinent to a perceptual emphasis and to environmental factors. The basic assumption of the studies is that onset of illness is the consequence of exchanges between individual characteristics and environmental qualities in the presence of a disease agent—a formulation similar to that of Dubos. Yet the research itself has not yet addressed such complexity. Until it is able to do so we can only assume that stressful life events have some connection to illness. "The important issues in understanding how life events interact with social, psychological, biological, and intrapsychic variables requires specification of *what* events influence *what* illness under *what* conditions through *what* processes" (Mechanic, 1974a, p. 87).

Another development that ultimately may cast light on the issue raised by Mechanic is the emergence of behavioral medicine with its conception of mind and body as two ends of a continuum. "The core of basic research in this field is an attempt to locate the specific neurochemical mechanisms by which subjective states—specifically those associated with emotional stress—lead to disease" (*Science*, July 25, 1980). So far there are only a few treatments or biobehavioral approaches associated with behavioral medicine. They include relaxation, biofeedback, and other behavioral methods directed to such disorders as hypertension, heart disease, migraine, gastrointestinal disorders, obesity, and chronic pain. This is a growing area of practice for social workers in hospitals and ambulatory settings. It differs from most behavioral modification approaches in that behavioral medicine casts the problems into a system or holistic framework of feedback loops and is concerned with the total person-in-environment.

A further observation, concerning the relation between stress and crisis, remains to be made. All crises are accompanied by stress, but not all stress connotes a crisis. By definition, crisis is a self-limiting state. Because the pain of crisis cannot be endured for more than a brief time, some sort of resolution inevitably occurs rather quickly. The duration of crisis is by no means clear, although there is some agreement on a period of six to eight weeks. Its resolution may lead to creative adaptation and growth, to the restoration of the precrisis state of adaptedness whatever its level, or to regression to a level of functioning below that of the precrisis state. The last may involve the solidification of maladaptive defenses; the relinquishment of an active, problem-solving orientation; and even extreme forms of ego disorganization. Crisis also appears to be characterized by the suddenness and immensity of the precipitating event, such as severe illness, disability, injury, or loss, posing a threat to life goals, valued activities, or bodily or psychological integrity.

The usefulness of crisis theory to social work was twofold. It clarified what occurs psychically during the actual crisis, including heightened anxiety and lowered defenses, when the individual or family is likely to be more accessible to help. Crisis theory therefore emphasized the importance of environmental supports for successful crisis resolution. These conceptions led to particular emphases in social work practice such as, (1) a rapid response to need, (2) an active approach by the practitioner, (3) help in cognitive structuring of the situation and in problem-solving, and (4) help in mobilizing social, emotional, and material supports. Moreover the term "crisis" is used by physicians to refer to the turning point in acute illness, where the patient is expected to take a turn either for the better or for the worse. Such usage has supported the idea of crisis holding the potential for challenge and growth, on the one hand, or slippage and regression on the other. So notions of crisis have been useful to social workers in health care where patients and families are regarded as being in crisis because of severe illness, injury, death, and other harsh demands.

Nevertheless, many so-called crisis states actually present long-term demands. The patient and family face a lengthy period of stress as one painful demand overtakes another through the course of severe illness, injury, disability, or bereavement. Patients facing degenerative or chronic diseases or parents of a newborn infant with serious physical and/or mental defects, for example, must devise strategies in anticipation of adaptive tasks to be faced at a future time along with those being coped with in the present. In such instances the loss of familial roles and the taking on of new roles of patient or handicapped person, prolonged and difficult treatment procedures, processes of physical and vocational rehabilitation, mourning, and a new view of the self are some of the long-term demands that are better understood within the concept of stress. Actually, the four emphases in crisis intervention, described above, are just as necessary, applicable, and helpful in stress. In this book stress is used to cover crisis situations as well, while noting their temporal dimension.

COPING

Just as adaptedness and stress express particular person–environment relationships, so too does coping. Its effectiveness will depend on both personal and environmental resources. The subjective experience of stress evokes coping responses—the special adaptations called upon to deal with the stressful demands. They may be physiological (for example, muscle tension, increased heart rate, release of adrenalin), cognitive (for example, avoidance or considering alternative solutions), behavioral (for example, resorting to alcohol or seeking support from friends), or all three. Effective coping reduces or eliminates the stress. Ineffective coping results in unrelieved or even intensified stress. If marked stress continues unabated, the consequence may be physical dysfunction, emotional disturbance, or social disruption in family and group life. These then lead to further stress in a circular feedback loop where stress arising from coping failure leads to additional stress. The newly added stress meets depleted coping resources, leading to further coping failure and more stress. Cause becomes effect and effect becomes cause.

Coping responses serve as feedback processes revealing how the organism is doing. As feedback they can affect the actual or perceived demand or capability, the appraisal of discrepancy, the stress experience, or the coping strategies themselves (Cox, 1978, pp. 18–21). For example, securing information might alter the demand by reducing it; the defense of denial might lessen it in the short run but increase it in the long run. Asking for network support might increase capability; resorting to alcohol might decrease capability. Environmental approval or disapproval of coping maneuvers might alter them in one direction or the other, for better or for worse.

Actual coping skills run the gamut of human adaptive efforts to master, tolerate, reduce, and minimize environmental and internal demands and conflicts among them (Lazarus and Launier, 1978). What is effective coping with a particular demand in a particular context by a particular person may not be effective in a situation where demand, context, or person is different. Mechanic (1974b) suggests that coping skills include various capabilities, such as self-directedness and problem-solving skills; motivation to meet stressful demands; and ability to maintain an optimal degree of inner comfort that will facilitate problem-solving, including defense against immobilizing emotions and a favorable level of self-esteem. These personal resources depend for their effectiveness on environmental resources. Mechanic specifies these as follows:

1. Societal provision of effective institutionalized solutions to the major stressors people face. Health care examples include social and physical arrangements that permit disabled persons to fulfill conventional roles successfully and the provision of home health care and

family-respite services to support the family's continued caretaking functions for the chronically ill or severely handicapped.

2. Adequate training by society's preparatory institutions (family, school, workplace, and so on) in the skills for dealing with common stressful problems and needs. Health care settings need to provide health education. Patients and family members can learn the skills required for coping with specific illnesses and disabilities.

3. Environmental provision of incentives and rewards are required to mobilize and sustain coping efforts. This refers to the kinds of behavior that are valued or condemned in a social system. As discussed in Chapter 3, the patient who seeks an active role in treatment by insisting on information and participation in decisions about treatment may be defined by staff as a troublesome patient. The docile, conforming patient may be defined as the ''good patient.'' Each is rewarded accordingly, thereby affecting the motivation to cope.

4. The management of painful emotions aroused by the stress and the maintenance of self-esteem require emotional and social supports by family, friends, and others. In the context of serious illness and disability this might also include inducing new role expectations and approving new goals and behaviors. Patient groups and relatives' groups provide support also. Certain demands and their attendant stress may even be beyond individual solutions, regardless of personal resources, and yet can yield to cooperative or group efforts. Self-directedness (sometimes termed autonomy) requires environmental provision of needed information, opportunities for decision-making and action, and ample space (metaphorically) and time for the development of coping strategies— congruent with physical and other capacities or limitations. The more dependent one is on the environment because of illness, disability, or age, the more important it is that even minimal self-directedness be encouraged and supported.

All four of these areas are directly relevant to social work practice in health care, as will be seen later in this chapter and throughout the chapters ahead.

Coping activity serves two *functions:* the instrumental and the palliative (Lazarus and Launier, 1978). The instrumental function is intended to modify the stressful person–environment relationship. The palliative function is intended to manage or regulate the emotional responses generated by the stress. The two functions can be mutually facilitating, as when initial denial buys the time needed to protect the severely burned patient, for example, from overwhelming emotional pain (Hamburg et al., 1953), so that problem-solving efforts may begin. But one function can also interfere with the other, as when denial of a serious symptom such as a lump in the breast leads to delay in the diagnosis of possible cancer.

Modes of coping include (1) gathering information required in modifying the stressful person–environment relationship, which can also be palliative in reducing psychic discomfort by imparting a means of control over the demand. (2) Innumerable and diverse actions may focus on the environment, as when a woman changes jobs in order to avoid an allergen prominent in her asthmatic attacks. Or actions may focus on the self, as when an adolescent suffering from diabetes changes his attitude toward dietary restrictions from rebelliousness to acceptance. In these instances the actions are behavioral, but they can be cognitive, as when a patient or family member considers what changes in physical arrangements will be needed to permit the disabled individual to return home (problem-solving). (3) Inhibition of action (as opposed to immobilization due to internal conflict and defense) refers to controls exerted against impulsive or dangerous action, as in the case of a cardiac patient who resists the yearning to smoke. (4) Intrapsychic modes of coping include unconscious mechanisms of defense and other processes used to maintain or restore internal comfort and a favorable level of self-esteem. In their adaptive form such processes not only make the person feel better but, because the individual feels more comfortable, she or he can undertake more effective action, inhibit action more readily, or seek information more productively.

In psychoanalytic thought, and now in common parlance, defenses are the ego's means for warding off danger or threat (anxiety). They constitute one class of adaptational strategies. As such they can be adaptive in supporting a good fit between person and environment, especially in the short term. Denial following a grave injury, for example, prevents overwhelming anxiety and depression that might impede efforts to withstand the early effects of the injury. But such defense can be maladaptive later by impeding coping with the attendant problems. Denial shuts out information from the environment and interferes with the development of new solutions required by a totally new situation. The stroke patient who cannot acknowledge to himself the extent of his disability is less likely to engage productively in rehabilitation.

The transactional nature of adaptedness, stress, and coping, as expressing person–environment relationships, fits well with the practice aims of a profession committed to a person-in-situation conception throughout its history. The next section will cast practice processes and principles in the adaptational model as described to this point.

Social Work Processes in Health Care Practice

The adaptational paradigm, with its concepts of adaptedness, stress, and coping, helps reshape basic social work processes to fit the practice demands specific to health care. This section will present a brief overview of the following basic processes and associated issues:

1. Phases of help
2. Unit of attention, the knowledge base, and the value system
3. Problem definition, goal-setting, and task allocation
4. Professional relationships
5. Reorientation of interventions to stress and coping

PHASES

Most conceptualizations of social work practice, regardless of approach or field of practice, include recognition of the phases through which client–worker activities proceed in achieving goals. Different terms may be used to describe this process as it moves across time. In this book the process is described as comprising initial, ongoing, and ending phases. The *initial phase* includes the processes of engagement, exploration, problem definition and assessment, contracting, goal-setting, and planning needed steps.

The *ongoing phase* refers to the activities undertaken by client and worker in order to achieve the agreed-upon goals. The *ending phase* refers to the processes of termination, perhaps referral or transfer, and evaluation of outcomes. The three phases are preceded by certain preliminary steps, which themselves follow upon preadmission planning, social work screening, or referral for social work service. The total process is depicted in Figure 4–1. These phases are more readily differentiated in theoretical discussions than in the actualities of practice. They are conceptualized as separable in order that their components may be analyzed, taught, researched, or examined in a book such as this. In health care settings the practitioner finds that the phases are frequently telescoped, especially in the short-term social work service provided most typically in acute treatment hospitals and some ambulatory settings. Such telescoping demands strong skills of the social worker, particularly in the tasks of the initial phase.

And as screening procedures move the worker into earlier stages of the patient role, the demand for competence is increased (Rehr et al., 1980). While referrals to social work by physicians and nurses usually ease the social worker's entry into the patient's or family's situations, early social work screening means the worker does not have that prop. She then must be especially clear about the social work function and roles and must be adept at explaining them to the patient/family in terms of their felt or anticipated needs. The ability to elicit and assess those needs under the immediate stresses of the hospitalization itself, the patient's pain and discomfort, the family's fears, and often the uncertainty of

FIGURE 4-1.   Phases of the Helping Process with Individuals, Families, and Groups in Health Care Settings

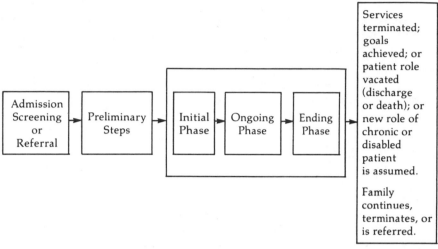

PRELIMINARY STEPS: Preparation for initial contact; offer of services; client acceptance of service. For group: securing organizational sanctions, planning group composition, etc.

INITIAL PHASE: Engagement; exploration; definition of need, and assessment; goal-setting; planning the actions. Mutual agreement on next steps.

ONGOING PHASE: Actions by client and worker to achieve desired goals and objectives, including reduction of stress and enhancement of coping. Mutual agreement on next steps.

ENDING PHASE: Planning for discharge, or for transfer, or for referral. Mutual evaluation of the work together. Carrying out the discharge plan, transfer, or referral. Followup. Dealing with another kind of ending: death and bereavement.

diagnosis and prognosis requires a high level of skill and sensitivity (Rehr et al., 1980).

Moreover, phases of help are not always in sequence. The relationship may grow as engagement develops through the initial phase, yet be ambivalently rejected at a later point. Needs or problems may be clearly defined in the initial phase, only to be continuously redefined as more data emerge, as client and worker respond to their joint efforts beyond the initial phase, as the patient's condition changes, and so forth. Therefore assessment must be understood as a process rather than a finished product. Assessment also is a state of mind maintained throughout the contact as the worker continually observes verbal and nonverbal behaviors, considers their manifest and latent meanings with the client, and reflects upon the nature of the client–worker exchanges and their reciprocal activities in achieving goals.

Clearly, also, the ending phase refers to the end of the relationship and the work together, yet in many instances the end is built into the process at the beginning by plan, is initiated by discharge planning, or is the result of the patient's death. Similarly, evaluation of outcomes is performed at the end, yet evaluation as a process is a part of every session in the sense that the worker keeps a vigilant eye on the joint effort, noting what is going well and what is going awry, and seeks with the client to determine the reasons. This is the value of contracting as a process. It is actually a periodic evaluation of where the participants are at any given moment with respect to their agreed goals and tasks. The old saw that treatment begins in the first contact and diagnosis continues until the last contact is more than a cliché. It expresses the notion of process and the untidiness of life processes when held up against neat paradigms like that shown in Figure 4-1.

So, while phases are orderly phenomena as discussed in this book, they are far less orderly in the real world of practice. Nowhere in social work practice is this more true than in health care settings, where the pressing issues of life and death scatter orderliness to the winds of constantly changing conditions. Yet this makes orderliness in the practitioner's thinking even more essential. The phases of helping and the practice principles and skills involved are the subjects of Chapters 6 through 9.

EXPANDING THE UNIT OF ATTENTION, KNOWLEDGE, AND VALUES

In the adaptational paradigm the field of forces to which client and worker must attend throughout the contact is conceptualized as the client's life space. Within the life space are included all the personal, environmental, cultural, and illness factors, and the health care organization itself. In such an expanded unit of attention a major task for the client and worker in the early phase of the contact is to select those salient features which are pertinent to the particular need of the particular individual or family in a particular situation, and also appropriate to the purpose of the particular health organization. As broad as this set of factors appears to be, the life space is not complete without taking account of the worker's presence in it, and this factor will be discussed below in connection with professional relationships.

Such an expanded unit of attention requires an expanded knowledge base. In addition to the general knowledge base of all social workers, the practitioner in health care must have knowledge about illness factors and their relationship to personal, environmental, and cultural factors; knowledge about the health care system and the health care organization; knowledge about patienthood and the patient role; and familiarity with medical terminology, routine tests and procedures, organ systems, syndromes, technological developments, and forms of treatment pertinent to the practitioner's particular setting or service. The social worker in a family planning clinic, for example, will need medical information different from what a worker on a hospital's neurosurgical unit or a worker in a geriatric facility will need.

Theory and knowledge develop so rapidly in the biomedical sciences that most health professionals feel overwhelmed without the perceived security of specialized responsibility, that is, knowing as much as possible about a particular area. This applies to social workers too. Within the specialization of health care social work the number of specialty groups is growing. Renal social workers, oncology social workers, pediatric social workers, perinatal social workers, public health social workers, ER social workers, and other groups are banding together on local, regional, and national levels. It is too early to assess the advantages and disadvantages of this movement toward subspecialities, but some fear it may lead to the splintering of the profession or at least of the health care segment, thus reducing the power of health care social workers vis-à-vis other health professions whose members already outnumber social workers anyway. Others believe it will enhance professional competence (including knowledge, skill, research capability), thereby elevating the status and influence of all social workers in difficult host settings.

In the field of health care the value system of social work is now beset by new conflicts in rights and new ethical/moral dilemmas arising from technological developments. These were addressed in Chapter 2 and will receive additional attention in later chapters.

PROBLEM DEFINITION, GOAL-SETTING, AND TASK ALLOCATION

Regardless of the practice approach favored by the practitioner, the way in which problems and needs are defined influences what is done about them. In health care practice the adaptational paradigm focuses the process of *problem definition* on the emotional and social consequences of the illness or disability for the patient and/or family members. Thus needs and problems are defined as problems in living. The problems are viewed as arising from the stress (harms, losses, threats) posed by discrepancy between the demands and the capabilities for dealing with them.

Client and worker must agree explicitly on the definition of the problem or need. Otherwise two covert agendas will be operating, and service outcomes will be disappointing to both. Sometimes the needs and problems may be manifold thus affecting the morale of both client and worker, and the worker must help set priorities among the needs and problems or help plan the sequence of addressing them so they do not exceed resources and undermine motivation, lower self-esteem, and so on.

If the agreed definition does not fit the organization's purpose or the social work purpose and domain of competence, then referral to another agency, service, or discipline may have to be arranged. In some of those situations, however, it may be possible to redefine the need or problem so that it does fit organizational and professional purposes and capacities.

Setting goals must also be a mutual process. The general professional purpose is to help improve the person–environment relationship by relieving emotional stress–internally or externally generated–aroused by illness, disability, or death. In addition, specific, individualized goals usually will be set by client and worker, reflecting individualized needs. These goals flow from the agreed problem definition. Often the worker's skill may lie in finding a common ground between the broad professional purpose and the specific goals of the client. Like problem definition, setting goals requires mutual decision-making, agreement, and explicitness.

Tasks for both client and worker flow from the specific goals and the general professional purpose. The tasks represent cognitive, emotional, or behavioral (action) steps necessary in mobilizing and sustaining personal and environmental resources for dealing with the stressors and/or achieving the specific goals. The processes of defining problems or needs, setting specific goals, and allocating tasks to client and worker may be directed toward changes in the statuses and roles of patients or family members as a consequence of illness or disability. For example, the mother of three young children was to return home after cancer surgery. In addition to her feelings of sadness, fear, and perhaps guilt or anger about her terminal condition, she faced an additional threat to psychological integrity. Her status as wife and mother and the associated roles had been engulfed by her new status of dying patient. Although she was able to return home, she was no longer strong enough to fulfill her familial roles. Before discharge she felt helpless and despairing, and these feelings would very likely impair her ability to cope with her physical condition and to experience the remaining time as positively as possible.

The social worker, after consulting with the physician, planned with the patient and her husband not only for home health services but also for a hospital bed to be placed in the family's living room. Here, for as long as her condition permitted, Mrs. Devlin felt less isolated from the activities of family life than she would have felt had she been hidden away in her upstairs bedroom. She was more able to retain some sense of effectiveness and an optimum level of self-esteem and self-directedness. She could maintain relatedness with her family and with the relatives and friends who came to visit. She did, indeed, remain a cherishing and cherished part of her family's life until the end.

These same processes are often applied to the relief of stress that predated the illness but bears on recovery or on the management of disability.

For example, a fifty-six-year-old woman, Mrs. O, had made a slow recovery from a heart attack. When discharge planning was brought up, she became withdrawn and depressed.

A social service consultation was requested by the house officer. In an inaudible tone, Mrs. O revealed that her problem was her senile, psychotic mother-in-law who had been Mrs. O's constant burden for the past ten years.... Mrs. O made numerous, but ineffectual, attempts to induce her husband to make other plans for his mother's care. Mr. O ignored her pleas, staying away from home as much as possible to avoid communication. [Sokol, 1976]

With Mrs. O's permission, the social worker met with her and her husband. Although in thirty years of marriage they had not previously risked open communication about their feelings and about the home situation, Mr. O was relieved to be able to discuss the conflict he had about placing his mother in a nursing home.

He knew that it was difficult for his wife, but just could not separate from his mother. These several joint meetings liberated their hidden feelings, and they began to talk about solutions. [Sokol, 1976]

Ultimately all the family, including two visiting daughters, met with physician, nurse, and social worker. The family problem was resolved, and Mrs. O was able to return home.

Studt (1968) suggests that clients' goals should be regarded as primary and the worker's goals as secondary, a useful view in health care practice. Clients therefore have primary responsibility for the tasks that must be completed to attain their specific goals, consistent with professional purpose, and the worker has secondary responsibility for providing the conditions that will help assure clients' successful completion of their tasks. As with problem definition and goal setting, the planning of tasks for both client and worker must be based on mutality, agreement, and explicitness. The worker's skill may lie in balancing client tasks with the individual's physical capacities, emotional readiness, and environmental resources (and in the case of the family members with the family's needs), so that coping will be enhanced and not undermined by inappropriate expectations. The secondary nature of the worker's contribution may therefore require much more worker activity—or even total worker activity—as the condition for task completion or goal achievement by the very ill, very old, or very young.

For example, Mr. O'Leary, was referred to the staff social worker by a nurse in an urban home health care agency. The worker's brief notes read as follows:

Patient, a former cook, is sixty-two years old, paraplegic following a stroke. He is single, and has two siblings living 30 miles away. He lives in a second floor, depressing apartment situated over a funeral home. It is inaccessible to a wheel chair, and Mr. O'Leary is depressed. He lies in bed, is not motivated to work with the therapists, and is making no progress. There are financial problems as well.

With Mr. O'Leary's permission, I referred him for senior citizen housing, and we soon accomplished his move to a complex with on-site meals and medical care. I referred him to Social Security for early retirement benefits, to the VA for a pension, and to the state for Medicaid (he did not wish to travel to the VA hospital). The financial problems were resolved.

Emotionally, Mr. O'Leary is making good progress. He is cooperating well with his therapists. He is happy and making friends, and is coping well. No longer isolated, he is now even involved with cooking at the center.

With more able patients worker activity may be less but is still related to the notion of secondary responsibility for providing necessary conditions for clients' successful pursuit of even quite modest tasks. These and other practice principles and skills associated with processes of problem definition, goal-setting, and task allocation will be examined in detail in later chapters.

PROFESSIONAL RELATIONSHIPS

A distinctive feature of the professional relationship in health care practice is its expansion to include processes of interdisciplinary collaboration, which will be considered in Chapter 8. The social worker's relationship with the client, however, is a significant element in all practice, viewed as the channel through which change is facilitated, growth released, and goals attained.

A general trend in contemporary practice is an emphasis on mutuality, honesty, openness, and genuineness in the client–worker relationship. Efforts are made to minimize the power differentials that arise from the practitioner's "control" over information and tangible resources and from the client's vulnerability imposed by the needy or problematic state. Efforts are also made to reduce social distance arising from differences in language or language facility, cognitive styles, coping styles, attributions of meanings, orientations to space and time, and values and norms associated with social class, race and ethnicity, religion, age, gender, and sexual orientation. Such efforts operationalize professional values of acceptance of difference and respect for individual dignity and worth.

Another trend, perhaps less prevalent, is a view of the client–worker relationship as a transactional field or a circular loop of reciprocal influences. Such a view assumes that each member of the relationship learns from the other(s). The client brings experiential knowledge and life experience, and the worker brings professional knowledge and experience (and life experience) to their encounter. It is not an egalitarian relationship, because the two sets of knowledge and experience are different, but it is a relationship best characterized by the property of mutuality. Together the participants achieve more than if either worked alone.

Just as the client brings her expectations and perceptions, norms and values, and definitions of what kind of help is helpful—derived from culture, past experience, and reference groups—so too does the worker. But, in addition, the worker brings into this transactional field his own and his agency's professional ideologies, preferred practice approaches, and the opportunities, resources, demands, and constraints reflecting the health organization's purpose and structure and the operations of the social work department within it.

Within this transactional field, then, each is influenced, shaped, and even changed as a consequence of their exchanges. Whatever the individualized goals are, many health care social workers share the hope that clients will emerge from their social work encounters with heightened self-esteem and a positive sense of identity and with greater capacity for relatedness, self-directedness, and competence, however modest such capacities might be in the light of the illness and disability. Many would also anticipate that, in their teaching, learning, and helping experiences with their clients, they will emerge from the same encounters with increased professional competence, a firmer sense of professional identity and pride in being a social worker, and greater capacity for self-directed practice (autonomous, accountable, and responsible practice).

ORIENTATION OF INTERVENTIONS TO STRESS
AND COPING

Helping processes will be briefly considered in the light of Mechanic's (1974b) specification of four requirements for successful coping discussed earlier in the chapter (pp. 67–68): incentives and rewards to stimulate and sustain motivation to cope with the stressful psychological and social consequences of illness and disability; adequate preparation and instruction in coping skills; support for managing painful emotions and maintaining self-esteem; self-directedness in meeting coping tasks; and societal solutions to common major stressors.

Each of Mechanic's requirements for successful coping has implications for social work practice. Table 4–3 (p. 78) shows the social work

TABLE 4-3. Social Work Tasks and Roles in Helping Clients to Cope With the Stress of Illness, Injury, or Disability

COPING TASKS OF CLIENTS	SOCIAL WORK TASKS	SOCIAL WORK ROLES FOCUSED ON THE CLIENT(S)	SOCIAL WORK ROLES FOCUSED ON ENVIRONMENTS
Motivation to cope with successive demands of the illness or disability	Providing incentives and rewards for coping. Influencing others to do the same. Dealing with ambivalence, resistance, and dependency	Mobilizer	Mobilizer
Problem-solving activities to deal with the demands of the illness or disability and other stress	Providing instruction in coping skills individually and in groups. Influencing the environment to do the same	Teacher Coach	Collaborator Mediator
Managing painful emotions and maintaining optimal self-esteem, to permit coping efforts to be made	Providing emotional support. Influencing the organization to be responsive to emotional needs. Organizing and working with natural support systems	Enabler	Organizer
Maintaining self-directedness	Providing information, time, and space for effective coping; opportunities for choice, decision-making, and action. Creating new programs and services to meet needs. Influencing organizational and outer environments to change when needed.	Facilitator	Facilitator Innovator Advocate

roles and tasks related to these coping requirements (practice issues regarding societal solutions are considered in the Epilogue).

Each coping requirement is associated with specific social work tasks, which are viewed as falling into two sets of practice roles. One set of roles is focused on the "self" of the client and one set on the environment, with due recognition that both are usually involved. The environment is further specified as referring to the health organization, including the health team, and the outer environment of community, support systems, and other impinging elements. The tasks and roles will be further defined by the practice skills associated with them, and these will be developed in Chapters 6 through 9.

In most situations, the patient, family, or group will be involved in all four requirements—almost at once sometimes, and sequentially at other times. Similarly, the four sets of social work tasks and roles may interact and overlap. Not all the tasks and roles may be carried out by every social worker in every setting or with every patient, group, or family in any setting. They are generalizations and so must be modified to fit personal, environmental, cultural, and illness factors in the particular situation as well as the characteristics of the particular setting. In many settings, for example, the tasks and roles are carried out in collaboration with other disciplines.

Lazarus and Launier (1978) specify three characteristics of coping in addition to that of function, which was described earlier. They are focus, temporal orientation, and modes. They too are useful to consider in helping people to cope with stress.

Focus is illustrated in a practitioner's work with a young couple following upon the birth of their first child. The baby boy was born with cerebral palsy manifested, so far, in a severe motor disability. The parents' happy expectations were shattered, and since they had moved to the community shortly before, they had no family or close friends to whom they could turn in the crisis. As a high school football coach, the young father was bitterly disappointed that their son would not be an athlete:

The social worker encouraged Mr. and Mrs. R to recognize their grief and to mourn the perfect child they had expected. Together they discussed the parents' prebirth fantasies and how these related to their feelings. The social worker also helped the parents identify the strengths they could use in coping with the situation. [Parks, 1977]

In this instance the worker is helping both parents to focus coping efforts on themselves. As their grief reaction and associated feelings of guilt and anger are effectively handled they will be better able to deal with the multiple tasks that lie ahead.

Their coping efforts must also be focused on the environment:

She told them of a community association for cerebral palsy where they could meet other parents with similarly afflicted children. Additional resources were discussed and investigated. As Mr. and Mrs. R became able to respond to the real needs of their child and family, they began to feel more comfortable in their new community and in pursuing present and future child-rearing issues. [Parks, 1977]

By keeping the importance of *temporal orientations* in mind the social worker can help patients and families move back and forth between present and future demands as needed, by helping them identify the required tasks, set priorities, and regulate the tempo of coping activity in light of the patient's condition and the family's needs. This is often the case in situation of terminal illness, when the social worker helps a dying patient and spouse toward more open communication of their present feelings of grief and mourning, while at the same time helping them undertake needed planning for the anticipated future needs of spouse and children.

Occasionally the patient's and family's efforts may not be well synchronized, causing strain. This can be observed, for example, when a patient is ready to face and talk about his terminal condition, but his spouse and other family members may not be ready, and continue to deny the seriousness of his condition. Here the social worker may help bring the efforts of patient and family members into closer alignment so they can be reciprocally supportive. In some instances the worker may help her clients recall successful coping in the *past* to encourage their efforts in the *present* stressful situation.

Social workers help mobilize and sustain coping behaviors in various *modes* including seeking information, taking action, inhibiting rash action, and drawing on psychic resources. They *furnish important information* to patients and families about entitlements and how to secure them and about community services designed to support their coping tasks. For example, Mr. G age fifty-one, had worked twenty years in an occupation where he was exposed to asbestos particles in the air. Five years ago he had been diagnosed as having asbestosis but had not been told by his physician that his condition might be work-related, nor did the doctor suggest he apply for Worker's Compensation. During an earlier hospitalization the social worker who worked with Mr. G had not recognized the work-related etiology or his possible eligibility for Worker's Compensation.

Mr. G returned to the hospital totally disabled from respiratory failure. At that time his case was referred to our Occupational Health Program by a nurse who was acquainted with the Program. Our clinical consultation team, which consists of an occupational medicine physician, an attorney, an epidemiologist, and a social worker, evaluated the case and immediately advised Mr. G of his rights to Worker's Compensation benefits. The clock had ticked by considerably since the time Mr. G was first diagnosed as having asbestosis and the statute of limitations in the Worker's Compensation law necessitated a prompt application for benefits.

The occupational health social worker assisted Mr. G to file for benefits. His wife, herself disabled and whom he had married just one or two months before while in the I.C.U., was given the names of attorneys and licensed representatives trained to represent workers' compensation cases. We then prepared his medical records properly for the Worker's Compensation procedure. [Shanker, 1983]

Mr. G remained in the hospital and died about ten months later; his wife received his retroactive disability benefits of $21,000 and $120 per week for the rest of her life. Medical benefits of $72,600 were also awarded to cover his hospital costs.

Some practitioners are in a position to share information about how others have successfully coped with the social and psychological consequences of a particular chronic disease or disability. Research reports reveal creative ways patients and families have been able to manage living with such chronic illnesses as rheumatoid arthritis, emphysema, colitis, cancer, and diabetes through their various stages (Strauss and Glaser, 1975). Measures that some patients develop for juggling time, energy, and personal and environmental resources in order to manage their disability is important information to impart to others. It can bolster morale and sustain the coping efforts of other patients where they are faltering.

Taking action is supported by the social worker in many ways. In an ambulatory setting, for example, he might help reduce a client's resistance to joining and participating in a self-help group such as Alcoholics Anonymous, help the client find more suitable and safer housing, and help other clients develop new interests or recapture old ones that are still feasible activities in light of the disability or chronic disease. Over time, he may help passive and inappropriately dependent patients to take a more active role in treatment, family life, work life, and community life. Sometimes this requires work with family members because their understandable fears or other personal features have led to overprotecting the patient. Mrs. W, age seventy-seven, suffered from cancer and heart disease. She was receiving home health care services but remained in her bed on the second floor of her house. Although her doctor indicated there was no reason she could not walk, Mrs. W maintained she was unable to do so.

The social worker explored the situation of the patient's husband and found that he had recently retired and was deriving great satisfaction from his role as caretaker for his wife. Because of this, he was not anxious to see her gain independence. In this case, the social worker was able to help the other members of the health team understand the situation. The social worker was then able to begin work with Mr. W, assisting him to realize that he would be helping in his wife's health care by encouraging her to walk. [Oktay and Sheppard, 1978]

In the following excerpt mothers of children on dialysis, in a group led by two social workers on the renal unit, are struggling with these same issues of activity and independence versus passivity and dependence:

> Those mothers who had become extremely limiting of their children's activities listened to those mothers who allowed their children to go to school, travel on public transportation, go to museums, take trips. One mother would exclaim in surprise when another described how her child took a full schedule in school, received good marks, while continuing to be dialyzed three times a week. Another mother would react in amazement when she heard that Mrs. X brought her child here for dialysis three times a week by bus and subway and that her child was surviving public transportation very well. Some of the mothers who were afraid to let their children go to school eventually sent them to school, with the support of the other mothers. Mothers who had kept their children in the house all day were able to see that this was not the way they had to live. [Glass and Hickerson, 1976]

The social worker may participate with the client in taking action, accompanying her in an intimidating official contact or working with patient and/or family on a disagreeable or difficult task necessary for effective coping. In other instances, instead of encouraging independence, the social worker may need to help the family accept appropriate dependence required by the patient's physical condition.

The social worker can help clients who have problems in *inhibiting rash actions* that endanger recovery or successful management:

A worker in a neighborhood health center formed a group for adolescents suffering from diabetes, many of whom gave greater priority to peer acceptance than to their medical and dietary regimens. The members, with her help, shared feelings about themselves, the disease, and its constraints on their activities and their futures. The members learned from one another how to cope with adolescent issues and the demands of diabetes in complementary rather than oppositional ways. They were then better able to resist rash eating of improper foods.

In the following, the practitioner is a social worker in a rural home health care agency in a very isolated area. The patient was Mrs. Honicutt, who had been receiving hospice care because of terminal cancer. Very suddenly she died at home of an aneurysm. Mr. Honicutt appeared to cope with his feelings through the funeral and over the next few days when a relative from another state came to help him. He then began to drink heavily.

He became verbally and physically abusive to his niece, and he was also threatening to take his life. I was told of his condition after transporting another patient to the hospital for a mildly acute condition. I rushed to Mr. Honicutt's home and attempted to defuse some of the hostility. The State Police and the Community Mental Health Center had been notified, but Mr. H refused to leave his home voluntarily for psychiatric treatment. I stayed with him six hours, encouraging him to talk of his grief, and he also expressed his shame and guilt. I legitimized his concerns and conveyed hope that his problems are solvable. I saw that he got to bed that night and promised to return early the next day. With his approval that morning, I arranged a voluntary visit to the nearest mental health center. We averted an involuntary admission, and he was able to maintain his job as security guard and his informal support systems of friends and neighbors, without major upheavals. [Heald, 1982]

And, finally, social workers in health care must be highly skilled in providing emotional support to psychic resources. They may also need to help patients and families draw on such environmental sources of emotional support as informal helpers, social networks, and self-help groups. Organized patient groups and relatives' groups, led by social workers, are also powerful sources of emotional support. Members help one another manage painful feelings, sustain self-esteem, and relax maladaptive ego defenses that may be interfering with medical regimens, participation in therapies, or forming an acceptable new body image.

In a rehabilitation center, a social worker meets with a group of ten patients. Five men are undergoing treatment for paralytic strokes, three men are recovering from leg amputations, one man has multiple fractures, and the tenth suffered a spinal cord injury, which has left him paralyzed from the waist down. The purpose of the group is to help the patients deal with the coping tasks arising from their disabilities through the development of a mutual aid system. Their common tasks include coping with a changed self-image, changes in familial roles, difficult treatment procedures, loss of function and sexual issues, and the psychic pain of anxiety, rage, and depression.

These three measures for emotional support (practitioner and organizational provision of support, informal support systems, and group approaches) derive their power from conveying to the individual that she or he is cared about and respected and is a valued member of a mutual aid system. Such support elevates and sustains self-esteem, the loss of which is typically a dynamic factor in the experience of stress and coping capability.

OTHER SOCIAL WORK TASKS AND ROLES

In addition to these many processes involved in helping individuals, families, and groups cope with the demands of illness and disability, social workers in health care carry many other responsibilities. These frequently include related activities such as screening and case finding; preadmission planning and discharge planning; and outreach to groups or individuals in high-risk situations.

However, many social workers will also be engaged in quite different tasks and roles, either in addition to their face-to-face responsibilities with clients or as an exclusive responsibility. For example, they may participate in legislative advocacy for health care policy and services at local, state, and even federal levels. They may help communities to identify health needs and to plan for health care services. They may provide instruction to social work students and participate in the education of students in other health professions and staff in training programs. Increasingly, health care social workers conduct social work research and collaborate in interdisciplinary studies.

> A social work researcher on the staff of a small health clinic, serving clients with a cleft lip and/or palate, undertook a study of client satisfaction, using 100 randomly selected adult patients and parents of young patients. He was interested in learning how clients view the services, the multidisciplinary staff, and the physical facilities of the clinic. He designed the interview schedule and secured 100 percent participation by providing full information and assurance of confidentiality. The results of the survey were analyzed by the social work staff, and a written report, of findings and recommended corrective actions in areas of weakness, was submitted to the executive director and the director of program development. The report was then discussed at a meeting of department heads, to which the president of the Parents and Adult Patient Group was invited.
>
> At the meeting plans for recommended changes were made, new procedures were subsequently set in place, and means were developed for monitoring their effects and then later implemented. [Starr et al., 1980]

By contrast, public health social workers carry quite different roles and tasks related to quite different functions. In a state or local health department social workers may carry planning and research functions, licensing and standard-setting functions, educational functions, and preventive services functions such as screening, genetic counseling, parent education in young parent programs, and crisis intervention.

The medical social work consultant from a state health department recently organized a regional workshop for social workers in maternal and child health. He invited ten social workers to form a planning committee. With the help of this group he secured funding for the workshop, and he enlisted the cooperation of the continuing education staff of the local school of social work in the arrangements. The committee, under his leadership, then planned the theme, topics, and speakers and work-group leaders. The three-day workshop was attended by fifty social workers in the region.

During the period of planning this workshop the consultant was also involved in working with staff and hospital colleagues on developing guidelines for social services in short-term hospitals within the state. Over the same period he also engaged in planning with other social work staff to improve coordination of the department's maternal and child health programs around the state; he wrote a grant application for a small research proposal; he collected data from social work designees and consultants in nursing homes as to desired educational content for a conference he was planning on social services in nursing home care; and he served as practitioner member of a school of social work faculty group developing a curriculum in health care practice.

A similar examination of functions, tasks, and roles of many other social workers in other kinds of settings would show other types of diversity, reflecting the purpose, size, and structure of the particular setting. For example, in a small rural health agency the director of social work, as the only staff social worker, may carry responsibility for as many social work functions and tasks as the organization will sanction and the director's time and energy will allow. In a large urban medical center, social work activities may be highly specialized, so that each practitioner may carry some functions, tasks, and roles, but not others.

Summary

This chapter presented an overview of pertinent theoretical concepts and how they reshape basic social work processes, functions, tasks, and roles in face-to-face services to individuals, families, and groups. Clearly, social work in health care is very different from what it was during the early years of medical social work, although the commitment of practitioners is the same. In general the major social work function in face-to-face practice is to help patients and their families deal with social and emotional needs and problems that may accompany or predate illness and disability. Attention is given to improving the person–environment relationship by easing the associated stress and enhancing internal and

FIGURE 4-2. Practice Paradigm

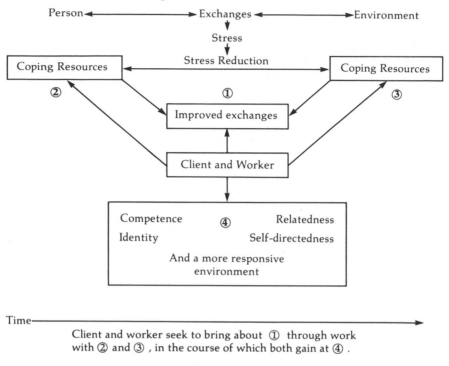

Client and worker seek to bring about ① through work
with ② and ③ , in the course of which both gain at ④ .

external coping resources for dealing with the associated stress. This adaptational paradigm for practice is illustrated in Figure 4-2.

This chapter also provided a brief description of social work functions, tasks, and roles carried out by social workers who may not be engaged in face-to-face services or, if they are, still undertake other kinds of responsibilities out of professional commitment or because of the nature of their assignments. These practice aspects are directed to research, policy, and program development and to organizational, community, population, societal, and other systemic factors bearing on health, illness, and treatment beyond particular clients.

The remaining chapters will examine the skills of face-to-face practice, of collaboration, and of organizational change and innovation. Chapter 5 begins the analysis with a presentation of the beginning phase.

PART TWO

SOCIAL WORK PRACTICE IN HEALTH CARE

CHAPTER 5

The Helping Process: Initial Phase

THE INITIAL PHASE includes the processes of preparation, engagement, exploration, problem definition and assessment, contracting, goal-setting, and planning next steps. Each of these processes will be examined in this chapter.

Preparation

Before the first contact with the client, certain preliminary steps can help ensure a successful beginning of the helping process. The social worker's first task is to prepare for the initial contact by readying himself for entering the client's life space sensitively, appropriately, and helpfully. Preparation involves anticipatory empathy, thoughtful reflection, and planning (Schwartz, 1976; Shulman, 1979; Germain and Gitterman, 1980). Affectively and cognitively, the worker seeks to anticipate and identify with what the patient/family/group is likely to be experiencing and feeling so that in the interview he will: (1) elicit and respond helpfully to their concerns, fears, and hopes and the needs created by the illness; (2) offer services appropriate to the needs as they are experienced by the client(s); (3) be sensitive to client–worker differences in age, sex, race, ethnicity, or social class and their potential impact on the initial meeting; and (4) be prepared for and better able to control his own subjective states aroused by the patient's condition, appearance, prognosis, and so on.

Seasoned practitioners carry out this preparation almost outside of their own awareness. It is already an integral part of their approach to

89

practice as they draw on their experience and knowledge. Perhaps it is experience with a particular setting (such as an intensive care unit, with the frightening impact of its machines and staff activity on patients and families), with particular illnesses or injuries (such as cancer or serious burns and their meanings to patients and families), or with a particular age group (such as children or the elderly, and their special needs). But for the student or the practitioner new to health care settings, the purposeful, conscious use of empathic and cognitive processes in advance of the initial contact is essential.

Affective processes in empathy include placing oneself "in the shoes" of the other in order to identify with what he is experiencing and feeling. It includes the effort to enter the world of the other and to sense from the "inside" what it is like for him in his world—to be *with* him there (Mayeroff, 1972). Such empathic identification also requires the ability to step back from the identification, not losing oneself in the other but holding fast to one's own identity. The worker, for example, does not have to be frightened in order to respond sensitively to the patient's fright. But, because she "feels" his fright from "inside" his world, she is able to convey her understanding of what it is like for him. These abilities contrast sharply with the process of overidentification, which may be unconscious, tends to distort one's perceptions, and interferes with the ability to see the world as it appears to the other while maintaining one's separateness.

Overidentification is the result of unconsciously projecting a part of oneself on to another person. In effect it is the loss of objectivity that is an essential part of empathy. The worker then views the patient or family member unrealistically as someone in need of rescue or reform. This often leads either to doing too much *for* the client or not enough. In overreaction to the part of the client that is most like a hated part of oneself, one responds punitively toward her because of her alcoholism—for example, her sexual orientation or even her particular illness or disability, age, or ethnic background. Another worker may instead project onto the client his own unconscious longings to be taken care of and encourage the client's dependence, passivity, and grateful devotion.

In health care practice, overidentification frequently takes two forms: (1) The practitioner is unable to perceive or understand the positions of others in the client's situation. This can lead to taking sides with the patient against the physician, a nurse, or family members in ways that do not advance treatment goals or the patient's ultimate well-being. (2) The practitioner feels the same degree of anxiety as the client and is therefore not able to be helpful. The case of the Butoni family is assessed later in this chapter. It is noteworthy that the seasoned and highly skilled worker in this family's situation reported occasional overidentification. Whenever Mr. Butoni's distress over his serious limitations became especially acute, she also became overanxious, feeling that she too had no options. Recognizing this pattern, she was able to pull herself back from the overidentification to an empathic identification that permitted her to find options for Mr. Butoni and the family to consider. The remedy for overidentification is continuous attention to the development of self-awareness (the recognition of one's own patterns of relating to particular client situations), aided by the use of consultation as needed.

Anticipatory empathy before actually seeing the patient and/or family readies the worker for empathic engagement in the first session. These affective processes are bolstered by the thoughtful review of knowledge and theory of the patient role, the impact of the illness and the hospitalization, and the demographic, social, cultural, and emotional factors pertinent to the particular situation. It is essential to guard against preconceptions of age groups, illness categories, or social and cultural groups, because preconceptions interfere with relating to patient and family members as unique individuals. An important safeguard is to check the preliminary cognitive review of generalized theory and knowledge against the unfolding actuality as the person's unique characteristics emerge in the contact. One seeks to anticipate the likely feelings, needs, and concerns of the particular patient, family, or patient group in advance of seeing them. Yet one remains sensitive in the session to all the ways the anticipation may be contradicted.

Such preparation helps assure openness to both the manifest and the latent content of communications in the session. The worker is then in a firmer position to offer a service that will fit the needs being experienced by the patient, family, or group. And, finally, these preliminary steps can aid in self-awareness. They are helpful to the student and new practitioner in preparing for their own likely responses to what may be new experiences with intense pain, unpleasant sights and smells, and the anguish of lost function or of bereavement. The weaving together of affective and cognitive processes needed for empathic caring is of critical importance throughout the entire helping process. But the following example illustrates the effort to achieve anticipatory empathy as a preliminary step before the helping process even begins:

Mrs. Ryan, age sixty, was struck by a hit-and-run driver on her way to work. She was rushed to the hospital with multiple injuries including a fractured cervical vertabra, fractured right leg, internal injuries, abrasions, and contusions. Because of the seriousness of the spinal injury; she was placed on a Stryker Frame, and a "U" clamp was screwed into both sides of her skull. The clamp was held in place by two 10-pound sandbags. Her leg was casted. Two days after admission the head nurse on the orthopedic service made a referral to the social work department explaining that the patient would probably have problems because of the nature of the accident. The nurse was also concerned about discharge planning.

The only information available to the social worker is that Mrs. Ryan is a widow and has worked in a textile mill for more than forty years. He prepares himself to see Mrs. Ryan, and writes of the process:

I thought first of the senselessness of the event and how in a single moment Mrs. Ryan's whole life and future is thrust into jeopardy. Even at best, both will be transformed. She must be in severe physical pain, and she is probably experiencing intense psychic pain as well; worried about her job and finances, her living quarters and belongings, fears about her condition and the already stressful nature of the treatment process. Perhaps she is already feeling rage at what has happened to her, but, if not, she will almost certainly feel that rage in the days to come.

The nurse is anticipating problems. I wondered if Mrs. Ryan is depressed and withdrawn? Is she being uncooperative or demanding or hostile with staff? If so, I will need to help them understand why, so that poor patient–staff relations do not get started.

I thought of Mrs. Ryan's age, and how it might make her physical recovery more difficult, yet her long life experience may serve her well in coping with the psychic tasks she will face. But she may have to face an enforced retirement long before she had wanted to retire; and I wondered how it will be for her, alone and unable to work — her job must have been an important part of her world for forty years. While I myself have never experienced a traumatic injury, I did find myself thinking of my mother, who is about Mrs. Ryan's age, and I could feel my concern for all she would be facing after an accident like this. Yet at least she would have my father and all of us to help her through it. So I thought again of Mrs. Ryan's status as a widow and wondered if she had children or relatives, or friends and neighbors who could be rallied to her support in the difficult weeks she faces. And, finally, I thought it might be hard for Mrs. Ryan to talk because of her pain and perhaps despair or even anger. Therefore, it will be important for me to convey my concern for her and my confidence that I can help her deal with the enormity of what has happened through tangible and intangible services, not the least of which will be listening to what happened, perhaps over and over. I will need to do all this in a way that won't threaten what I anticipate will be strong feelings of personal independence.

The worker was indeed able to convey his concern and a sense of hope, and he presented his function and role in a way that was responsive to what concerned her. Mrs. Ryan accepted him and his offer of service. He was able to listen to the outpouring of details about the accident and to understand that this was an important means for her to begin to master the trauma of the accident and of having been abandoned by the unknown stranger responsible for her massive injuries.

Preparation before the initial contact is equally valuable in work with family members. In the following example from an outpatient setting, a terminally ill cancer patient and his wife have been referred to the social worker by the physician. Mrs. Kahn will not let the doctor tell Mr. Kahn his prognosis. The physician is concerned because the patient is severely depressed and isolated, while Mrs. Kahn maintains a cheerful, optimistic façade in front of him. Mr. Kahn is receiving chemotherapy, but his condition is deteriorating and he will soon need to reenter the hospital, perhaps for the final time. Before seeing Mrs. Kahn, the worker attempts to enter into her world and to sense from the "inside" what that world must feel like. In this way, she hopes to be ready to help Mrs. Kahn to cope with her husband's illness and impending death so that, together, she and Mrs. Kahn can help her husband. From inside Mrs. Kahn's world, the worker writes:

"My husband is so depressed and I don't know what to do to help him. He lies in bed all day and won't talk to anyone—he's shutting out the world. He's shutting me out, and that hurts me. I feel like we're so far apart now, but I don't know how we can get close to each other again. Since the cancer was diagnosed, there's been such a barrier between us. I wish he would open up and share his feelings with me. I wish I could tell him what I'm feeling inside—how much I love him, how much I'll miss him, how terrified I am that he's dying. There is so much to say and so little time left. But I'm afraid to talk to him now, to tell him what I'm feeling—I don't think we could bear it. At least if we don't talk about it, we can pretend that all this isn't really happening. So I try to put up a cheerful front all the time—I keep all my feelings inside and just make small talk about the unimportant things. I feel so terribly alone. This whole thing is like a nightmare that I can't wake from: One day I'm a normal wife leading a normal life, and the next day it's like I've been handed a death sentence. It's so unfair—he's too young to die. We had so many plans for the future. And I'm so afraid for myself. I don't know if I can cope with being alone."

The worker draws on what she understands of the meaning and impact of cancer on families and her knowledge of what is likely to lie beneath Mrs. Kahn's façade of cheerfulness. She wants very much to "be there" for Mrs. Kahn, in her world of anguish, although she also recognizes that this anticipatory picture of that world must remain tentative until the first session—or perhaps even later than that. But she is ready to bear Mrs. Kahn's pain—and also her own—as she tries to help.

These same affective and cognitive processes of empathy are essential in preparing for the initial meeting with a formed group, whether it is a group of obese patients in an HMO, a group of wives of paraplegic patients in a rehabilitation center, or a group of elderly patients in a nursing home. Preparation for meeting the group, however, requires additional preliminary steps if the group is to be successful. These include (1) assessment of need for a group service; (2) clear definition of the group's purpose; (3) securing organizational sanction for the group approach; and (4) planning the group's composition and size, its temporal and spatial arrangements, and the recruitment of its members.

The plan to form a group must rest on an identified need (shared by the potential members) that is not otherwise met or that can be met more effectively by a group approach. For example, a worker in a rehabilitation center writes:

The more I observed the Stroke Club, the more I saw that the wives there occupied a confusing status. The wives either stayed during the Stroke Club, talking among themselves which distracted the men, or they went out for coffee. So I am interested in forming a group for the wives. I think many of them feel helpless in dealing with the severity of their husbands' handicaps. Some seem to have a good store of knowledge about strokes that might help in dispelling the myths held by others. I have also noticed that the women are at different levels of adaptation to the stress of disability, so I think those farther along will be able to help those who are just now encountering the tasks.

The purpose of the group is, of course, connected to the assessment of need. In the above example, the implicit purpose is to create a mutual aid system through which the women can provide support and learning to one another. The social worker's clarity of purpose beforehand will aid in the recruitment of members. Later, when the group is actually formed, the purpose—clearly conceived by the worker and explicitly expressed to the group—will become the basis for their work together. A social worker in a hematology clinic prepared to form a group of adolescent patients suffering from sickle-cell anemia. She was aware that they had many personal and social concerns and needs that were not being met by the clinic's focus on medical aspects. The group's purpose was formulated in terms of (1) increasing the members' knowledge of the disease and (2) helping them deal with feelings about themselves and their experiences at school, with their families, and with peers, as these were affected by the disease. Without the worker's clarity about the group's purpose, the members will not understand what is expected of them, what to expect of the leader, and the role of the setting in their joint efforts. Without a sense of purpose, they may continually test the leader for limits, may continually question, "Why are we here?" Most unfortunate of all, a group that lacks a clear purpose may never develop a mutual aid system through which the members encourage and support one another and learn and grow together.

Because the social worker in health care practices in a multidisciplinary setting, it is imperative that the other disciplines and administration be engaged in the planning for a group service.* Physicians may have questions about the impact of the group on their patients. Nurses may be concerned that their own roles in patient care will be

---

* This aspect is discussed more fully in Chapter 9.

usurped. They may worry that they will have "to clean up afterward," that is, to manage members' feelings, demands, and behaviors aroused by the session's content. Administrative personnel may have concerns about space, time, and other resources required by the group service.

Engaging staff participation in advance planning for patient and family groups can eliminate many common obstacles. Without such participation, physicians may refuse permission for their patients to participate in the group. The worker may find that the meeting space has been reassigned, the patients have been scheduled for other activities, or the group sessions are interrupted on a variety of pretexts. Some social workers advance the provision of group services by meeting individually with other staff members to present the need for the group and its purpose, clarify perceptions and expectations, and invite suggestions. Others find a general meeting for all pertinent staff can achieve those aims and also promotes the exchange of ideas and encourages more open communication among key staff. Sherman (1979, p. 29) suggests (1) taking a positive approach. The worker is not asking permission. Instead she presents the need—and herself as capable of meeting the need. (2) Relating to the specific interests of each discipline is helpful. Where it is an accurate description, the group can be presented as a means of increasing adherence to medical regimens, for example, or of reducing the demands on nursing staff or administration, or, in the case of a relatives' group, as a means of enhancing the public image of the institution. These presentations help generate favorable responses. (3) Feedback sessions demonstrate the worker's sensitivity to the group's impact on staff. Distributing periodic brief summaries of the group and inviting comments maintains the interest, cooperation, and even the involvement of the other disciplines. The reports (or more formal presentations) and chart entries increase the visibility of the group and enhance the potential for institutionalizing the service.

Other preliminary steps in preparing for the group include decisions about composition and size; the frequency and duration of meetings; and physical arrangements. These decisions need to be made in the light of the assessed need, the purpose, and the nature of the setting. In acute care, for example, hospital stays tend to be short, so open-ended groups with shifting membership and waiting room groups of varied size are prevalent. In ambulatory care and chronic care settings it is possible to have closed groups. Depending on their purpose such groups may be kept small (six to nine members) in order to foster intimacy and sharing for growth and task achievement. They may be much larger, however, if the purpose is more educative. Group composition, theoretically, should provide a fine balance between sameness and difference with respect to illness category, stage of illness, age, sex, ethnicity, social class, and so on. However, worker judgment is important in each instance and with respect to each of these factors. Patients who are farther along in the recovery process (for example, in a postmastectomy group) offer models for coping to patients whose coping tasks are only just beginning. But in some incurable illnesses (for example, diabetes), the presence of patients whose illness has progressed to later stages of blindness or amputation may frighten newly diagnosed patients. Age and sex differences may be more important to consider with children and adolescents than with adults. Diversity of race, ethnicity, and social class is valuable, although no member should be alone on these or other factors if it can be avoided. Where the common need is strong, however, as in life-threatening illness, differences in social characteristics tend not to interfere with members' ability to identify with one another. Indeed, a valued unplanned outcome may often be the members' growing acceptance of diversity.

The number, frequency, and length of sessions must take into consideration not only the group purpose and the nature of the setting, but also the ages and physical states of the members. The actual hour set for the sessions must be carefully selected to avoid conflicting with diagnostic or treatment activities. In the case of relatives' groups, the time arrangements may have to be part of the contracting in the actual first session because of members' work and child care responsibilities.

Meeting space must be arranged with regard for the physical comfort of the members, ease of access, continuity of the space across sessions, availability of needed supplies or equipment, and arrangements for refreshments when deemed advisable. Leadership issues also should be settled before the group begins. Co-leadership has advantages and disadvantages in any setting. In a health care setting, a social work group co-led with a physician or nurse may defeat the group's purpose of dealing with feelings about the illness. Instead the group may focus on medical aspects. Some practitioners set aside time for both sets of activities on the assumption that a focus on feelings in the first half will enable members to raise informational issues in the second. Others work in the preparatory sessions with staff to clarify the different purposes of groups led by different disciplines and to encourage the formation of different groups with different purposes.

With these preliminary steps completed, the worker is ready to invite potential members to the first meeting. The usual form of recruitment for patients' groups is through a personal interview in which the group's purpose is explained and any misperceptions of a group experience can be clarified. The same method can be used for relatives, especially on a service where most family members are already known to the social worker (for example, pediatric oncology). Or a more impersonal method may be used, such as distributing flyers and posting announcements in waiting areas. This open invitation elicits voluntary participation, because, unlike a personal invitation, it exerts little or no pressure for acceptance. It results in a self-selected group with attendant advantages and disadvantages. It is not likely to bring in those who are uncertain or fearful about what a group experience entails (Gitterman, 1979). The methods of recruitment must be weighed for their fit with need and purpose. Both may be used productively, as in the following example. In a perinatal intensive care unit of a university health center, the social worker decided to offer a continuing open-ended group for parents. This structure was required because some babies are discharged quite soon after birth, and others remain for as long as six months or even a year. The worker writes,

Parents of babies currently in the unit are invited to attend an informal meeting every other Thursday evening for one and a half hours. The parents are invited by either the primary nurse caring for the infant or by me. In addition, a sign is posted the week before the meeting to give parents early notice and in case we are not able to reach them personally. We also extend the invitation to grandparents, and we let parents know they may bring a friend if the spouse is unable to attend or if the parent is a single parent.

So not only do preliminary steps with groups include the same affective and cognitive processes required for successful entry into the life space of an individual patient or family, but advance preparation for a group requires additional steps as well. The effort involved is repaid with a successful group and its contribution to quality patient care or to meeting the unmet needs of patients' families.

The more successful the social worker's preliminary steps are in achieving anticipatory empathy, reviewing pertinent knowledge and theory, and coming into touch with her own likely responses to particular situations, the more likely are the tasks of the initial phase to go well. These tasks are engagement, exploration, definition of needs/problems, assessment, goal-setting, and planning.

Engagement

Engagement refers to the establishment of a working relationship with the patient, family, or group, through which client tasks and worker tasks toward goal attainment can be successfully completed. Steps in developing such a relationship begin with the worker's offer of service and a clear presentation of his function and role. Relatively few patients and their families request social work service, although this is changing as more departments of social work in health care settings distribute brochures describing their services. So, in presenting his function and

role, the worker must also explain his relationship to the patient's physician, the nursing staff, and other team members. He must carefully
describe how his service can aid the patient and family by helping them
to deal with illness-related stress, to locate resources for meeting practical
concerns, and to plan for discharge.

In the following illustration the patient was admitted to the hospital
following a stroke at home. Five days later he was transferred to the
Skilled Nursing Facility. The social worker immediately telephoned the
patient's wife to schedule the customary appointments with the
therapeutic team for information about her husband's condition, and
with herself to begin planning for discharge. The facility expects a timely
and effective discharge to take place within the limits of patients' insurance coverage in order to avoid overstays without insurance
coverage. The social worker seeks to humanize this concern by engagement of the patient and family in realistic planning for discharge. This requires not only a skillful *focus* on the needed information but an equally
skilled *responsiveness* to the feelings and concerns about what has happened. Sometimes these can be conflicting requirements. The pressure
of time is often an advantage since it helps worker and clients to focus on
discharge goals and tasks. Yet the time pressure must not be allowed to
interfere with providing the support the clients need for coping with the
stress generated by the illness or disability. In the initial session, and continuing throughout the contacts, the worker also needs to gather information that will be useful to the rehabilitation team in engaging the patient's strengths and in understanding any negative responses to the
rehabilitative processes. The stress of impairment from a stroke may
cause reverberations in customary family patterns and roles, which then
react back on the patient to affect his participation in the therapies. Preex-
isting maladaptive relationships may result in feelings of guilt or anger
that may also interfere with rehabilitation.

Mr. Boyer, the sixty-four-year-old patient, is retired from a federal job as a skilled
tradesman and receives a pension. Four of the five adult children reside out of the
state, and one son lives nearby. Mr. Boyer has right-side weakness and severe expressive aphasia. Full evaluation of his comprehension has not yet been completed. He transfers in and out of bed with the assistance of one person. Prognosis
for ambulation, probably with a cane, is good. His endurance is good. His right arm
is seriously affected, and Mr. Boyer is not able to write. He requires long-term
speech and occupational therapy, but physical therapy will be needed only for a
short time.

In the context of her experience, knowledge, and awareness of her own
response tendencies, the worker had already considered these data and

had prepared herself affectively and cognitively for the first interview with Mrs. Boyer:

After introductions and settling Mrs. B in the chair of her choice, I repeated what I had said on the telephone about the purpose of our meeting together. She said she understood our purpose and was eager to talk with me. She was warm and friendly, but I noticed she clutched her purse tightly to her body and seemed quite tense. She said her children have been wonderful, and three of them are trying to spend as much time as possible with their parents right now, and also accompanied her to the meetings with the therapists. She began talking rapidly about their accomplishments as teenagers and beyond, and I commented that it was easy to see why she was so proud of them. I asked how the sessions with the therapists went. She said they were helpful, especially for the children, "as I am an LPN (licensed practical nurse)." I said it was fortunate she had a knowledgeable background, but nevertheless I hope she would feel free to ask any questions of me or of the other team members. She nodded.

I asked what thoughts and feelings she has now about Mr. B's stroke. She said she was a little nervous about the thought of leaving him alone at home. She works three late night shifts a week at a local nursing home and would hate to give that up, although she said she will if she has to. I acknowledged that could be a difficult decision but suggested she defer making it until a clearer prognosis is available and the team can evaluate Mr. B's abilities for late night self-care, telephone use, and so on. She relaxed at that.

I asked about Mr. B's interests, activities, and employment just prior to the stroke. She said he retired two years ago because of a heart condition and had some odd jobs since. He has a workshop in the cellar and spends much time there; he bowls regularly with the senior citizens' league, and he is crazy about his dog, which he bought when he retired. "They do everything together and walk about two miles a day. The dog misses him like crazy." I commented she hadn't mentioned anything she and Mr. B do together. She began playing with her purse and said there really isn't anything they enjoy doing together. She began talking rapidly and said she likes to go to the beach on vacation, but he doesn't because dogs aren't allowed. "But I don't care. I go and rent a cottage by myself for a few weeks during the summer. I suppose that's out for this year, which is all right. I don't mind. Staying home with Allan is more important."

Noting the apparent lack of mutuality, I asked how she thinks Mr. B will react to her taking care of him? She said she wasn't sure.* I said that in a few weeks we could arrange a day for her to come in and spend the day giving him care, if she thought that would be helpful. She said it would be. I said she had mentioned retirement and I wondered if she had any concerns about finances. She said the only

---

* It would have been useful and helpful to pick up with this uncertainty.

thing is that they have separate checking accounts and his retirement checks go into his account. She pays some bills and he pays others, but now she doesn't know how to draw on his account. I described the power of attorney instrument and said I could help her with that if she wishes. She seemed relieved. I then asked about the physical set-up at home. She described it in some detail and ended with the statement that she would lock the cellar door to prevent Mr. B's going down unassisted. She seemed tense again as she said this, opening and closing her purse. So I commented that it sounds as if she can't trust his judgment. She replied, "Well, he's a drinker, and that's where he hides the stuff. I don't know if he'll try to find any once he's home. And I don't know if I can find all the bottles because he hides them so well." Her voice rose in pitch and she seemed on the verge of tears. I wondered if she could tell me more about his drinking. She said he drank all through the years when the children were young. She described the children's anger and their later gradual acceptance, as well as her own fears and several separations. For three years they both attended AA, and she was disappointed when he stopped going three years ago. She mentioned occasions when she returned home from work to find him drunk and other times when she had to go out late at night to look for him. Her biggest fear is that he will continue to drink in spite of his physical impairment. She wept, and I reached over to touch her arm. She said God worked in strange ways and perhaps this was His way of finally stopping the drinking. I agreed God worked in strange ways but added that at some point we will have to address the problem. She nodded and said she felt OK about doing that.

I acknowledged how difficult it must have been for her to tell me all this and how important it is for us to know about it. She said she felt better "now that you know." I asked if the doctor knows about Mr. B's drinking. She isn't sure, and I indicated I will need to share the information with him and the team and, at some point, with Mr. B. She said that was fine. I also explained our Alcohol and Drug Abuse program and indicated that the ADA counselor would be available to her after our own work together is ended at discharge. She seemed receptive. I said that because of the drinking problem we will probably want to have Mr. B stay in the facility as long as possible to ensure maximum rehabilitation and to design good supportive services, so we will need to check on insurance coverage. Mrs. Boyer said she would do this.

Our time was up, so I summarized what we had agreed upon. Our plan is that Mr. B will return home and that Mrs. B, tentatively, will continue her work. Two days from now we will obtain the power of attorney if Mr. B is agreeable. Mrs. B will look into the insurance, and begin rearranging the ground floor of her home, obtaining a commode, and so forth. As soon as Mr. B's condition permits we will begin dealing with the drinking problem. We then agreed on (1) joint sessions with the therapists every two weeks so that Mrs. B will have current medical information, and (2) weekly sessions with me on our goals and tasks. I said I will meet with Mr. B tomorrow to explain my involvement on the team, the purpose of my meetings with Mrs. B, and the need for the power of attorney. I added that at some point the three of us may wish to have joint sessions. Mrs. B seemed quite relaxed with all this.

The worker carefully observes nonverbal behavior and notes when anxiety appears. She "listens" to both the manifest and latent content of what is being said and picks up on cues that all is not well with the marriage. As Mrs. B feels supported she lets the worker know about the drinking problem. Both the marital relationship and the drinking are critical to the rehabilitation process, so both need careful evaluation in the few weeks before discharge.

The worker has succeeded in engaging Mrs. Boyer in the initial phase of their proposed work together, and they have a tentative agreement on their next steps. The worker is aware that many areas will need exploration before she understands the situation and can help Mr. and Mrs. B cope with the physical, emotional, and interpersonal demands facing them. For now, however, Mrs. B feels supported, encouraged, and hopeful. Two days later,

I introduced myself to Mr. B, put the bed rail down, and pulled up a chair beside the bed so that we could be at eye level with each other. Then I indicated my awareness of his speech problem and said he needed only to give me yes/no responses. I then explained my function in the skilled nursing facility and on the rehabilitation team, and described the purpose of my meetings with his wife. He responded, "OK." Then I mentioned the immediate problem of paying the bills and told him of the power of attorney procedure and its temporary nature until he regains writing skills. I asked if he felt comfortable with that, and he said, "Yes." I explained that we would try to do this inexpensively and I will meet with them both to handle the details. He said, "Good," and I asked if he was receiving all the medical information he would like? He said, "No." I asked if the doctor had been in to talk with him, and he said, "No." I said I would pursue that, and he said, "Good." I added that he and his wife will also be meeting with the team for medical updates and for more definite information about his length of stay. He should probably plan on no less than four weeks. He shrugged. I acknowledged it might seem like a long time, but time and therapy are two things he needs right now. He said, "OK." I said I understand his goal is to return home, and he said, "Yes." I also mentioned that his wife had told me about his dog, and a little later we can plan to take him out to the lawn to visit with her. He smiled for the first time and said, "Great." To sum up, I said I will come to see him at least once a week to keep him posted, and perhaps we will have Mrs. B join us on occasion. I said I will work on the power of attorney, request the doctor to see him before the weekend in order to discuss the stroke, and will talk with him next week about the dog's visit. I asked how all this seemed, and he said, "OK."

An aphasic patient with limited speech and often with little comprehension or writing skills presents a challenge to the social worker. Verbal communication is critical to much of practice, and without it the skills of the worker may be sorely taxed. With her knowledge and empathy this worker was able to see into the inner world of Mr. Boyer and to anticipate at least some of the questions and concerns he might have. She related to him as a fully competent adult, able to participate in decision-making, which helps allay his anxiety about his present helplessness and enforced dependence. She surmounted the lack of feedback in one-word responses, which, in more ordinary situations, often leave us frustrated and at peril of unproductive silences (Schroeder, 1980). She was careful to make this interview brief and supportive, knowing that aphasic patients can become easily frustrated and fatigued.

There is beginning engagement achieved through empathy and respect for Mr. Boyer's dignity and autonomy as an adult. Because the worker assumes comprehension until an evaluation proves otherwise, there is no tinge of condescension in her verbal or nonverbal behaviors. While the power of attorney represents a loss of control, she is careful to say the arrangement is temporary until he regains his ability to write. Her decision to remove the guard rail and to sit at eye level is also supportive of Mr. Boyer's capacities. A physical barrier to interaction is eliminated and a human mutuality replaces the power position inherent in a professional's standing above the supine, helpless patient. The worker was aware that withholding the information she had about the drinking problem undermines the sense of control she wishes him to maintain. Her rationale was the need to plan with other team members for therapeutic timing of this intervention. Mr. Boyer may be feeling guilty about the drinking, along with expectable fears about his impairment and the changes it will mean for his way of life. This will complicate worries about helplessness and dependence on his wife's care, so timing is important.

Similarly, Mrs. Boyer's background as a licensed practical nurse, while it lends comfort to her in this medical setting, may lead to her being "too clinical" in her approach to Mr. Boyer's care. She will need help in individualizing his needs, fears, and frustrations and help in handling her anger at him, so that her caregiving role does not result in further deterioration of their already strained relationship. Thus the plan for trying out their new roles in the facility emerges out of the worker's sensitivity to the potential strains for both. The tentative plan for her continued night work will help keep some part of her life separate while seeking and sustaining a new quality of mutuality.

Engagement proceeds through the worker's sensitive response to the clients' questions about the service, their concerns, and any ambivalence about taking help, during which full account is taken of nonverbal behaviors and incongruences between them and verbal communications. Ambivalence in this context refers to feeling two ways about the social worker's offer of service or the referral by other staff. On the one hand there may be relief that someone is there to help. But on the other, there may be fears that accepting help will be construed as a sign of weakness or will mean relinquishing control of one's affairs to another. Accepting help may arouse long-standing fears of being disapproved of or disliked or old feelings of distrust toward others, along with the almost universal fear of the unknown. It is helpful to verbalize for the individual, in an empathic way, the ambivalent feelings that are conscious or just beyond immediate awareness. For example, "Perhaps you have some thoughts about my suggestion" or "It's hard to think about needing help" invites the expression of doubts or concerns, conveys the idea that it is all right to have misgivings, and begins to build trust in the worker's understanding and genuine interest.

This level of ambivalence may also be apparent in response to the offer of family sessions or a group service. In addition to the fear of the unknown, there may be fears about the loss of privacy or confidentiality, fears of exposing oneself to strangers in a group or of exposing family weaknesses and "secrets" in family sessions. Where such feelings of doubt and concern are apparent they need to be handled also, by verbalizing them, exploring them, clarifying the nature of the helping process, and addressing the issue of confidentiality.

People have the right to refuse a service, and that right must be respected. But it is desirable that such a decision, like all decisions, be based on information rather than assumptions. Therefore it is important that the worker be as clear as possible in her description of the purpose of help and how it is carried out. Then, if the individual refuses, it is also important, without feeling personally rejected, to convey acceptance and respect for the decision, while indicating one's availability should there be a change of mind.

Engagement reaches its desired beginning level when worker and client agree to work together on a mutually defined need or problem. The agreement may be only tentative until exploration and assessment can clarify the nature of the client's situation, so that goals can be set and tasks allotted. Clearly, engagement is a process that supports the achievement of other tasks of the initial phase. But it is, in turn, strengthened by their successful achievement. The relationship makes the work possible, yet it depends on the work for its development.

As noted earlier, groups in health care settings are often of short duration, open-ended and, unstructured, as in waiting room groups and single session groups. Such groups must be quickly engaged, which places a special demand on the social worker's skill in clarifying why they are meeting and what the nature of their shared illness-related tasks is. The following example of a waiting room group, led by a social worker, comes from a weekly diabetes clinic in an outpatient setting. The population served are anxious about and frustrated by their illness. Many experience difficulty adhering to their diet and achieving optimal weight, or complying with the regimens of urine testing and insulin injection.

Most are discouraged by the fact that even careful adherence does not assure immunity from deterioration or complications such as insulin shock, visual loss, circulatory problems and amputation, kidney failure, and loss of sexual potency. Clinic staff felt that even one-session waiting room groups might help the patients in their efforts to cope with the stress of their illness.

The waiting room was full, and I asked how many were there to attend the Diabetes Clinic. About ten people raised their hands. Most were seated in the same area. One man sat at a distance, but he later moved to join the others. I introduced myself and said I was a social worker who would be meeting each week in the waiting room with those who are attending the Diabetes Clinic. I mentioned that often people seem just to "wait" in waiting rooms without talking with one another. Yet people with the same disease may have encountered the same kinds of problems and concerns about it. So the clinic staff thinks that an opportunity for patients in the waiting room to talk together about their experiences can be helpful. I added that even though clinic staff can answer questions, it's often helpful to talk with others who face the same concerns. One woman then asked if I meant "like talking about what happens when you get diabetes?" I nodded, and someone else said, "How scared you feel, like your whole life has changed." One woman said she recently fell on the street. Several people helped her get up and asked if she were all right. She indicated she was, but immediately fell again. She explained to the group that she had felt too embarrassed to tell her helpers that she had diabetes. One of the other patients responded, "That's why it's good we can talk so you can see that other people have it too." The woman next to her patted her knee and said, "See, we're all in this together." Then a man began to talk about the need to face the fact that you have diabetes. "Otherwise you can get sick and people won't know you have it, and you could die in shock or in coma." He said that's why he wears a bracelet that says, "I am a diabetic," and carries a card with medical information about his condition. This led to a discussion of the consequences of cheating on diets, and members shared ideas about how they handle their frustration about food. At first they directed their questions and comments to me, but I encouraged their interaction with one another. This proceded well, and additional themes included eye problems and the incidence of diabetes in families. At the end of the hour when appointments were called, I asked for their evaluation of the meeting. Comments included, "I learned a lot," "This was fun," "I think everyone liked it, we're so lonely." I said I was glad they felt good about it. Someone said she'd see me again, and I replied I will be here weekly, so whenever they need to come to Clinic I will look forward to being with them.

The patients clearly became engaged with one another and with the worker. However, as the groups continued, it became evident that the open waiting room was dysfunctional for the group's purpose. Yet the groups seemed to gather momentum as some patients returned to later sessions. Staff felt the groups were beneficial, so the clinic then in-augurated a series of four-session closed-end groups in a separate room, led by the social worker. These were well attended, even though they meant extra trips to the clinic for this largely poor population.

Not only are all tasks of the initial phase telescoped in such single-session groups, but aspects of the ongoing and ending phases are also. To facilitate the quick development of mutual aid, the worker must be continuously aware of the level of anxiety, depression, and other affects, and sure-footed in discouraging the expression of feelings that is not con-structive or productive and in dealing with disruptive behavior, since members for one-session groups are rarely screened. He must know when to be active in structuring the discussion in order to maintain a focus on its purpose and when to rely on the group's ability to do this, when to answer questions and when to redirect them to group members, and how to avoid the temptation of offering solutions and instead to en-courage interaction and work by the group. The worker must also be able to affirm the group's achievements so that members leave with a sense of having been helpful to others and having themselves been helped—however modest the achievements in a one-session group can be. Such knowledge and skill are developed and strengthened by experience with groups that are more structured and by observation of successful leaders of one-session groups.

But even in more structured groups the engagement process rests first on a clear statement of purpose. Since the members must become en-gaged with one another and with the worker if an effective mutual aid system is to be developed, most group leaders find that the self-introduction of the members and a brief description of their experience with the illness that brings them together are important at the outset. The purpose can then be more clearly enunciated in relation to the common concerns that emerge from these statements. The process of identifica-tion with one another thus begins.

In a regional pediatric cancer center the social worker offers a six-session evening group to mothers and fathers of children suffering from cancer who have just been discharged from inpatient care. The group is timed to coincide with the early (diagnostic) stage of the illness in order to help the parents cope with the meaning and impact of their children's grave condition. This is an important entry point before maladaptive pro-cesses appear or become frozen in place. The group serves as an effective vehicle for promoting adaptive behavior patterns and effective coping skills. In the diagnostic phase of the illness the parents' coping tasks in-clude telling other family members, considering what and how to tell the patient, arranging for the care of other children, evaluating financial resources, and so forth. They now focus on themselves as parents of a seriously ill child (Ross, 1979). As they grapple with these tasks, "they are developing psychosocial 'tools,' mechanisms for surmounting stress. These tools, acquired during each phase of the child's illness, are necessary to resolve the stress of the next phase. When there is a failure to develop such tools, each successive phase of the illness is experienced as if it were the first and the obstacles to adaptive coping may be compounded'' (Ross, 1978).

The leader opens the first session by repeating what she has told them individually about the group's purpose: to provide members an opportunity to share their common concerns as parents of a child who has cancer. She mentions that other parents have found such groups helpful. The parents are asked to introduce themselves and to tell the group their child's name, diagnosis, and time of onset of the illness. She then invites them to respond to the group's purpose with their thoughts about attending. Frequently the parents feel it might be depressing to talk about the illness. She acknowledges the validity of that concern while pointing out that they can help one another with the feelings that are already there, since they are all learning to live with the situation. She suggests they might share their beginning experiences with each other. ''As each parent describes the first days and weeks, the group begins to change and many parents relax and sometimes become more animated. The social worker stresses the commonalities and points out that they have already begun to find ways of coping. By this time the participants are beginning to ask each other questions and are raising issues'' (Ross, 1979, p. 385).

The group's purpose had been discussed with potential members at the time of recruitment. But if it is not restated in the opening session nor opportunity given for responses by the group members and for their participation in further specifying the group's purpose, it is likely that members will not feel safe. They will not then become engaged with the worker or with one another. Instead, they may constantly raise the question verbally or through behavior, ''What are we here for?'' The work will not be focused, and a mutual aid system may not develop. The skills of engagement, then, are needed across levels of human organization: individuals, couples, families, and groups. They are summarized in Table 5–1.

Exploration, Assessment, Planning, and Contracting

Exploration, assessment, planning, and contracting in most health care settings are characterized by the need for rapidity in gathering needed life space data, assessing their meaning, and developing a plan of action based on their meaning. Except in long-term care and some ambulatory settings, social worker and client in health care do not have the luxury of

TABLE 5-1.   Skills of Engagement

1. Connecting the offer of service to the particular illness and individualized situation, presenting clearly the social work function and role, and the worker's relationship to the physician, nurses, and other staff
2. Responding sensitively to clients' questions about social work help, their concerns related to the impact of the illness such as finances, child care, transportation, job, the stress of the patient role, plans for discharge, and so on
3. Responding empathically to cues and signals of distress with acceptance of feelings, respect, support, and realistic hope
4. Recognizing nonverbal behaviors that are incongruent with verbal communications and responding to the latent content
5. Clarifying next steps to be undertaken by clients and worker, including when, where, and with whom
6. Managing initial ambivalence and resistance (issues of motivation)
7. Checking out the validity of one's expectations and perceptions tentatively held prior to the first session—especially those related to age, sex, race, ethnicity, and social class—and assumptions based on theoretical perspectives
8. Encouraging interaction among members of family or group, making sure that each one has the opportunity to participate

covering needed information in several interviews. Instead, they must quickly reach agreement on mutually set goals and the tasks by which to meet them. Sometimes exploration, assessment and contracting, goal-setting, and planning must all take place in the first interview. Also, it takes a high level of skill to judge how much an ill and possibly frightened patient can participate in exploration and planning, and to help families understand the need for certain kinds of data when they are the principal informants.

It is particularly important to understand how personal, environmental, and cultural factors interact with the illness factors to produce added stress. This requires the worker to consider carefully the patient's developmental stage in the life course, inasmuch as the associated life tasks will affect the tasks of coping with the illness and will be affected by them. Chronic illness, for example, affects the developmental tasks of a child or youth in significant ways bearing on the development of a sense of competence, peer relations, identity formation, appropriate degrees of autonomous functioning, and so on. In turn, how these tasks are or have been handled will affect how the individual copes with the illness. A young adult head of a family or a single parent has a different set of life tasks that may make coping with the consequences of illness or disability very difficult. The self-concept, life goals, and significant statuses and roles in family, work, and community life may be adversely affected by the illness. Similarly, an elderly person who may be coping with losses of family and friends, the relinquishment of the work role, and changes in financial arrangements may find the loss of physical health and vigor or the demands of chronic illness particularly hard to bear.

It is equally important to consider the developmental stage of the family *qua* family in its own life course. The associated family tasks, interacting with individual members' life tasks, will provide clues to the likely impact of the patient's illness on the functioning of the family and its other members. Frameworks have been developed for delineating family developmental stages and tasks (Rhodes, 1977; O'Connell, 1972). While helpful, they must be used with caution, because they refer to the prototypical nuclear family of the middle class and may not fit other family forms.

This caution underscores the need for the social worker to take into account newly emerging family structures and the possibility that such structures may face exceptional life tasks in addition to those they share with nuclear structures. The added tasks of coping with the illness may therefore be even more difficult. Such structures include but are not limited to one-parent families, reconstituted (step) families, two-career families (often maintaining two geographically separate homes/work sites), and same-sex families. The last-mentioned may be based on sexual preference or on ties of friendship or kinship.

All families, regardless of their structure, must maintain an adaptive balance between the imperative for constancy as an identifiable entity over time and the imperative for variability in response to changing internal and/or external conditions. Families that are unable to change their structures and functioning in response to the changing needs of members as they develop, mature, age, and decline, or families that are unable to change in response to external pressures such as work or school demands, changing norms and values, and illness itself, are likely to find their functioning impaired or in danger of impairment. Similarly, families that are unable to maintain needed stability in the face of the shifting winds of fate, the ups and downs of family life, and the vagaries of community and societal life are likely to have dysfunctional relationship and communication patterns and to experience difficulties in meeting the pressures and opportunities presented by the environment.

The family is also embedded in a culture or subculture derived from group affiliations such as race, ethnicity, social class, religion, and occupation. Besides, it creates its own unique culture out of the shared experiences of its members over the life course. The two cultures blend and are manifested in the values and norms by which the family organizes and governs itself, structures its statuses and roles, allocates tasks and functions, patterns its internal relational and communication processes, and guides its relations with the outer world.

The impact of illness and disability is likely to reverberate throughout the family's structure, shaking up the spousal, parent–child, and sibling

subsystems, upsetting established patterns of communication and relationships, dismantling old coalitions and alliances, or providing impetus
for the formation of new ones that may be more or less adaptive than the
old ones, and creating pressures for the reallocation of statuses, roles,
and tasks. Illness may diminish the quantity and quality of nutritive exchanges in some instances. Some families may have functioned well
before the illness but be unable to cope with the multiple stresses the illness poses. Such inability may be related to the family's own
developmental stage and tasks, to problems connected to its structure
and functioning, to the patient's own developmental stage and the tasks
and roles she or he occupied within the family, or to the absence of external coping resources. Other families may not have been functioning
adaptively even before the illness, and the added stress of illness may
push the family toward disintegration, increasing the stress on all
members.

The social worker in health care has to explore the structure
of the family (statuses, roles, and subsystems such as spousal, parent-
child, and sibling), its functioning (tasks, interpersonal processes),
and its culture (values, norms, goals, and attitudes toward health,
illness, and disability). The skills of exploration are summarized in
Table 5–2 (p. 110).

The following situation illustrates the complex interplay between the
tasks of coping with illness and the tasks associated with individual and
family life stages. Mr. Butoni, forty-eight, of immigrant Italian parentage, suffers from multiple sclerosis, diabetes, deteriorating vision and
hearing, and depression. He was hospitalized in a VA hospital and then
discharged for rehabilitation to a blind center, where he worked hard but
soon reached a plateau because of his disabilities. He is now home. The
worker on the neurological service, also attached to the blind center, is
able to follow him and the family. She describes the situation:

Because of MS and diabetes, Mr. B can now only walk short distances before
becoming fatigued. He is grossly overweight and shuffles along unsteadily,
supporting himself with a quad cane. He cannot raise his arms or carry even a light
object without severe pain. He has no peripheral vision and can see only a few feet
straight ahead. He is losing his ability to think and remember, and he is embarrassed at not being able to follow a conversation or to retain information. He wears
a sad and bewildered expression, and poured out his sorrow to me, his dread of
total blindness, his fear of losing his mind, and his rage over his helplessness. He
held two jobs in a service occupation until the onset of MS a year ago, and now he
has to depend on his wife who instead is working two jobs. He feels he is a burden
to his family, and though he asserts she won't he fears his wife will leave him. He
said he had not been such a good husband in the past and there had been much
quarreling. He added he always admired her intelligence, aggressiveness, and hard-

TABLE 5-2.   Skills of Exploration

Mutually with the patient and-or family:
1. Eliciting the patient's and family's beliefs about the nature of the illness, its etiology, the personal meaning attached to it, and ideas about effective treatment/help (see Ch. 3)
2. Scanning the life space to ascertain (a) coping resources; (b) preexistent problems in living that may impede coping with the illness; and (c) actual, potential, or feared impacts of the illness on personal, interpersonal, and environmental areas for patient and family
3. Noting the quality of affect, including anxiety, guilt, and depression; the level of cognitive-sensory-perceptual functioning; self-concept; the nature of interpersonal processes; and initial coping efforts including defenses
4. Providing emotional support to ease or contain crippling levels of anxiety, depression, guilt or other immobilizing affects by the use of engagement skills noted in Table 5-1
5. Eliciting and weighing the social and cultural factors (race, ethnicity, social class, religion, occupation) that may influence perceptions and expectations regarding the illness experience, the patient role, treatment/help, and coping patterns
6. Eliciting and weighing age and gender factors with regard to individual and family developmental stages and tasks, and their implications for successful coping
7. Scanning the physical and social environments for the availability of concrete resources, information, social network support, and responsiveness of the health care organization to the particular needs of patient and family, and noting the need for adjustments/changes in the physical setting
8. Exchanging pertinent information with team members (with clients' informed consent or, at the least, with clients' knowledge)

working nature and thought her superior to him. He hopes she will accept the love he feels for her now. He is not close to his two older sisters or to his two children, daughters aged twenty-two and twenty-one, and has no close friends. He was the youngest in his family and was very close to his mother, who died when he was twenty-four. He said he lost his only protector and so quickly looked for a replacement in his wife, whom he married one year later.

Mrs. B, age forty-two and also of immigrant Italian parentage, when interviewed quickly admitted that she did not love her husband and would leave him if her religion and sense of duty permitted. She had felt very unsupported by him throughout the marriage. She described him as self-centered, verbally abusive, and never there as a father or husband. She added that she had depended on her father to help her. She cried as she revealed she was her father's favorite, but he had died fourteen years ago, and her marriage had gone downhill ever since. She has a hostile relationship with her mother, and she tired of pleasing someone who is prouder of the two older sisters and fonder of the younger brother than of Mrs. B, the more dutiful and successful daughter. Bitterly, she said her mother always referred to her as the "dumb, unreliable one," making her feel inferior to her sisters. She is a college graduate and holds a professional position.

Mrs. B, angry at her husband's helplessness, said her own needs have always been submerged in the service of her husband's. She complained that she always came second after his sisters. Mr. B protested that he has never been close to his sisters but can't change their ways and doesn't want to cut off the tenuous relationship he does have. It was clearly an old, unresolved issue, about which they had been in marital counseling earlier, to no avail. Mrs. B appears to project her relationship with her mother and siblings onto Mr. B and to be unable to appreciate that he cannot change his sisters.

The older daughter, Eleanor, lives out of state but comes home each weekend to be with the family. She has not been seen, but Mrs. B says she is rebellious and does little to help at home since she feels she gives enough by coming home each weekend. From Mrs. B's description, she has no friends, is withdrawn, and is less favored by mother than her sister. The younger daughter, Louise, a college graduate like her sister, works and continues to live at home but at present is at home full time recuperating from an auto accident. She reports that whenever she goes out now, leaving her father alone, his anxiety makes her feel terrible. She wants to move out but feels guilty about it because of the needs of both parents. She fears her mother will feel abandoned, will drive herself still more, and might have a heart attack (her heart is said to be weak) and die. Louise describes her mother as a martyr. She also says that she herself has no social life because male friends are given the third degree, which prevents her from having even a casual relationship.

The extent and gravity of Mr. B's disabilities are sufficient to cause inordinate stress in almost any family. But the Bs have long-standing marital and parent–child issues, which make coping with the consequences of his disabilities very difficult indeed. Mr. B and every member of the family is suffering. He is grieving for the loss of his health, vigor, mobility, vision, hearing, cognitive powers, status, self-concept, and ability to work and to support his family. Mrs. B has apparently always viewed herself as a reluctant martyr and now experiences her husband's illness as intolerable. Long-standing conflicts are resurfacing, or in some instances continuing, and interfere with the partners' abilities to deal with the reality issues of the illness.

Ethnically derived norms and values, as they influence the couple's marital roles, self-concepts, and expectations of their daughters, will have to be explored. There may also be a social class difference between the spouses, reflected in Mrs. B's educational and professional status, possibly affecting their relationship. These are unusual accomplishments in first generation Italian-immigrant women (Rotunno and McGoldrick, 1982). Nothing is yet known of the family's religion (probably Catholic) and whether it is a potential source of strength to draw upon. Family ties must also be explored. They are of great importance in Italian families, yet Mr. and Mrs. B are both alienated from their families. He is the younger brother of two older sisters and favored by his mother. Mrs. B is the older sister of a preferred (by her mother) younger brother and favored by her father. Each partner seems to look to the other as a replacement for the lost idealized parent. Doomed to continuous disappointment, they seem unutterably lonely and isolated, made the more so now by the horrors of Mr. B's illness. Mrs. B feels trapped in a hopeless situation, and Mr. B has a tremendous fear of being abandoned once again.

As young adults, both daughters are affected by their father's serious illness. Eleanor seems cast in the role of unfavored daughter and Louise in the role of good and devoted daughter, perhaps a reenactment of their mother's own perceived experience. In the larger culture, young women their age are expected to be more independent and even more liberated in terms of living away from home, with freedom to engage in cross-gender relationships and to take direction of their own lives. These norms are at variance with those of many Italian families. Thus the daughters may be struggling to free themselves from the culturally and psychologically based needs of their parents. Too little is yet known about each daughter and their own sibling relationship, but the tasks of young adulthood are clearly threatened by those parental needs to keep the daughters close—now greatly intensified by the serious illness. This conflict adds to the stress.

As work continues with this family, Mr. B will need help to rediscover his own strengths and interests. The worker has already arranged for Talking Books and for attendance at the local senior center, where Mr. B enjoys the activities and socializing. She plans to consider with him his interest in an animal companion to assuage his loneliness in the long days when he is alone. It is also possible that a group offered through the local MS society can provide both social interaction and support for coping. Similarly, Mrs. B will need support in meeting the demands her husband's illness realistically places on her. Respite services or a support group for spouses of MS patients will be considered with her.

Once more is known of the family's culture, it may be possible to bring some pleasure into the family's life together by encouraging a return to previously loved ethnic and religious rituals and celebrations (Laird, 1982); by mobilizing natural helpers through the church and

Italian community for companionship, respite, and as coping resources; or by reconnecting family members to past pleasurable activities. It may be important to give support to Louise in her wish to leave home. If that is the case, work will have to be done to help Mr. and Mrs. B deal with still another loss.

Fortunately, there are many strengths to work with, despite the long-entrenched dysfunctional relationship patterns. Mrs. B has a secure position she enjoys that provides her with self-esteem. Mr. B works cooperatively with the health care system and now with the worker. He is responsive to support and encouragement and has a fighting spirit. Despite his understandable depression, his motivation to deal with his losses has continued. He works hard in physical therapy and is eager to keep busy. And, for the time being at least, there are no serious financial concerns. Eventually it may even be possible to work with selected extended kin since these relationships seem to be a strong interfering factor in the Butonis' struggle to reach an adaptive family balance, both in the past and now in the face of Mr. B's incurable illness (Hartman and Laird, 1983). It is very important that the policy of the hospital permits the worker to continue with the patient and family even though he is now at home.

In this illustration, exploration and assessment are both evident, particularly as assessment points up the need for further exploration, which in turn may change the assessment. Thus assessment considers how personal, environmental, and cultural factors interact with illness factors to influence the degree of stress and the quality and amount of coping resources of both the patient and the family. These content areas are summarized in Table 5-3.

TABLE 5-3.   Content of Assessment

1. Illness factors, including diagnosis, prognosis, and likely sequelae
2. Personal factors, including patient's developmental stage and associated tasks connected to age and gender; statuses and roles; emotional and psychological features, social and cultural features
3. Interpersonal factors, including the family's developmental stage and associated tasks; communication and relationship processes; structural aspects
4. Environmental factors, including obstacles and resources in both the physical and social environments
5. Cultural factors: norms, values, goals, and attitudes toward illness, all as derived from race, ethnicity, social class, religion, and occupation
6. Interplay of the five preceding sets of factors in the creation and/or maintenance of stress, and the absence or presence of coping resources (internal and external)

However, assessment is to be approached not only from the stand-point of *content* areas to be explored and understood by client and worker; it is also a *process* that advances from moment to moment throughout the contact. It is a cognitive and empathic process on the part of the worker, but its findings must be frequently checked with the clients for their validity. It is continuous, as worker and client together review and handle pertinent information—thoughts, feelings, and experiences related to the illness as well as life space material. The process is essential for gaining mutual understanding of the individualized situation in order to undertake effective action. It is the basis on which the worker tests out the impact and effectiveness of her moment-to-moment verbal interventions and keeps in touch with her own feeling responses to the client situation. Basic steps in diagnostic thinking for ecostructural family therapy, as developed by Aponte (1979), are adapted for the *process* of assessment in health care social work. These are summarized in Table 5–4. They apply to both the patient's and family's overall need-situation and the issues occurring in any given session, and they offer a way of thinking/responding throughout the contact.

Aspects of exploration, assessment, and planning can be seen in the Boyer case, analyzed earlier in this chapter. The worker next met briefly with Mr. and Mrs. B in order that Mrs. B could secure the power of attorney for Mr. B. Four days later the worker and Mrs. B met for their scheduled session. After some opening discussion of discharge plans, the worker again raised the possibility of alcoholic counseling. Mrs. B remained silent. The worker commented on this, and Mrs. B said she hated even to think about the "what-ifs" in case her husband started to drink again. The worker acknowledged this was a difficult area to think about and wondered if Mrs. B had some feelings about it too?

TABLE 5–4.   Basic Steps in Clients–Worker Mutual Processes of Assessment

1. Identifying the nature of concerns/problems/needs to be addressed
2. Collecting relevant data, reported by patient, family, and staff, and derived from transactions within sessions
3. Developing tentative hypotheses about personal, interpersonal, environmental, and illness-related factors in 1, with particular reference to theory, knowledge, and experience
4. Setting tentative goals, immediate and long-range
5. On the basis of the first four steps, deciding on immediate intervention that will lead toward goals
6. Observing effect of intervention to confirm or discount hypotheses about effectiveness of intervention and accuracy of hypotheses. With the last step the cycle begins all over again, a moment-to-moment process.

On the verge of tears, yet remaining in control of herself, Mrs. B told me of the events leading to the hospitalization. Mr. B had been in the cellar "working" all day and had refused to come up when she called him for meals. Finally, when it was late enough for her to go to bed she went down to see "what condition" he was in. Beginning to weep, she said, "He was in one of his stupors. So I put my arm around him and pulled him up, but could not maneuver him up the stairs. He was no help at all and totally unresponsive. I was so angry at him I did something I had never done before. I left him on the cellar floor all night and called him a no-good bastard. Can you believe anyone could do such a thing, to leave him all night on the floor?"

I said, "Yes, I can. It is extremely frustrating living with someone who is a heavy drinker." She relaxed a little, and said that when she woke up that morning she went down to the cellar and found that he had vomited all over himself. He was still in a stupor, but she managed to undress him and then brought a bucket of water downstairs, washed him, and redressed him. "It never occurred to me, even then, that he had had a stroke; and I'm supposed to be a nurse." I commented she is being hard on herself, as she had had no reason to think of a stroke. She had been concerned about finding him in that condition and had tried to make him more comfortable. She nodded.

Mrs. B continued, "I don't know how I did it, but with him helping a little I got him up the stairs and settled on the couch. It still didn't occur to me it was taking him an extra long time to sober up. But a few hours later I began to be suspicious. When he still couldn't speak and he kept trying to tell me something, pointing to his mouth, I finally said, 'My God, Allan, I think you've had a stroke.' That was when I brought him to the hospital. Imagine all that time and nothing had been done for him." I acknowledged her worry and fear about what she had done and not done. We sat quietly for a moment, and then I asked if she and her husband had yet talked about this. She said no, but he was even more affectionate with her now than before, and so she thinks he doesn't blame her. I wondered if she could bring it up with him, so she could tell him how she feels about it. She said she wasn't sure. When I mentioned that the ADA counselor could be helpful with this, Mrs. B said she would think seriously about accepting a referral.

The worker's earlier hypotheses concerning lack of mutuality in the marriage and problematic drinking behavior on the part of Mr. B receive additional support from the data yielded by this interview. The problem of alcoholism is now understood to be serious. Because she will not be able to stay with the Bs after discharge in four or five weeks, the worker presses for entry into alcoholic counseling. Her intervention, based on the hypotheses, is met by Mrs. B's resistance. But the supportive comment on the silence frees Mrs. B to unburden herself further. The hypotheses are confirmed.

A new hypothesis is now entertained that Mrs. B is feeling guilty (and probably is also angry at her husband for the circumstances giving rise to her guilt) about how she handled the situation at the onset of the stroke.

The worker accepts the feelings and points, realistically, to the care Mrs. B did give her husband before she recognized the stroke. More important, she suggests to Mrs. B that it will be helpful to her and her husband to talk about it. If it is hypothesized also that Mr. B may be feeling guilty about his drinking and any perceived connection to the stroke, such communication between the couple will be beneficial to him as well.

Since Mrs. B is planning to be the primary caretaker after Mr. B returns home, the worker concluded this interview by inviting her to attend a conference on the present situation and postdischarge needs, with the whole team. Mrs. B accepted and repeated her hope that she could keep her part-time evening job. She said their son, John, had agreed to stay with his father on those nights. The worker supported this idea on the assumption (hypothesis) that the couple will need some spatial and temporal distance from the intensity of giving and receiving care. Their new roles are likely to have repercussions for both as Mr. B is forced to become dependent on his wife and she is forced to interact with him more intimately and more continuously.

Next the worker conferred with the treatment team about the material elicited in this session that bore on the rehabilitation process. The physician acknowledged he had known about Mr. B's drinking and had warned him about the likely impact on his health, but eventually he had concluded persuading Mr. B was hopeless. Other team members were sympathetic regarding all that the couple now needed to deal with. They suggested that Mrs. B be invited to participate in Mr. B's daily living activities once a week so that team members could be alert to any areas of personal and interpersonal stress on the part of either. It was agreed that the worker would not discuss the drinking directly with Mr. B for another week, when it was expected that his speech would be somewhat clearer and comprehension more completely evaluated. All team members supported the plan for Mrs. B to continue her part-time job.

This conference with the team underscores some of the dilemmas experienced in team practice, particularly issues of confidentiality. Mr. B's drinking is being discussed and analyzed without his knowledge or consent. The worker, feeling the urgency of providing alcoholic counseling, introduces the problem perhaps earlier than she had to and therefore before Mr. B's readiness to participate could be ascertained. On the other hand, her rationale could well be that the team's decision about when to introduce it had to precede his permission to have them know. These and other dilemmas of team practice are taken up in Chapter 8.

So far, then, the assessment has uncovered maladaptive patterns of relationship and communication between the spouses, attributed to Mr. B's excessive drinking. Viewed transactionally, the drinking may be both cause and effect of the marital conflict. The conflict predates the illness but is a critical factor, because it is likely to affect the couple's ability to cope with the stress of the disability. Mr. B is facing the role transition of becoming a chronic invalid, with all its implications for him in terms of his self-concept, style of life, feelings about dependence and independence, possible guilt that his drinking caused the stroke, and so on. When his speech improves, it will be necessary to learn from Mr. B what personal meanings the stroke has for him. With that information in hand the worker will be in a better position to help Mr. B by enhancing personal and external coping resources. Mr. B's return to drinking seems to have predated his retirement by a short period. One might therefore hypothesize that the loss of the work role and the enforced togetherness that retirement means for some couples were difficult. He did develop his workshop and bowling interests, but they will probably no longer be accessible, so he faces many losses in addition to the grievous loss of functions and health.

Before the illness the couple had handled their conflict and maintained their marriage by separateness and distance. They had separate bills and financial accounts and took separate vacations. Mr. B became involved with his dog, and Mrs. B visited friends and worked outside the home. Their only bond, it seemed, was their shared interest in their children. The availability of the children and their apparent caring represent important strengths in the present situation, although the quality of their relationships to their father is not yet known. Mrs. B apparently is now fearful of having to relinquish her independence and separateness in order to provide the intimate physical care her husband requires. This may be especially hard in the face of her old anger at him for his drinking and her new guilt surrounding the onset of the stroke.

With respect to planning, the tentative assessment suggests the importance of helping the couple to reopen clogged channels of communication, giving Mrs. B "permission" to leave Mr. B in the care of a son three nights a week for her respite in a job she enjoys, and rallying the support of their children. A little later, after Mr. B has been involved in discussion about the drinking problem and communication between the Bs has improved, more work can be done toward a referral for ongoing counseling and a search for activities of interest to Mr. B and appropriate to his capacities.

With respect to contracting, agreement has been reached that the couple will work together in a controlled, supportive environment on Mr. B's basic needs and Mrs. B's complementary tasks; both will participate in planning and carrying out the steps needed to make the house ready for Mr. B's return; and joint sessions will be held in the time remaining before discharge so that the worker may support their talking together about critical issues in their adaptation to the disability.* It is expected

---

* The interview with Mr. B, in which these agreements were also made is not recorded here (nor is the session where Mr. B's dog was brought to the hospital for the promised visit on the grounds—which brought much pleasure to them both and also to Mrs. B).

that these activities will also yield further needed information on adaptive patterns and degree of resilience in each partner, external coping resources, and movement toward or away from a new marital balance that will support their joint tasks. Moreover, the points of agreement (contracting) also will provide focal points for periodic review of progress, evaluation of next steps, the need for renegotiating any points such as goals and tasks, and so forth. The skills of contracting are summarized in Table 5-5.

In this illustration the initial phase has proceeded smoothly, but that is not always the case. Resistance during this and later phases may obstruct the helping process. In the initial phase it is most frequently due to conscious and preconscious factors related to personal, social, and cultural differences between client and social worker. These include age and gender differences as well as differences in social class, ethnicity, and even religion. Although the individual, family, or group may have accepted the offer of or referral to social work services, full participation in the processes of the initial phase seems to be blocked. In addition to ambivalent feelings mentioned earlier, the elderly may feel that a young worker will not understand the problems facing the ill and disabled old person. The adolescent patient may feel similarly about an older worker. Women may anticipate that a male social worker will be unsympathetic about the impact of certain illnesses and disabilities on a woman. Men likewise may not trust the knowledge and skill of a female social worker or may view her mainly as a sex object.

Previous unhelpful relationships with a social worker may have led to stereotypes about all social workers. Among the poor and otherwise oppressed persons, the expectation of being treated as inferior or in an authoritarian, or even paternalistic way may be strong and, unfortunately, reality-based in life experience. In some cultural groups, strong norms exist against sharing personal and family matters with an out-

TABLE 5-5.   Skills of Contracting

1. Reaching agreement on the nature of the problem/need, in transactional terms
2. Reaching agreement on realistic, appropriately ranked goals, directed to reducing stress and enhancing coping resources (internal and external)
3. Reaching agreement on next steps (clients' tasks; worker tasks) required for achieving the goals, appropriately paced
4. Reaching agreement on modality or modalities to be used (individual, family, and/or group), and temporal and spatial arrangements for sessions
5. Renegotiating agreements as needed, for example, when conditions change or new data are processed
6. Using points of agreement for periodic evaluation of progress made in both client tasks and worker tasks

sider. In other cultures one is expected to behave toward authority figures with deference and submissiveness, which runs counter to the professional values of self-determination and active participation by the client.

Such attitudes and expectations and perceptions (except for cultural norms), *when they are present*, are potential obstacles to effective help. They are of a different order from the resistances that may appear later. Resistances of the initial phase are usually more readily handled. Responsiveness to verbal and nonverbal evidence of their presence is necessary. Within an empathic, nonjudgmental, and accepting context, the worker must comment on them or verbalize them and encourage their open expression. "Perhaps you're wondering if someone so much younger can possibly understand what you're going through," "Have you had any experiences with a social worker before?" "What was that like?" and "Sometimes it's hard for a black person and a white person to feel comfortable with each other" are ideas to be conveyed in the practitioner's own words and style. The preliminary steps of preparation would have included the anticipation of such obstacles, but they may not be present in any given instance, in which case comments will be gratuitous and should be avoided. Indeed, they could well evoke resistance!

Cultural norms and values about communication and relationships with professionals must, of course, be respected and their accompanying expectations met. This requires of all social workers that they become familiar with cultural patterns of the population groups they serve. The processes of help may be slowed while trust is built, but if cultural norms are not observed, effective help will be impossible.

Newly developed tools of exercises and simulations are available for use in the initial phase (and can also be used instead as later interventions in the ongoing phase). Among them is the eco-map, devised by Hartman (1978; 1979). When used dynamically with a family, couple, or individual, it can engage the cognitive, perceptual, and emotional functions, thus helping to mobilize coping resources. Deceptively simple, the eco-map shows the clients and the worker the strengths and obstacles in their transactions with the environment. It highlights the nurturing aspects and the conflicted aspects of those transactions, as well as the presence or absence of environmental instruments of help. The eco-map may suggest to clients, quite graphically, an explanation for their stress or for their coping difficulties. It may also suggest possible changes they may wish to make in their situation. On occasion it can even clarify for the worker how the boundary around her unit of attention should be expanded. This was an unanticipated benefit in the following example, a case presented for social work consultation by a social worker assigned to the patient:

Mrs. X is a thirty-six-year-old married mother of three children. She is a patient in a large research-oriented cancer center in the Southwest, 1,500 miles from her home. Eighteen months ago Mrs. X was discovered to be suffering from leukemia. Chemotherapy was unsuccessful, and her only hope now is a bone marrow transplant. Mrs. X's husband is expected to arrive soon and will be able to stay for a short time following the transplant. Just now he is at home arranging for a sitter for the children, ages fourteen, twelve, and ten.

Living in the same city as the hospital is Mrs. X's mother, divorced, remarried, and then widowed. She is distraught with worry about her daughter, but she is also preoccupied with complaints about all her daughters' neglect of herself. Staff has experienced her as a trial to them.

The patient's sister, Elizabeth, is willing to be a marrow donor, and the match is excellent. She flew in from her home on the East Coast and immediately was subjected to a medical examination at the hospital. This revealed undiagnosed emphysema and a lump in one breast. A mammogram was negative. Elizabeth was upset by all this, so her husband joined her and will be able to stay a week. She herself will have to stay six weeks in case the marrow is rejected. Her first husband died of cancer at twenty-four.

Because of the need for familial blood, the father of the three young women was located. The patient had seen him only once in the past thirty-two years. He was said by the mother to have been an alcoholic who was abusive to his children and therefore never permitted to see them after the divorce. The mother was upset at the need for his reappearance. Yet, curiously, she had known precisely how to locate him. During the period prior to the transplant Mrs. X and her father found intense pleasure and meaning in their visits together.

The patient is on a special research floor that is usually not staffed by a social worker. Because this life-threatening procedure is new in this center and the psychological and physiological stresses in such patients are very great (six hours' total body irradiation, inability to eat for several days, high fever, and so on), the attending physician asked for social work participation in helping the patient muster her coping resources. Other staff involved, besides the attending and house physicians, are nurses, mental health nurses, and physical therapists. The patients on this floor are a cohesive group because of their shared research status, and the housekeeping staff are also important in the now constricted life space of the patient.

The eco-map in Figure 5–1 shows a life space that has now contracted literally. Yet metaphorically it has expanded. Spatial dimensions stretch across the United States, and time dimensions reach back to a relationship completely cut off thirty-two years ago. Also highlighted are the patient's psychological and social needs juxtaposed with the medical ones, and the illness-related vulnerabilities of husband, children, mother, sister-donor, and estranged father. Organizational and team needs and investments, derived from humane concern for the patient and deep

FIGURE 5-1. Eco-Map

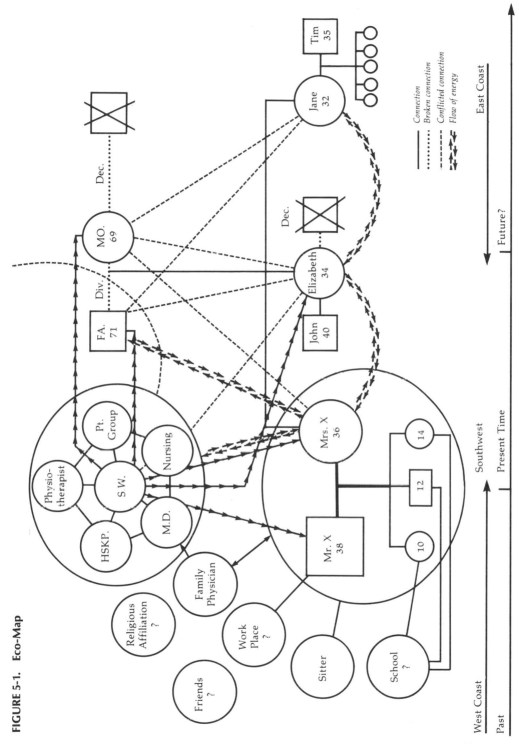

Connection
Broken connection
Conflicted connection
Flow of energy

East Coast

Future?

Southwest

Present Time

West Coast

Past

121

commitment to research outcomes that will support life are also made visible. While there are many strengths lacing the life space, one must be attuned to the many conflicted relationships and to the actual and potential sources of depletion in each of the transacting systems. From that point of view the eco-map shows that all of these transacting forces can be rightly considered part of the social worker's professional unit of attention.

A line drawn around the entire eco-map shows that those forces all do, in fact, become "the case," in which the social work function expands beyond helping the patient to cope with the treatment procedure:

1. The patient's husband and mother will need help with practical concerns as well as with coping with the stress of Mrs. X's illness and the treatment. They may also need to be helped to understand the risks involved and to deal with the possibility of the patient's death.

2. The donor is seen only as donor and not as a person with needs arising from the interaction between her own history, new physical findings, and the physiological and emotional stress involved in the painful procedure of taking the bone marrow. In Elizabeth, the hospital created partly a new patient who receives no care and partly a lifesaving colleague who receives no attention.

3. The patient's father is thrust into an unusual situation: After thirty-two years he is pulled back into the family in the role of lifegiver, which may offer an opportunity for atonement of any guilt he may have felt over the years in his earlier roles of father and husband. In any event, his presence has great meaning for the patient and for himself but is stirring up considerable anger and protest in the patient's mother.

4. The patient's children also need the social worker's attention, through her encouraging Mr. and Mrs. X to maintain telephone and mail contact with them and through work with both parents around the children's need for help with their fears, grief, and loneliness/isolation from what is going on so far away.

5. Because the patients are very much involved with Mrs. X and will be caught up emotionally in any untoward outcome, they may need the social worker's attention then or, perhaps, even now.

6. Finally, because of staff's intense involvement with Mrs. X, only their third patient for this procedure, and their intense commitment to its success, they may need the social worker's empathic help in dealing with loss and a sense of personal and professional failure should Mrs. X not survive. But even now they need support in dealing with the emotional demands involved in caring for her. Beyond that, because they are not used to having a social worker on their team, they are not receptive to her entry into what they see as their territory—the psychosocial needs of the patient. Sensitive work must therefore be done with them to gain their

acceptance and cooperation, not only on behalf of this patient but for future social work staffing on this important research floor, where patients' needs are very great but social work is absent.

Summary

This chapter has examined the practice principles and skills associated with the initial or opening phase of help to individuals, families, and groups in health care settings. The significant processes of this phase include preliminary preparation (anticipatory empathy) and planning (especially for groups), engagement, exploration, assessment, goal-setting, and task allocation—each with its characteristic content and techniques. Setting, personal, environmental, and illness/disability variables determine the duration of the initial phase. But whether it involves several sessions or is compressed into a single session, its associated skills are directed to the critical tasks of (1) establishing a beginning working relationship with the client that conveys empathic concern, respect, and hopefulness and encourages as much self-directedness as age and capacity permit; (2) managing issues of initial resistance and ambivalence; (3) exploration and assessment of relevant factors bearing on coping needs and resources; and (4) reaching agreement on goals and tasks. Throughout, the worker must strike a balance between a focus on needed data and responsiveness to client concerns, feelings, and nonverbal cues.

The principles and skills described in this chapter are not limited in use to the opening sessions alone. They may be called upon throughout the contact whenever changes in illness, personal, or environmental factors require additional exploration, reassessment, and/or the setting of different goals and tasks. As social work moves toward greater autonomy in case finding and in defining psychosocial needs for service through screening mechanisms, it is likely that these skills will undergo further elaboration and refinement. Moving into situations early when the medical diagnosis and prognosis may not yet be known requires (1) a high level of sensitivity to patients and families experiencing fear and dread (or sadness at the institutionalization of an aged member); (2) clarity about the social work function and role in the health organization when services are offered to clients or described to colleagues; (3) and interpersonal skills for moving into the situation confidently and empathically, becoming neither overidentified nor underinvolved. Data must be quickly gathered, a beginning relationship established, and immediate help given to ease powerful, often overwhelming feelings—and all at once before many facts are yet in.

Whether the opening phase is long or short and whether it comes early or late in the client's contact with the organization, its consistent purpose is to lay a carefully wrought base for effective helping and for providing the team with relevant psychological, social, and cultural data needed for effective interprofessional treatment planning. When the base is sound, activities of the ongoing phase will flow logically from the work of the initial phase, however tentative its findings may yet be. The skills of the ongoing phase are examined in the next chapter.

CHAPTER 6

The Helping Process: Ongoing Phase

INTERVENTIONS IN THE ongoing phase flow out of the client's and worker's assessment of the situation and their agreement on goals and tasks, which were achieved in the initial phase. These initial assessments and agreements are melded with the continuous shifts in understanding as the illness proceeds through its stages, other conditions change, and new data appear. Patient, family, or group tasks in the ongoing phase include:

1. Sustaining a hopeful attitude
2. Mobilizing and maintaining coping efforts despite personal or environmental obstacles
3. Directing those efforts to personal and/or environmental issues or to present and/or future demands as changes in the illness or in environmental conditions require
4. Shifting from one coping mode to another as required by need, situation, goals, tasks, and so on
5. Reshaping coping activities in the light of reappraisals of demands or capabilities, or internal and external feedback

The social worker's tasks in the ongoing phase are intended to support the client in fulfilling his or her goals and tasks by helping to reduce stress, strengthen personal and environmental resources for coping, manage painful feelings aroused by the stress, and improve the person–environment relationship disturbed by the illness or disability. In particular, the tasks include:

1. Sustaining the motivation to cope and, when present, helping with issues of ambivalence and resistance
2. Teaching, guiding, and modeling coping skills
3. Providing emotional support to restore or enhance self-esteem, support adaptive defenses, and relax maladaptive ones
4. Providing needed information and opportunities for choice and decision-making, action, and relatedness and dealing with issues of dependency and independence

With such varied tasks, it is helpful to view them as interventions associated with particular practitioner roles. The roles are *mobilizer, teacher, coach, enabler,* and *facilitator* when interventions are directed to client capabilities for, or personal obstacles to, effective coping. They are *mobilizer, facilitator, mediator, organizer, collaborator, innovator,* and *advocate* when they are directed to environmental resources for, or obstacles to, effective coping.* In the sections that follow, the social work roles and practice skills are described in relation to the four main components of coping: motivation, problem-solving, maintaining inner comfort, and self-directedness.

Client Motivation and the
Social Work Role of Mobilizer

The coping requirement of motivation depends in part on the environment's provision of incentives and rewards for coping efforts. Hence the social worker calls on the skills of the *mobilizer* as she seeks to generate or sustain the client's motivation and to motivate organizational staff and the outside environment to support the client's motivation. The patient, family, or group manifested motivation in the initial phase by their very acceptance of help. In the ongoing phase, however, discouragement often sets in and motivation flags when medical treatment has become difficult or progress stops. New problems confronting the patient or the escalating demands of the illness itself may dampen motivation.

The social worker helps to mobilize and sustain motivation throughout the course of acute illness or over the long term in order to manage chronic illness and disability successfully. He does this by helping the patient, family, or group members to sustain hope and to confront changing demands. If possible, he may open up, locate, or identify additional options that will conserve energy, morale, time and other resources. Affirming and reaffirming client strengths, partializing problems or demands into manageable pieces, regulating the pace of demands and of coping efforts if possible, or even renegotiating agreed-

*The roles of collaborator and advocate are not described until Chapter 9.

upon goals and tasks to reduce pressure all help to reestablish and sustain motivation. Encouragement, identifying areas of coping effectiveness already demonstrated, commending efforts, and reiteration of likely gains from continued efforts are important. Interpreting new demands, redefining coping tasks, and clarifying misperceptions of the actual demand–capability balance are additional skills of the mobilizer role.

The factors identified so far that affect motivation adversely are, for the most part, conscious. Other obstacles to motivation may be unconscious. They show themselves in verbal and nonverbal expressions of anger toward the worker and other staff that have no discernible base in reality, or in silence or garrulity, or in acting-out behaviors ranging from missed appointments or tardiness to rash, impulsive, and even dangerous actions, particularly of a self-destructive nature (for example, flouting a diabetic diet, overactivity in a cardiac patient). Such resistance, designed to protect the person from otherwise unbearable anxiety, effectively blocks motivation to move ahead on coping efforts. It is more frequently observed in ambulatory settings than in acute care settings, but it is found in both. Resistance—either conscious or unconscious—can also be a group phenomenon in family or group sessions, blocking motivation to move ahead.

Noncritical, nonhostile comments on the resistive behavior may lead clients to discuss what is bothering them. An observation such as, "Something is getting in the way of our moving ahead—any ideas about what that could be?" can elicit the client's verbal expression of what is difficult or fearful, or what has provoked the behavior. And then reminding her of her strengths and what has so far been achieved, empathy regarding the difficulty and encouragement to proceed with the difficult coping tasks may be enough. Reframing a problem or a task in a way that will preserve self-esteem or providing face-saving alternatives may sometimes be useful. In the case of rash or impulsive action, it can be useful to point out the discrepancy of the behaviors with the client's avowed goals. Obviously, people have the right to abrogate goals; but in a caring context confronting them with the negative consequences of dangerous actions or omissions that jeopardize recovery or disability management can help reduce the anxiety and restore controls. Similarly, in family and group sessions resistance must be commented upon by the worker, with an invitation to the group or family members to look at what's going on and to work on the issue getting in the way of continued progress.

Sometimes resistance is generated by negative feelings toward the worker. In general they should be met with an empathic comment on their presence, inviting exploration and discussion so that movement toward goals can proceed. One must, however, distinguish between momentary annoyances with the worker that are not impeding the work and more pervasive negative feelings that are barriers to progress. They may be based on the reality of something the worker did that was inappropriate or something she did not do that should have been done. Such errors should be acknowledged authentically and with concern for their impact on the individual or group. Negative feelings toward the worker may instead be unrelated to the reality of the relationship. It may be possible to clarify the reality by sharing how the worker is experiencing the relationship and her positive regard for the client. It may be necessary to connect the feelings to those previously described by the client in the context of other relationships as a possible pattern to be examined. Because of the vulnerability created by illness, this must be done especially carefully, with acceptance, gentleness, and tentativeness. But it is important that the effort be made to dispel persistent negative feelings; otherwise, helping efforts will fail.

There are, of course, different theoretical explanations of the observable behaviors cited here. The interested reader is referred to *Practice Digest* (1982, pp. 5–16) for a debate on the meaning of resistance and its handling by social workers representing seven different theoretical and practice positions. Issues of excessive dependence or independence may arise and also block motivation. Measures for handling them will be considered in discussion of the *facilitator* role.

In addition to mobilizing motivational processes, the worker must also make certain that the impinging physical and social environments support the motivation to cope. Where they do not, the worker draws on the skills of the mobilizer role to intervene with team members and other health care staff in the health organization. Interventions may include interpreting client needs and behaviors, making suggestions for the management of difficult behaviors, helping staff to recognize coping efforts and to reward coping activity even if it causes inconvenience to staff, and interesting staff in changing easily changed procedures that increase stress, reduce motivation, and inhibit coping activity. Effectiveness in mobilizing staff motivation depends on an attitude of collaborative problem-solving and empathic communication, assuming consensus on the goal of quality patient care.

With respect to the outer environment, the worker may need to mobilize community services and social networks to provide needed resources to sustain client motivation. With respect to community services, interventions may include skilled referral, follow-up to make sure the connection has been made, and engaging the interest of the agency in meeting the client's practical needs. With respect to social networks, interventions may include helping members of the client's network develop measures to support or restore the motivation and arranging for referral to self-help groups where appropriate.

The skills of the mobilizer roles in providing incentives for coping are illustrated in the following example: Mr. Conway's brother called the department of social work in a local hospital demanding that Mr. C be readmitted to the rehabilitation unit. Mr. C, aged sixty-five and suffering from diabetes, had had a below-knee amputation one year before. He had been fitted with a prosthesis and had been discharged after rehabilitation was completed. Mr. C, never married, lived alone in a small apartment. His brother and sister-in-law, who live 100 miles away, visit on weekends. Homemaker and visiting nurse services had been arranged, but once home Mr. C refused to use his prosthesis. He became increasingly depressed, belligerent, and uncooperative. He would forget to take his insulin and then refuse to admit the nurse or the homemaker into his apartment. A social worker, nurse, and physical therapist from the hospital made a home visit to determine with Mr. C if readmission were appropriate. The social worker writes,

Mr. C was fairly lucid and very charming. He was also angry and fearful about the threat to his independence, and insisted that no one was to put him in the hospital. We offered him outpatient therapy inasmuch as he had also said he wanted to be able to walk again. Mr. C agreed, so transporation was arranged and therapy begun. Neither his brother nor the visiting nurse agreed with this plan at the outset, believing that Mr. C would be safe only in the hospital.

Once Mr. C was involved in therapy, I introduced him to the Adult Day Care program at the hospital, because he had been complaining of isolation and loneliness in his apartment. He quickly developed relationships with others in the program and derived satisfaction from helping those who were more handicapped than he. His medication could now be regularized on a daily basis, and his physical condition began to improve. Within a month Mr. C, who had been poorly functioning and whose condition seemed to be deteriorating, became an alert and active man, working effectively toward his goal of walking again. He was able to maintain his independence and to develop a strong supportive network of friends and professionals.

The social worker and her colleagues helped Mr. C achieve a better person–environment fit so that his psychological discomfort was reduced and his coping capabilities strengthened. She responded to his signals of distress by understanding the latent messages of his maladaptive behavior and converting them into a therapeutic plan. The team created an additional option for Mr. C, and the worker focused on the environment's responsiveness to his coping requirements. She helped him to shift from taking no action, so dangerous to the management of his chronic illness and disability, to taking constructive action. The shift was supported by appropriate arrangements of services and follow-up. In this instance the worker did not have to seek out possible intrapsychic barriers to motivation, since the environment's responsiveness set in motion a new circular feedback system. It contributed to Mr. C's sense of competence, autonomy, and relatedness to others and restored his self-esteem. It interrupted the previous loop of despair, hopelessness, and nonnutritive environmental responses. The newly found network not only provided validation of Mr. C's worth and fulfilled his need for human contact, but it aided the process of social comparison. He could see others who were coping well with handicaps, so optimism and confidence about his own future were reinstated, and his sense of effectiveness was boosted by helping others worse off than himself.

In the next example mobilizing the motivation of staff as environmental support for the client's motivation is illustrated. In this hospital the social workers still do not screen patients for service but wait for referrals from physicians and nurses. Ms. O, age seventy, had been admitted to the hospital for amputation of a gangrenous toe. She was suffering from multiple ulcers on both legs and diabetes mellitus, and had had an arterial by-pass. Her right knee was flexed at 90°; she was incontinent and emaciated but alert and oriented. Her treatment was nearing completion, and the physician referred Ms. O to the social worker for discharge planning because he felt she would need nursing home care.

The social worker learned that Ms. O had lived all her life in the same small town. Unmarried, she had supported her widowed mother until the latter's death at age ninety-three, a brother mentally retarded at birth, and another brother who received a psychiatric discharge during World War II and had not worked since. She had two years of college and worked as librarian until seven years ago, when she suffered two heart attacks. Her house, where she and her brothers continue to live, is paid for. She receives Social Security and a small pension. In starting to plan with Ms. O for her discharge, the worker encountered her strong resistance to nursing home care. He quickly discovered that she was in severe conflict with the nursing staff. Until that was resolved, the worker felt that Ms. O would be unable to cope with the demands presented by the present stage of her illness.* He writes:

When I spoke with the nurses about Ms. O they referred to her as "that cranky old lady" and stated she was difficult and probably senile. I noticed a paucity of nursing notes in her chart, and the short ones present referred only to the work the nurses had performed. This is unusual, for nursing notes usually comment on how the patient is feeling, what she said, how she looks, and so on. In my contacts Ms. O was warm, friendly, and interested. She had a strong desire to get better. In spite of extreme pain, she welcomed my visits. She sees herself as an independent woman, and it is important to her that she continue to be independent. However, there are

---

*Other work done with Ms. O is not included in this excerpt.

many things she is not permitted to do in the hospital. Staff does not want her to move her arm because of the tubes, so she has to be fed. This embarrasses her. To avoid embarrassment she tries to feed herself. The nurses tell her no, and she feels angry. Rather than saying anything when the nurses order her to do something she doesn't like, she withdraws and refuses to do anything. Then the nurses write in her chart, for example, "Patient refused physical therapy" or whatever. Ms. O complains also that the nurses are very impersonal and uncaring. She said, "Listen, Ron—can I call you Ron? I've been pretty healthy all my life. I never looked this bad till a year ago, when I really got sick. All this happened in one year. I looked at myself the other day and started to cry. I look so bad, so old, and it all happened in just a year. I don't know what's happening to me, one day you're OK and then all of a sudden you fall apart. Now I have to sit in this room and they tell me I have to put up with everything. They came in a while ago to change the dressing on my foot and they hurt me, so I yelled at them. They really hurt, look at my foot, look at those sores. They hurt so much, and they pick up my foot like it was a nothing. They don't care about *me*."

While he worked on all this with Ms. O, accepting her feelings but also considering with her some ways she could help the situation, he also tried to convey to the nurses how she was feeling:

It was the discrepancy between my perception of Ms. O and theirs that made me feel something was wrong. I brought it up in rounds and also spoke with some of them individually. I know that some patients can be difficult and demanding, so I was careful to avoid any note of criticism and instead empathized with the stress they felt in caring for Ms. O. I wondered with them if she had told them anything about herself and how she was experiencing all that was happening to her? When it was clear she had not, I mentioned some of the reasons for her behavior and also said I was working to help her understand the reasons for the restrictions she was fighting. There was improvement after this, as Ms. O became more willing to allow others to do for her, and the nurses tried to be more patient and accepting.

The worker's aim was to help the nurses understand the sources of Ms. O's maladaptive coping efforts, on the assumption that changes in their responses would support her motivation while promoting more effective coping activity. He drew on principles of good communication such as respect, empathy for their concerns, and acceptance of their feelings. Above all, he avoided casting blame for the interpersonal impasse, which then permitted the nurses to "hear" and respond to what he said about Ms. O.

While not covered in this excerpt, the worker was also concerned about the wellbeing of Ms. O's brothers while she remained in the hospital or was transferred to a convalescent setting. Network figures were mobilized to help sustain Ms. O's motivation. He contacted a friend of Ms. O—with her consent—who agreed to visit daily to make sure that meals and household maintenance are proceeding adequately. He also talked with a nun at Ms. O's church who is interested in the family, and she would also look in on the brothers. If things do not go well, she agreed to contact the worker so that alternative arrangements, drawing on community services, could be made.

The skills of the mobilizer role are summarized in Table 6–1.

Client Problem-solving and the Social Work Roles of Teacher, Coach, and Mediator

In the roles of *teacher* and *coach,* the practitioner may teach patients and families problem-solving skills, interpersonal and communication skills, skills in securing services and entitlements, and skills in dealing with the psychological and social consequences of illness—especially chronic disease—and disability. Such teaching can be done individually or in groups and is often collaborative (frequently with a nurse and/or physician). Teaching techniques range from the didactic to the experiential: (1) Brochures and films about the illness are useful ways to impart information. (2) Direct instruction can be used to help parents, for example, prepare a child for surgery by describing expectable age-specific reactions. Parents can learn how to help their child express his feelings and fears and how to help him during the hospitalization (Coleman, Lebowitz, and Anderson, 1976). (3) Teaching can also be done by modeling desired behaviors, as when the social worker models the ways in which a client might be more assertive with a physician or effective ways of dealing with a governmental bureaucracy concerning entitlements.

In the following example of a prenatal group of Hispanic women, teaching is done by the social worker and group members. The work is also an illustration of eliciting culturally based conceptions of a physical state (pregnancy) and its possible outcomes. Staff of the prenatal clinic were concerned about the poor communication between them and Spanish-speaking clients, which resulted in the women's being ill-prepared for labor and delivery, misinformed about childbirth, and seemingly unwilling to follow medical regimens. A group service was designed to meet these problems and to provide comprehensive prenatal care of a higher quality. The group was led by a bilingual American-born Puerto Rican social worker on the staff of the prenatal–obstetric unit and the neonatal intensive care unit. It had the full support of the nursing and medical staffs and administration (Cooper and Cento, 1977):

Once members felt support from their peers in the group and from the group leader, they were able to ask team members their questions and, even more impor-

TABLE 6-1. The Skills of the Mobilizer Role in Supporting Client's Coping Task of Sustaining Motivation

CLIENT'S COPING TASK	SOCIAL WORKER'S PRACTICE TASK	SOCIAL WORK ROLE	SOCIAL WORK SKILLS
Motivation	Provision of incentives and rewards for coping efforts; dealing with ambivalence and resistance	Mobilizer	*With client:* Conveying hope; providing encouragement and managing despair; partializing demands into manageable pieces; inviting and handling expression of ambivalent feelings, handling resistive behaviors when they obstruct moving ahead on the coping tasks
	Influencing the environment to provide incentives and rewards for coping efforts	Mobilizer	*With staff:* Interpreting client needs and behaviors; helping team and other staff to recognize coping efforts and to reward coping activity even when it causes inconvenience to staff; interesting staff in changing easily changed procedures that inhibit coping
		Mobilizer	*With outer environment:* Establishing linkages to community services and resources when needed to sustain motivation; arranging referrals and following up on them. Encouraging support by social network.

133

tant, remember staff members' answers and explanations. . . . Members asked questions about signs of labor, hospital and clinic procedures, stretch marks, varicose veins, episiotomies. . . . and infants' positions during delivery. Many thought the vagina was too small for a baby to come through and had no idea that it stretched. They were also confused about and fearful of anesthesia; the staff and group leader designed a printout in Spanish that described every procedure used. The sheet was then used by staff and patient in the clinic and delivery room, and communication was facilitated. [pp. 694–95]

In addition to learning from staff, members also helped one another to learn strategies for handling such practical concerns as weight control and getting to the hospital on time for delivery.

Coming from twelve Spanish-speaking countries, many of the women had cultural backgrounds that included reliance on superstition, lay healers, and folk medicine. It was important to elicit culturally based ideas about pregnancy and childbirth. These were respectfully listened to. For example, one member said,

"You can't look at a defective person or your baby will be defective; if you look at a horse, you baby's head will be like that of a horse." [She said] that she knew these were probably superstitions but these admonitions still bothered her . . . . The group leader said that many pregnant women worry about their babies not being born normal . . . that it's natural to be afraid. [p. 698]

Such culturally based ideas, however, were supplemented with information derived from Western medicine. The new information then became group property and was used by the members themselves to instruct new members:

Mrs. T, a Puerto Rican woman, said that if one touches or cuddles one's abdomen during pregnancy, the baby will be born retarded. The other members said that this was not true, and each demonstrated how they caress their abdomens.

In addition to the benefits of emotional support, social contacts, and improved staff–client relationships and communication, the team and the clients agreed that gaps in knowledge had been filled, misconceptions clarified, and superstitious fears allayed so that the women were better able to cope with the demands of pregnancy, labor, and childbirth.

White (1974) maintains that practitioners should offer suggestions about strategies for coping with stress rather than seeking to develop insight on the assumption that only insight leads to behavioral change. White reminds social workers that often changed actions lead to changed feelings about oneself, others, and the stressful situation. Indeed, in health care social work an overconcern with internal phenomena and the past may lead to regressive preoccupations. Practitioners helping people to cope with illness and disability can be more effective by encouraging a consideration of present realities and future alternatives, which fosters an optimistic and realistic attitude in the patient or family member. A social worker and cardiologist suggest that helping the myocardial infarct patient with problem-solving should begin in the coronary care unit and continue right through convalescence and rehabilitation (Obier and Haywood, 1972):

> The patient should be encouraged to talk about the future, to meet appropriately his immediate problems, to make decisions, and instruct his family in carrying them out, and to begin to plan for convalescence and rehabilitation. Use of this technique will help to prevent excessive preoccupation with the cardiac condition or with morbid thoughts of self or death. . . . Alternatives to living life as a "cardiac cripple" should be discussed. . . . Realistic concerns and problems should be responded to by giving the patient and his family information regarding available community resources. Knowledge of sources of help can serve to alleviate undue anxieties and fruitless activity. . . . Misconceptions held by the patient or the family regarding the effect of the cardiac disease on his continued functioning should be clarified. . . . Patients often need support in asking the physician questions and they should be referred to the physician for medical clarification regarding their cardiac condition.

Nevertheless, teaching in the context of stressful demands must be rooted in awareness that cognition and emotion are interdependent. Each affects the other, and an undue emphasis on one at the expense of the other is likely to be ineffective. Social workers sometimes tend to focus on the emotions and to overlook the role of cognition in coping with illness. To right the balance, the cognitive-sensory-perceptual capacities must be brought to the fore. But care must be taken that the opposite error is not committed, focusing only on the rational, overlooking the irrational forces in the feeling realm of human life. Effective coping with the continuing demands of illness requires awareness of one's internal world of biological and emotional needs *and* clarity about the demands of the external world. The social worker as teacher and coach must be able to reach out to both.

Problem-solving is taught best in a climate of support, with the provision of pertinent information for problem-solving at a pace and in a cognitive form (visual, auditory, verbal, doing) most suited to the patient's or family's readiness, needs, and cognitive style (Bruner, 1966, pp. 15–11). Some learn more easily in an action mode by doing, as in an advance visit to the labor room, delivery room, and obstetrical unit arranged for the fearful pregnant woman. Some learn more easily through imagery by viewing pictures and films. The dynamic use of such diagnostic and treatment tools as eco-maps and genograms (Hartman,

1979, 1978), adolescent grids (Anderson and Brown, 1980), and children's time lines (Court, 1980) combine doing and imagery. Still other people learn more easily in the conceptual mode of verbal and written materials. Most people benefit from a mix of all three. Newly acquired learning is bolstered by opportunities to try out the new behaviors, attitudes, and knowledge in both old and new environments and by feedback from staff, other patients, family members, friends, and the social worker.

Based on their work with severely burned patients, polio patients, and parents of leukemic children, Hamburg and his colleagues write that patients and families benefit from specific information about the demands of illness and disability and strategies for handling the demands (D. Hamburg, B. Hamburg, and deGoza, 1953; Visotsky, Hamburg, Goss, and Lebovits, 1961; Friedman, Chodoff, Mason, and Hamburg, 1963). Hamburg has long held that practitioners should study how successful copers manage the demands of illness and disability and then teach their strategies to others—if appropriate to age, sex, and ethnic group. Consideration must be given to the risks, costs, opportunities, and benefits associated with each strategy in each situation, within particular cultural and subcultural settings (Hamburg, Adams, and Brodie, 1976).

Mechanic (1977) also argues that management of a specific illness or disability requires specific information and skills for dealing with the social and psychological consequences, which transcend the medical aspects. For effective teaching, however, such materials must be broken down into component parts and made highly specific, in contrast to the usual generalized admonitions, "take it easy," "avoid stress," and the like.

Strauss and Glaser (1975) and their colleagues have studied the demands of such chronic diseases as childhood diabetes, rheumatoid arthritis, and ulcerative colitis and the strategies patients develop for meeting them. In emphysema, for example, the chief demand is the management of scarce energy due to limited oxygen reserves. Two key issues are symptom control to prevent energy loss and the balancing of the demanding regimen against other considerations. How one juggles resources of time, money, and energy depends on one's supply of these resources, the availability of other people's resources for purchase or otherwise, and one's life-style and life situation. One must continually gauge oxygen requirements for physical mobility and sociability and then set priorities by deleting or restricting aspects of life-style so as to live within one's energy and oxygen capacity. Obviously, as in all chronic illness, everything is made much more difficult by a declining course, advanced age, and being poor, all of which shrink options and maneuverability.

The range of strategies developed by patients to meet these demands can be taught to other patients: for example, recruiting natural helpers for difficult mobility requirements; condensing activities into the shortest time by anticipating and planning routes, gauging time and energy to get to the bus stop, and taking roundabout routes to avoid hills; locating "puffing stations" such as walls, telephone poles, and mailboxes where one can lean and "recoup oxygen" instead of creating a public scene by sitting on the curb; avoiding going out on windy, cold, or smoggy days; and planning hourly, daily, and weekly expenditures of energy in order to spread the demands.

Teaching these and other coping strategies can be done with individuals by a social worker attached to a home health agency or with groups by a social worker in a hospital's or clinic's lung service. Parry and Kohn (1976) suggest that groups for those suffering from emphysema foster an interchange among members about their illness that leads to knowledge and information for how to manage it. These social workers also brought in educational programs and resource people to supplement member-induced learning.

The role of *coach* is a variant of the teaching role, having more of a dimension of directiveness, advice, or suggestion than the role of teacher. The worker, for example, may coach a client in the steps for task achievement:

Mrs. Beech, age seventy, a retired registered nurse, suffered a severe stroke four months ago. She is in a skilled nursing facility in the small New England town where she and her husband have lived all their lives. Mr. Beech, age seventy-two, a retired salesman, is alone in their small apartment. The couple had no children and no real social network. They have always been, as he puts it, each other's best friend. He spends nine hours a day with Mrs. B, and because he felt useless, I have arranged concrete tasks to do with her that he feels comfortable doing, such as setting up her trays, reading to her, and so forth. His movements are quick, and he always appears anxious. He is polite and seems afraid to use too much of anyone's time. He has never had medical problems and is on no medication.

Both hold to the typical New England "work ethic," and it is difficult for Mr. B to discuss alternatives to their self-sufficiency. Again, typically for New Englanders, he does not wish to disclose what they have in savings. Finances are a private matter. In addition to this cultural aspect, Mr. B often stagnates on agreed upon tasks (e.g., insurance forms). I find I need to structure such tasks very carefully, while still giving him space and time for maintaining autonomy.

The inevitable change in their financial situation due to long-term illness is already intensifying Mr. B's stress and his fears of losing self-reliance and independence. The problem is acute, because Mrs. B recently lost her Medicare coverage through the federal regulation that the patient must show continued improvement. She still needs months of rehabilitative services and institutional care.

The situation is further complicated because the state bureaucracy is insensitive and the application process is frequently dehumanizing. Until Mr. B is ready to give me more information, the situation is likely to become still more difficult. At his request, he and I have submitted an appeal to Medicare, and he is aware of its dubious outcome. I have given him a full explanation of the Medicare and Medicaid programs so that he understands the system. I keep him informed of Mrs. B's bill and have asked the business office to send him monthly notifications of current charges. With his growing trust in me, I am now coaching him in small tasks to prepare him for future needs. He responds well, and when he stagnates he doesn't seem to mind my directions to get him started up again. For example, I had him telephone the welfare department to verify the information I had given him, in the hope of creating a beginning relationship for him there. I also had him drive past the welfare office to minimize his fears about the bureaucratic system. I used my influence with the agency to find out what workers he would be seeing so I could give him their names, thereby personalizing the organization for him a little bit. I also gave him a copy of the application form so he could take it home and read it. Because I knew that Mr. B wished his finances to remain private from me, I showed him how he could divide the couple's savings account so as to preserve 50 percent of their savings and gave him some examples of how welfare would allow the remainder of the money to be spent.

Last week, after six weeks of working on this issue, Mr. B felt ready to make an appointment and actually went to the welfare office to discuss his future application when his diminishing savings reach the amount specified by welfare regulations.

The directiveness involved in the role of coach, tempered by recognition of cultural norms and personal qualities, succeeds in aiding Mr. Beech to cope more adequately with a future threat of harm, even though he is coping with present demands. It required a shift in temporal orientation.

In addition to the roles of teacher and coach and their interventions directed to personal aspects, the social worker has a complementary responsibility in the role of *mediator* to make certain that the environment supplies needed resources for problem-solving. Mediating interventions in this context* include (1) influencing team members to be responsive to clients' questions, to participate in group services for conveying medical information and the teaching of medically oriented coping strategies, and, where needed, to collaborate in the teaching of the psychosocial management strategies just described; (2) arranging for, and helping patients and families, as needed, to accept and follow through on, referrals to agencies and institutions, such as rehabilitative settings or family service agencies for learning new roles and new ways of managing illness-

---

*The skills of the mediator role are examined in more detail in Chapter 9.

induced changes in other areas of the life space; and (3) helping clients to locate and recruit natural helpers needed for illness/disability management.

The last-named intervention is demonstrated in an example from the files of a social worker attached to a visiting nurse association in a remote and isolated rural area:

Ms. Jacklin, age forty-eight, had been discharged from a local hospital after a nine-week stay following surgery to remove tumors from her back. She had worked nine years in a local plant as inspector, despite being unable to read or write. She lived in a decrepit trailer that was structurally unsound, strewn with litter, unsanitary, and reeking of animal wastes. She has four cats and a dog, who void wherever they please in the trailer. The pipes freeze continually, and the electric wiring is unsafe. Ms. J's widowed mother lives in a nearby village, but both wish to live alone. An only sister lives in another state, and Ms. J appears to have few friends, although members of the Morman church have recently taken her under their wing. She has considerable difficulty with personal and household care, made more difficult by the deplorable housing, but she insists on retaining her independent living arrangements.

Ms. J's health required immediate change of housing. Although the social worker worked with her on other issues as well, the following excerpt is concerned only with the housing issue. Mutual goals and plans were made for establishing a safer and healthier environment, and then:

Together we assessed her financial and work situations. We had Mr. Archer come to assess the value of her present trailer and to discuss the costs of a new one and of moving both units. He also evaluated Ms. J's lot to determine how he can get the old trailer out and a new one in. Next, Ms. J, her mother, and I drove over to inspect the variety of mobile homes Mr. Archer has at his sales center. She made her selection of a refurbished unit, and we drove to the bank to discuss financing. The loan was approved several days later. Meantime, with Ms. J's consent, I organized a work party to ready the lot for the installation of the trailer. Wood, litter, and snow had to be removed, and some excavation was also required. I secured volunteers from among the neighbors and the members of the Morman Church and arranged for an electrician to come and upgrade the service. The old trailer was removed and the new one installed, and the next day I organized a group of youngsters in the area to help clean up the lot.

In most rural areas, great store is placed in neighborliness and mutual help. Maintaining one's independence is also a prevalent norm. The worker was fully aware of these values. As a social worker living and working in the rural area, sharing its life and sensitive to its social systems, he was able to rally a natural helping network to support Ms. J's problem-solving effort to create a health-promoting environment for herself. As mediator, he helped each to reach out to the other.

The skills of the teacher, coach, and mediator roles are summarized in Table 6–2.

Client Self-esteem and Management of Painful Emotions and the Social Work Roles of Enabler and Organizer

The client's maintaining internal balance or psychic comfort involves the regulation of negative feelings aroused by the stressful demands of illness or disability and the retention or acquisition of a favorable level of self-esteem. Achieving these states requires both personal and environmental resources. The social worker in the role of *enabler* can provide emotional support and encourage other staff to do so.

Supportive interventions include helping the client to manage painful feelings, preserve the self-image or create a new one that takes in the reality of illness-induced changes, and sustain self-esteem. Defenses may need to be reinforced or relaxed, depending on the illness stage and other conditions, including medical treatment and rehabilitation procedures. Such feelings as anxiety, depression, guilt, shame, anger, and despair have to be sufficiently controlled so as not to interfere with recovery or with motivation, problem-solving, or self-directedness.

Thus the skills of enabling comprise supportive measures (including commendation, realistic reassurance, advice, suggestions, acceptance of feelings) and various forms of therapeutic communication (Hammond, Hepworth, and Smith, 1977). Some of them are demonstrated in the work with Mrs. Kahn, whose husband is dying of cancer. Her situation was briefly introduced in Chapter 5 as the worker prepared for her entry into Mrs. Kahn's life space. In the material that follows, some details of several interviews with Mrs. Kahn are reviewed to specify certain skills of the enabling role. Within a context of support and empathy, the enabling role often calls for *interpretation* of what is transpiring and *clarification* of personal and environmental components. In general it is considered more helpful if the client can be led, by tentative questions and supportive comments, to make her own interpretations and to recognize her own patterned ways of responding. By pointing to some consequences of her behavior, the worker hopes to help Mrs. K recognize that she is inhibiting her husband as well as herself from coping more effectively with his impending death. The aim of the worker's enabling interventions is to free Mrs. K from her need to avoid, intellectualize, project, and deny the implications of Mr. K's death for her own future.

TABLE 6–2. The Skills of the Teacher, Coach, and Mediator Roles in Helping Clients to Use, Gain, or Improve Their Problem-solving Capabilities

CLIENT'S COPING TASK	SOCIAL WORKER'S PRACTICE TASK	SOCIAL WORK ROLE	SOCIAL WORK SKILLS
Problem-solving	Providing instruction in coping skills, individually and in groups	Teacher Coach	*With client:* Helping to identify possible actions and alternative solutions and their likely consequences; teaching needed skills for achieving the solution; providing group experiences for such learning; providing advice and information as needed; devising tasks and providing feedback on performance; providing opportunities for trying out new skills; carrying out role rehearsal, modeling, and anticipatory coping activity for skill acquisition
	Inducing the environment to provide instruction in coping skills	Mediator	*Agency Environment:* Encouraging staff to participate in group services to provide for the learning of illness-related coping strategies; to furnish medical information needed for coping to patients and family members
			Outer Environment: Helping patients and families to accept referrals/transfers to agencies (rehabilitative settings, family service agencies, etc.) for learning new roles, new means of coping with illness-induced changes in other areas of life

The Kahns, both fifty-four, have been married thirty-five years. They are of the upper middle class; Mr. K occupies a responsible position while Mrs. K works part time in a job she enjoys. Two adult children live in other states. Mr. K has had a rapid downward course. His lung cancer was discovered less than three months ago. Outpatient chemotherapy was ineffective, and he has been readmitted to the hospital with metastases to other organs. Nothing further can be done, but Mrs. K still refuses to allow the physicians to tell her husband he is dying. They have therefore told him that they are trying to control his disease and that he has an 80 percent chance of recovery. Mrs. K has not told their children or Mr. K's parents that he has cancer. She continues to maintain a cheerful, optimistic façade while visiting him but complains to the worker that he doesn't talk to her and seems depressed. In fact, the situation was referred to social work by the physician because of his concern about Mr. K's depression. It seemed to the worker when she talked with Mr. K that he was aware of his terminal condition and felt very isolated.

In this interview, the worker helps Mrs. K to realize that she and her husband need to mourn their impending loss and to share their feelings of sorrow, pain, and anger. Because of Mrs. K's apparent fear of intense emotions, the worker tries to help her manage her own feelings more appropriately so that she can be more supportive to her husband as he attempts to cope with his. It is hard going for both Mrs. K and the worker. There is so much pain and so little time, because the referral to social work came late in the illness, and Mr. K's condition is deteriorating rapidly. They talk about what life will be like for Mrs. K after her husband's death. She speaks in an intellectualized way of how she is able to make the best of things, which reflects denial of Mr. K's actual dying: "I know that I'll get through this like I've gotten through everything else. . . . I'm going to work more afterwards. And I'm not going to allow myself to stay in the house and feel depressed. . . . I plan to continue going out and doing things."

Mrs. K was smiling and speaking in a matter-of-fact way. The worker tells her that her life won't be over, but it will change. She has been with her husband the longest part of her life, and losing that relationship will not be something that she can adjust to overnight. Maybe she will need time to sit in the house and be depressed. That would be natural for anyone who has lost a cherished person. Mrs. K says she knows it won't be easy, that it will take time. And the worker points out that she will have other people available to help. Mrs. K agrees and refers to her children, sister and brother-in-law, and friends.

The worker was encouraging Mrs. K to allow herself to mourn in an anticipatory way, to be in touch with her own feelings of grief. Mrs. K continues to control them, however, by intellectualizing and isolating them from her thoughts about her loss. The worker continues by giving her permission to grieve and *legitimizing* grief and mourning as both natural and necessary. But the discussion remains at the intellectual level. As important as that level is, remaining there will not help Mrs. K to integrate her feelings with her thoughts so that she can help her husband (and herself). If Mrs. K and her husband are to deal with their enormous stress more effectively, Mrs. K must be helped to reduce her fears about losing control of her feelings, and to relax that control (defenses). The worker now tries to help Mrs. K see that her husband actually needs and wants to talk, and that her wish to avoid painful feelings is preventing him from doing so. The efforts are made in a context of empathy, support, and realistic reassurance:

Mrs. K said, "What good will talking do at this point? I know it's only a matter of days or weeks. I talk to the doctors every day, and I know there's no hope left. So what's the point—it won't make it any better." Her eyes filled with tears, but she controlled them and did not cry.

The worker explained that talking would not take the pain away, for nothing can do that. But Mrs. K has been upset about Mr. K's being so depressed and keeping his feelings aside. What does she think those feelings might be? Mrs. K replies, "He's worried about his voice and not being able to keep up at work. I've told him he can retire now if he wants to, we can manage."

The worker wonders aloud if there isn't a lot more on his mind than his voice, "From what you've told me, I imagine he's very worried about whether he's going to make it or not, and that's why he is so depressed." Mrs. K asked, "But why does he have to know he's dying? What good will that do?"

The worker *confronts* Mrs. K with the reality, saying that wasn't the real question, since he already does know. She points out that the real question is how Mrs. K can talk about it openly with him, even though it is so very painful. Mrs. K responds that he doesn't know how poor his prognosis is. With support to Mrs. K for how difficult this is, the worker gently *clarifies* that Mr. K has seen his condition deteriorate very rapidly and that many patients are aware at some level that they are dying despite what doctors may tell them. The worker suggests that Mr. K is aware that he is dying and is frightened and depressed, just as Mrs. K herself is. Again, Mrs. K asked why he has to know he is dying, what good will it do? Recognizing the projection, the worker makes an *interpretation,*

"But that's not the question since he already knows. I think your question is, Why do you have to come out and talk about this in the open? You want him to open up and talk about what he's feeling inside, but you don't really want to be there when it happens?"

Mrs. K agrees, and says she thinks it will be easier for him to open up with a stranger. Her being there will inhibit him, and if the worker were there alone he might say what he's feeling. The worker responds with a clarification that he doesn't need to tell the worker those feelings, he needs to share them with his wife. Right now each is bearing the pain alone.

Again, Mrs. K asks how talking can make it better, and again the worker responds that it won't take the pain away and won't make them feel all better, but it will help them to share the burden of the pain.

Some patients do not really want to know or to acknowledge that their condition is hopeless, and practitioners have to respect this. But in this instance the worker's assessment was that Mr. K knew he was dying, wanted to talk about it, and to express his grief, fear, and concern for his wife and family. But he needed the permission of his wife to do so.

Then the worker moves more directly and asks if Mrs. K is afraid that all the feelings that might come out will be too overwhelming, too upsetting to deal with? But Mrs. K is not ready for this interpretation. She says, "No, I don't think so." In reflecting to herself, the worker thinks that more opportunity should have been given to Mrs. K to *ventilate* her fears that such talking might confirm the fact that, for her (and for Mr. K), he really is dying. While probably an accurate evaluation, an opportunity does come up later in the interview.

The discussion then shifts to Mr. K's parents, who haven't been told that Mr. K has cancer. Mrs. K explains that they are eighty years old, and her brother-in-law doesn't want to upset them. She also hints that he is not taking his brother's illness very well, and she herself can't take on the task of telling the parents. The worker offers to talk with Mr. K's brother, which Mrs. K appreciates. Then the worker talks a little about what it might be like for the parents not to know that Mr. K is seriously ill and then to hear of his death. She suggests, "This is their son, and they might want to be spending more time with him now. They might feel very angry that this was kept from them and they weren't told the truth sooner. If they are told now they will be upset, but this way they'll be able to assimilate and adjust to it gradually, a little at a time." She adds, "They can begin to grieve now, which may make their grief afterward less intense."

At some level, this clarification spoke to Mrs. K's own avoidance of feelings. She suddenly began to cry intensely, and in a pleading way sobbed, "Why does he have to grieve? He's dying—dying. Isn't that enough?" The worker empathizes with all the pain, and then says:

"Right now you and your husband can't talk with each other about what's really on your minds, and that's keeping you apart. You can't have that emotional closeness that you need right now. If you want to share what you're going through and support each other, then you have to talk about painful and upsetting things." Mrs. K said, "Yes, I understand what you're saying." The worker continues, "The price of becoming closer is that you have to bring all your painful feelings out in the open, and the price of not talking together about your feelings is the barrier that's between you and your husband now."

Mrs. K responds: "I want us to be close now. I would like us to be able to share and support each other. But I don't know if it's worth the price. I'll try to talk, but I don't know if I can. Don't blame me if I can't."

The worker answers that she won't blame Mrs. K if she can't do this difficult and very painful thing; they can talk some more and try it again. As they get up to leave for Mr. K's room, Mrs. K asks for reassurance, "I just have to ask, what do you think of me?" The worker patted her back gently, and said she is doing the best she can with a very difficult time.

In general, the worker as enabler is seeking to clarify the situation and its tasks and to encourage the expression of Mrs. K's feelings. If there had been more time, the worker would have moved more slowly, given even more support, and would have helped Mrs. K to reach her own interpretations and conclusions. Diagnosis of the illness and its rapid downward course have taken place in less than three months, so Mr. and Mrs. K may still be experiencing remnants of numbness. Until the present readmission Mrs. K's coping efforts had been directed appropriately to maintaining hope for husband and herself. Now, however, the coping strategies of avoidance, denial, and projection are not adaptive. Hence the worker, in a context of empathy, chips away gently at the avoidance and begins to free Mrs. K from the constraints she has imposed on her feelings. The worker holds Mrs. K to the tasks of confronting the imminent loss so that she may help her husband and herself to share the burden. But she also adds an additional temporal orientation by asking Mrs. K to anticipate and deal with future demands. Through clarification she stimulates Mrs. K's cognitive, perceptual, and emotional awareness of the implications of Mr. K's death for her future. It is a future-oriented consideration of the impending life transition of widowhood. It exists side by side with the demands and harms posed by the present life transition of grievous loss. Finally, the worker confronts Mrs. K with the two alternatives of avoidance and openness, and their respective costs. Mrs. K makes her own choice as she reappraises demands and resources.*

As the work of enabling continues, Mrs. K will require much support from the worker and others to deal with her grief and possible depression, anxiety, guilt, and other painful feelings. Work will involve rallying the support of various environmental components: family members, friends, and, if necessary, hospital staff. All of these persons may also have a reciprocal need for support, so that the worker must be ready to provide them with support herself as well as help them to reach out to one another. Later, it may be necessary to help Mrs. K accept a referral to a community-based service for help in coping with the new and stressful demands of widowhood.

* The joint session with Mr. and Mrs. Kahn that follows the choice is reviewed in the next chapter.

The part played by *informal support systems* in the alleviation of stress and even in the prevention of stress is a focus of growing interest in health and mental health. In the health field the research literature points to an association between natural support systems and vulnerability to noninfectious disease (Cassel, 1976, Pilisuk and Froland, 1978; Rabkin and Struening, 1976) and between such systems and reductions in the amount of medicine required, compliance with medical regimens, and more rapid recovery (Cobb, 1976). For example, a social worker on the staff of an urban home health care agency writes,

Reverend Lester, a sixty-five-year-old retired Baptist minister, was referred by the nurse because he is not taking his medication. He recently was retired by his church and was replaced by a young minister who is doing very well with the congregation. After consulting with the new minister, I referred Reverend Lester to the home visiting program of another church. He became involved and gained purpose and a sense of usefulness again. His anger and depression were reduced, and there have been no further problems with taking the medication.

Cobb (1976) defines social support as information that conveys to the person she or he is cared for, loved, esteemed, and a member of a network of mutual obligations. A social worker who became gravely ill two years before entering a graduate school of social work writes,

I was hospitalized with a high fever, chills, and a sore throat. The symptoms were unresponsive to normal treatment. After a series of tests was run, I was diagnosed as having Acute Myelogenous Leukemia. At that time I was a preschool teacher turned potter; I was living alone in a small house in rural Vermont. After my initial shock and numbness, I had the desire to tell everyone I knew I had cancer. I made many phone calls, and I was amazed at the response. There was an outpouring of love from my family and friends. This love supported me through the crisis of my illness, and I began to realize the importance of the support of other people in my life. Still I felt alone with the cancer. During chemotherapy, I was confined to a private hospital room for five weeks to minimize the risk of infection. Amidst this time of complete isolation, I received a letter from the mother of a child I had taught. This woman had had cancer several years before and had been considered "terminal"; she hadn't died. The letter was a gift of sunlight into my darkened existence. She spoke to my fear and my pain; I sensed that she knew how I felt. I wasn't the only one who had been through this experience.

Meanwhile the chemotherapy continued. There were moments when I came very close to dying. I expected to die. When I was told I was in remission and was going to live, I felt deflated and frightened. I wondered what life would be like with cancer. I had been prepared to die and now I found myself afraid of living. I talked with friends about this, and one woman who had been involved in women's support groups suggested I would benefit from meeting with a group of people who had been through a similar experience. . . . I asked my doctor about it and found that no such cancer support group existed in the area. . . . Five months later, a psychiatric nurse and I started such a group. Since then the group and the people in it have been a large and an important component of my life. The members have played a large part in my continuing integration of the illness, and learnings that accompany it, into my life. [Schweizer, 1979]

The concept of natural support systems includes the intimate social network of family, friends, neighbors, and colleagues; informal caregivers in the neighborhood such as bartenders, druggists, and hairdressers, and private persons who are known for their pragmatic wisdom and willingness to help (Collins and Pancoast, 1976). Strauss and Glaser (1975, pp. 8-39) refer to such helpers as "agents" upon whom the chronically ill individual and the family can call. There are helpers "who act as *rescuing agents* (saving a diabetic individual from dying when he is in a coma), or as *protective agents* (accompanying an epileptic person so that if he begins to fall he can be eased to the ground), or as *assisting agents* (helping with a regimen), or as *control agents* (making the patient stay with his regimen)", as "*redesigning agents,*" who work out ideas for compensating for the disability and reshaping social interaction, *treatment agents* (as in home dialysis), or *mobility agents* (helping with transportation). Recruiting and maintaining such natural support systems call for certain social arrangements. "People's efforts must be coordinated—with all the understandings and agreements which that necessitates. Thus disabled patients have standing arrangements with neighbors and friends who do their grocery shopping for them," take pets for a walk, or even do garden and farm chores. The following are examples of such helping uncovered by Swenson (1981):

A Neighborhood Helper: This is a middle-aged postmistress in the local post office, who is known locally as a "weigher" of babies—she uses the postal scales. Many young mothers stop by to see this grandmotherly woman and receive support In addition to the weighing.

Friends: A deaf man, single and about fifty years of age, is going into the hospital for surgery. It is expected that his walking will be limited for a few weeks. Two friends, also deaf, who live nearby plan with him that when he returns home they will stop in daily to visit, bring food, take care of him, and so forth. The three friends report a long-standing relationship with much mutual support and help over the years.

Neighbor: Mrs. Adams, age sixty-eight, helps Mr. Stern, seventy-two, who was just discharged from the hospital. They live in an apartment complex for the elderly. Even though a visiting nurse, a home health aide, and a physical therapist are providing services, there are still things to be done, and Mr. Stern has no family. Mrs. Adams has learned how to change the dressings on Mr. Stern's leg ulcers. She takes him on daily walking exercises and acts as a mediator with Meals on Wheels when needed. Mr. Stern becomes easily confused, so that he doesn't always remember nurses' instructions, and Mrs. Adams makes sure that he doesn't miss his meals and medications. Her help has made it possible for Mr. Stern to remain out of the hospital *and* to avoid nursing home placement, which was his dearest wish.

By contrast, the loss of a network can be devastating:

Tom, age thirty, was injured in a skiing accident and was now paraplegic. He lived in an urban independent living center for those with similar diabilities. The residents developed their own style and "in-language" such as referring to the non-disabled as "walkies." They supported one another, went places together, and adapted to their severe handicaps through the mutual aid system they had developed. They taught each other how to survive in the environment of the non-disabled by sharing effective coping maneuvers. Tom moved from his group setting to a small college town, 150 miles away, in order to attend the university. There, he was unable to find a group of people like himself, and had to make do with a "walkie" as a personal care attendant. "Walkies" were uncomfortable with him and often avoided him. There were many places and activities that Tom wanted to visit and participate in, but they weren't wheelchair-accessible. Having been athletic, the confinement to a wheelchair was stressful anyway—but now the stress was intensified by the loss of his informal support system, its culture, life-style, and reciprocity. Previous coping resources were no longer available, he resorted to alcohol, eventually dropped out of school, relinquished his goals, and returned to the city.

Positive exchanges with natural support systems nurture the sense of relatedness, self-esteem, competence, and self-regulation of all participants. In the role of organizer, the social worker can recruit helping "agents," mobilize natural systems, help them extend the nature and scope of their support, and help match their properties to individualized client need. In the following example a social worker in a rural home health agency created an informal support system for isolated elderly suffering from chronic illness. To do this he engaged the interest of faculty and students in the district high school:

I went to see the school principal and sociology teacher at the high school, and told them of my idea to develop a network of relationships between some young people and our elderly patients. They liked the idea, and the students then invited me to a session with the two sociology classes. I talked with them about home health, aging, and what a social worker does. The students filled out a questionnaire on the elderly, which stimulated good discussion about myths and stereotypes concerning the aged person. I described the planned program of visiting by the students to the homes of elderly patients to relieve the loneliness and isolation they now experience. The emphasis is to be placed primarily on the social nature of the interchange and secondarily on doing tasks or errands, valuable as this may be. Sixty percent of the class volunteered to participate. Next I spoke with our nursing staff and secured the names of older individuals who could benefit from the program by virtue of being homebound, without significant others, and receptive to visits by a young person. Sixteen elderly persons were nominated. I visited fourteen of them and telephoned the other two to describe the program and ascertain their interest. I then enlisted sixteen students, and we planned for the time, date, and place where I would personally introduce them to their respective older friends. Students are meeting a course requirement through their participation in the project. The expectation is that the student will visit his or her older companion on a weekly basis at a time and day that is convenient for both of them. Students will also be responsible for submitting to their instructor a slip each week describing the last visit and plans for the next one. I will be available to them by telephone, along with adjunct staff, on a round-the-clock basis. Each student was given a sheet covering the points we discussed in the planning meeting: the purpose of friendly visitation, suggested activities (talk, games, music, walk, and so on), conversational topics (yourself, your family, your older friend, his or her family, weather, current events, things of interest observed in the home), observations to be made of the older friend (mood, attitude, physical condition, grooming, dress, items of importance such as pictures or objects), what to do if there is a problem (submit it to the course instructor or, if it can't wait, call the social worker).

In each instance both the young and older persons seemed quite anxious prior to the visit, but this dropped away after the introduction. I was pleased to see the sensitivity shown toward each other. Each student and older person embraced after this initial visit. I have been amazed at the enthusiasm shown by both. Most students had decided to visit during their weekends, and the older people tell me that weekends are the hardest times for them to get through. Although the students' academic obligations to this project will cease at the end of the school year, I hope the relationships will continue if that is the wish of the participants. We at the agency will provide continued support during the summer. So far, I am encouraged to see how the reciprocal needs of each participant are met. The older person's interest in reminiscence provides the youthful listener with a link to the past and a glimpse into the future as it relates to his own aging. The youthful listener, in turn, assuages the pain of an elder's loneliness, and her respectful interest in past achievements and experiences restores the elder's self-esteem and connectedness to the present.

Informal support systems may serve as early referral systems to health care, as discussed in Chapter 3. Frequently they may be preferred over professional services (Mayer and Rosenblatt, 1964; Croog, Lipson, and Levine, 1972; Finlayson, 1976; Swenson, 1979). Strong support systems are found among poor blacks (Stack, 1974; Valentine, 1978) and other urban poor (Shapiro, 1970), and they help make coping with harsh environments possible. They constitute important sources of help in rural areas (Patterson, 1977). Mizio (1974) refers to the mutual obligations and emotional ties in the Puerto Rican extended family and to ties and obligations outside of the kinship structure: "The *compadrazgo* is the institution of *compadres* ('companion parents'), a network of ritual kinship whose members have a deep sense of obligation to each other for economic assistance, encouragement, support, and even personal correction" (p. 77).

Among American Indians, the tribe is an interdependent social system. It is "certainly nothing less than a big self-help organization that is designed to help people and meet the psychological, spiritual, and economic needs of its members" (Wilkinson, 1980). Each member has duties and obligations to others in their tribe, and "tribal alliances are also called upon . . . in an urban setting" (Goodluck, 1980).

Among Asian and Pacific Islander Americans, also, high value is placed on family obligations and responsibilities. One study suggests that among Japanese Americans and Korean Americans it is difficult for formal services to locate handicapped members because of the norm of family self-reliance in their care (Kushida, Montenegro, Chikahisa, and Morales, 1976). The islanders, in particular, being now far from home, seek out and maintain warm ties of friendship and cooperative social relationships, looking out for and looking after each other (Munoz, 1976). In considering the importance and availability of natural support systems, their culturally patterned relationships, and their emotional significance, it is essential that the social worker become knowledgeable about in-group and intergroup differences, including differences between the generations because of immigration and the value conflicts spawned by the larger culture.

Animal companions (and plants) are often significant network resources. In addition to the services dogs, cats, and monkeys perform for blind, deaf, and paraplegic individuals, pets of all kinds are reported to have a beneficial effect on the one-year survival rates of coronary heart disease patients (Friedman, Katcher, Lynch, and Thomas, 1980). Friedman and colleagues suggest that pets may have a soothing effect. They offer an unambivalent exchange of affection, attention, and contact comfort without the bargaining or supplication that characterize some human relationships. They also do not demand talk as the price of companionship, and speech raises blood pressure.

Pets have been used in the treatment of psychiatric patients and to relieve the loneliness of elderly persons. Horseback therapy is used for seriously physically disabled children, including those with muscular dystrophy, paraplegia, spina bifida, and cerebral palsy (Curtis, 1981). Programs for taking pets from shelters to visit hospitals, nursing homes, and geriatric facilities are spreading. At Children's Memorial Hospital in Chicago, for example:

Even though many of the children are very sick or badly injured, almost all are eager to hold the pets. A beautiful child in pigtails sees the volunteer in the hall and her eyes grow wide. Her mother props her up. The little girl cannot speak and lacks motor control of her arms, but she manages to draw the volunteer's hand close to her face so she can nuzzle a kitten.

A quadraplegic boy of about 12 is asked if he would like to see a dog. "Yep," he whispers. The pup's warm body is held against the boy's cheek. He smiles.

A wisp of a child attached to bottles and machines lies in her mother's lap in another room. Quietly we ask the mother if the child would like to pet a kitten. We are abashed in the presence of so much pain. But the child smiles, raises her hand to run it over the kitten. [Curtis, 1981]

The importance of remaining in touch with the natural world through animal companions or gardening (horticultural therapy), especially when one is chronically ill, suggests that the social worker should consider the use of pets and introducing programs such as those described as an environmental dimension of the enabler role. Bikales (1975) urges social workers in health settings or in other practice fields to help clients plan for the care of their pets when they face hospitalization. In emergency situations, the worker may even need to arrange for such care. Otherwise, many patients who live alone may refuse or delay hospital entry, or else their loving concern about the pet's wellbeing may create additional stress after hospital admission.

The concept of informal support systems also includes self-help groups. They reflect the growing readiness of all people to take control of meeting their own needs or solving their own problems and predicaments without professional leadership. They may use a professional as a resource person, but the members control resources and policy. The groups range from unaffiliated or loosely affiliated local ones to highly organized national associations having a network of local or state chapters across the country. Most such groups have varying functions: fundraising, changing public attitudes, consumer advocacy, and personal help to the members. Most serve more than one function and perhaps all four. A BSW social worker on the staff of a local chapter of the National Multiple Sclerosis Society describes the work of her organization, and her place within it:

The organization's three main objectives are: (1) to support national research leading to the causes, prevention, alleviation and cure of MS; (2) to aid individuals who are in any way disabled as a result of MS or other related diseases; and (3) to obtain and disseminate information about MS. The second objective is handled by the Patient Service Coordinator, which is the position I hold. Such services are provided without fee to our clients and I am currently responsible for servicing the needs of approximately 500 individuals living in two counties.

Such services include help with securing insurance payments, state aid and other entitlements, homemaker and other services, walkers, wheel chairs, Talking Books, and so forth. Among the programs this worker has arranged are monthly socials for MS persons and their families, weekly discussion groups for both the MS persons and their families, a ten-session "MS Home Care Course" for family members, a young adults' group, and an educational series for patients on "Living with MS."

The role of the social worker with mutual help groups includes making referrals to them, providing consultation when invited to do so by existing groups, serving on professional advisory boards, and initiating or helping to develop new mutual help groups (Silverman, 1978, pp. 46–55). Health care social workers now serve as consultants to other community caregivers, citizens' advisory groups on health matters, and consumer advocacy groups, in addition to the mutual help groups.*

The skills of the enabler and organizer roles are summarized in Table 6–3.

Client Self-directedness and the Social Work Role of Facilitator

The coping activities pertaining to motivation, problem-solving, management of emotions, and self-esteem are all relevant to the fourth component of effective coping, self-directedness. Hence the interventions specified for them apply as well as to self-directedness. In addition, however, in the role of *facilitator* the social worker draws on interventions that are quite specific to self-directedness. They are designed to help clients take a more active role in the treatment of illness or in the management of chronic disease, disability, or fatal illness; to manage issues of time and space as these bear upon their control of their own lives; to secure information about present and future practical needs and resources; to manage issues of dependence/independence, passivity/activity, and episodes of regression; and to influence the environment to be responsive to the need for self-directiveness.

These issues play themselves out to some degree in all illness and disability, but never more poignantly than in situations where patients are dependent upon machines or transplanted organs for continuing life (Abram, 1970; Abram, Moore, and Westervelt, 1971). Renal dialysis, in particular, is an area where the capacity for self-directedness is sorely taxed. Patients in coronary care units or other intensive care units may deal with similar concerns, but only temporarily. Many renal patients

* The skills of consultation are examined in Chapter 8.

TABLE 6-3. The Skills of Enabler and Organizer Roles in Helping Clients to Manage Painful Emotions and Maintain Self-esteem

CLIENT'S COPING TASK	SOCIAL WORKER'S PRACTICE TASK	SOCIAL WORK ROLE	SOCIAL WORK SKILLS
Maintaining psychic comfort, including optimal level of self-esteem	Providing emotional support. Handling resistance and excessive dependency or excessive independence when these are interfering with recovery, disability management, or effective coping	Enabler	*With client:* Responding to signals of distress; affirming strengths and self-worth; eliciting and handling feelings; legitimizing concerns; allaying anxiety, guilt, and reducing depression; providing contact comfort to children, the elderly, and the dying, or to family members; setting limits as needed; helping group and family members communicate more openly and directly; clarifying their discrepant perceptions, expectations, and incompatible coping strategies; supporting adaptive defenses and helping to relax maladaptive ones; providing advice, suggestions, and reassurance as appropriate
	Influencing the organization to be responsive to emotional needs	Organizer	*Agency environment:* Interpreting patient's and family's needs and strengths to other team members; influencing the staff to be more responsive to needs and coping tasks
		Organizer	*Outer environment:* Organizing natural helpers to increase the scope of support and exchange; where absent, organizing mutual aid systems and self-help groups; serving as resource person as needed; making use of animal companions and plants when appropriate

153

may be on the machine a long while awaiting a kidney transplant. Many more face a lifetime of dependence on the machine, up to twenty or thirty hours a week at a dialysis center, and less if patients dialysize at home or are able to use the new portable machine.

The role of dialysis patient tends to undermine the self-directive function at every turn. Hooked to a machine, being a slave to the machine, has a negative impact on the sense of identity and selfhood for many patients (Abram, 1970). Some patients feel they are less human and more machine—to the point of a disturbed body image. The sense of competence is undermined by the daily living with a life-threatening illness that prevents full and satisfying functioning in one's accustomed roles of spouse, parent, child, sibling, worker, or friend. Role losses in work and family and other realms of the life space, which erode the sense of control over one's life, create severe stress.

Independent decision-making and action must give way to dependence on the staff and the machine, reawakening old conflicts about dependence and control. These are replayed with staff, sometimes exceeding the limits of their acceptance and their understanding. The patient is told what to do and how to live his life. He is expected to cooperate and comply. Yet he is also expected to lead an independent life, to carry on work and family roles despite complications, symptoms, and environmental problems (Abram, 1970). Many patients can accept and handle the conflicting messages. Others rebel and don't follow medical regimens. Still others embrace the sick role, becoming passive, helpless, and dependent. They make excessive demands for staff attention, which may result in harshness or withdrawal on the part of some staff, thereby increasing the dependency and the demanding behavior. The whole process escalates in a circular feedback loop.

The capacity for relatedness may also be threatened as the machine comes to replace human contacts and social activity. Networks may contract, as friends, neighbors, and work mates withdraw, or the patient withdraws from them. More important, marital conflict, including sexual dysfunctioning, and disruption of the parent–child relationship may arise as consequences of the disease, its treatment, and its uncertainties. The very capacities required for coping with dialysis in ways that will sustain self-directedness—sense of identity and self-esteem, competence, autonomy, and relatedness—are often themselves undermined by the stress it generates. The social work tasks, then, involve simultaneous work with the patient, the family, and the environment, including the staff.

As in any situation of illness, disability, or injury, it is usually easier for the patient and family to unburden their feelings of anger, depression, helplessness, and despair to the social worker than to the medical and nursing staff on whom they depend for their lives. The social worker as enabler elicits, accepts, and then helps the individual to manage those feelings. But, in addition, the social worker must often help staff members understand the sources of the patient's troubling behavior so they can deal with the patient in ways that will soothe the dependency conflicts instead of escalating them. This enables the nurses to feel more competent, restoring their own self-esteem. The demands on nursing staff in any illness where the treatment regimen is difficult are heavy. In many instances the social worker becomes their support source, or she may help staff form their own support system.

In a severe chronic disease or disability, issues of time come to the fore. For the dialysis patient and family, the time waiting for a transplant and the time spent on the machine go on for so long that they may seem to swallow up all time. There is neither time nor energy remaining for activities of family life, work life, and community life. Some may experience having too much time because their condition does not permit the activities that formerly filled their time, and they have not been able to discover or invent valued substitutes (Strauss and Glaser, 1975). Time spent on the machine becomes dead time for some, who come to see themselves as socially dead if not yet biologically dead (Kalish, 1968). And finally, scheduling is an important temporal dimension in dialysis, and patients may act out their depression and anger by coming late for treatment or skipping treatment. As with other difficult behaviors, this may lead to a feedback loop of poor patient–staff relations.

With respect to time, social workers in the facilitator role may help patients and families to deal more adaptively with issues of scheduling and to learn to pace activities in tune with energy patterns, and may encourage activity and social relationships. In any chronic illness or disability, family members may be overprotective, controlling the patient's use of time and activity and thereby subtly undermining self-directedness. The social worker can be helpful in gradually raising patient's and family's awareness of these patterns and in reducing them.

In the following example the patient needed the social worker's help in achieving greater independence and a more active orientation:

Mr. Grant, age thirty-four, suffered kidney failure from juvenile onset diabetes. He has lived all his life with his parents in their present house. After ten years' employment, he was laid off from his factory employment about one year ago, before going on dialysis. He is hopeful of receiving a transplant. Since being on dialysis, he is driven to the hospital-based center by his mother. He doesn't feel up to driving or taking the bus.

At first, Mr. Grant tried to appear as if dialysis would not make a difference in his life. This has not been the case, of course, and he continues to need reassurance and support on a weekly basis. He has many medical complications. His toes have been amputated, and his feet appear deformed in his special heavy shoes. His vision is blurred, and he is unable to read or watch TV. He has few visitors. Both parents work, and he has so far refused permission for the social worker to see them. The staff is concerned about his passivity and despair. He is also very angry and displaces his anger onto the staff and the machine. He says the doctors and nurses don't help him, and the machine makes him sick. He seems to deny that diabetes is the primary disease and expects that a kidney transplant will cure all his problems.

The worker's intent is to relieve some of the despair and anger and to encourage Mr. Grant to identify some realistic goals, involve himself in action, and regain a realistic sense of control over what is happening to him.

I said that he will soon regain some of his physical energy and can get out to do more. I asked about the things he enjoyed doing. He told me that he had played drums in a band. Relaxing a little, he said one band started in high school and they stayed together seven years, playing clubs and summer resorts. He belonged to another band which broke up only six months ago when two members moved away. I wondered if he thought of finding another group, and he said it would be good. So I asked what he would need to do to find such a group and then to affiliate with it.

Here the worker is attempting to bolster the faltering sense of independence by focusing on planning for action possibility. Although Mr. Grant did begin to improve physically, his anger and depression continued. He vomited frequently on the machine and threatened to stop eating while at the center. He was angry with the dietary regimen and increasingly hostile with the nurses. She encouraged him to express his anger and his depressed feelings. They talked also about his diet, and she helped him see that it was not too different from what he had been long accustomed to. They also talked about how his refusal to eat while at the center would cause problems with the diabetes. Her empathy with his feelings apparently allowed him to continue with the regimen, and the vomiting stopped. Again,

We talked about his behavior with the nurses (swearing and obscenities). He blames this on one nurse who has to put the needles in too many times, so she bothers him and he bothers her. He said he feels miserable, has no appetite or energy, "so what's the use?" I tried to relate his feelings and behavior to the length of time he's been waiting for a transplant. He became angry at me and said he didn't want to be reminded of that. I acknowledged it was painful,* and he admitted he worries about being on the machine. I asked him what he worries about. He had trouble finding the words, and finally said, "Just coming here and being on this machine makes me realize my situation, the condition I'm in." He quickly added that he doesn't mind operations, just this machine. I reassured him that it takes time for most people to adjust to dialysis. He responded that he guessed some could get used to it, but he is sure he won't. He then said that coming here three times a week to be on the machine had changed his whole life. I agreed that it is very difficult, but he has been able to do it.

The worker's inviting the expression of feelings and her acceptance of them are intended to sustain Mr. Grant's motivation to cope with the demands that dependence on the machine imposes on him. In the context of renal disease, moving him toward action, productivity, and self-directedness will also require careful work on issues of passivity, dependency, and the angry exchanges with staff, including the worker. Work will also need to be done with the nurses to increase their understanding of Mr. Grant's behavior, thereby reducing their retaliatory anger. It is a transactional problem. For that reason, too, if Mr. Grant consents, it will be desirable to speak with the parents. The worker had just learned from Mr. Grant that his brother was killed in an automobile accident a year ago. That, together with the juvenile-onset diabetes, suggest the possibility of parental overprotectiveness, a transactional phenomenon that could be contributing to the passivity. Nor does the worker yet know the impact of that event on Mr. Grant himself. The aim of such interventions is to facilitate his rediscovering his capacity for self-directedness and to enhance his management of the chronic illness.

The skills of the facilitator role are summarized in Table 6–4 (p. 158), while general issues regarding dependency and passivity (and excessive independence) will be discussed in the section that follows.

Issues of Dependence and Independence

Adaptive functioning includes the capacity to be appropriately dependent and appropriately independent as situations in life require. The situation of illness or disability challenges such functioning. Pain, anxiety, and fear stimulate the need to be cared for and cared about on both emotional and physical grounds. A certain amount of dependence on the medical caregivers and passivity in the face of prescribed procedures is necessary. Yet at the same time preservation of autonomy through active participation is required for effective coping, at least when the emergency and most acute phase of the illness are past. Maintaining an adap-

---

* This was intended as an empathic response, but it might have been more useful to stay with Mr. Grant's anger at the worker. Their relationship can be an arena for work on his passivity, dependency, and associated anger which are obstacles to effective coping with his chronic illness.

TABLE 6-4. The Skills of the Facilitator Role in Helping Clients to Maintain, Achieve, or Sustain Self-directedness Consonant with Physical State

CLIENT'S COPING TASK	SOCIAL WORKER'S PRACTICE TASK	SOCIAL WORK ROLE	SOCIAL WORK SKILLS
Self-directedness	Providing information, time, and space for effective coping; opportunities for choice, decision-making, and action, consonant with physical state; meliorating excesses of dependence or independence	Facilitator	*With client:* Providing information in the appropriate cognitive mode at the appropriate time and in the appropriate amount; providing opportunities for decision-making and action by opening up options; reframing coping demands; managing episodes of regression; regulating the pacing, rhythm, and timing of worker–client activity; providing space and time to develop and try out coping strategies and to deal with losses; managing issues of dependency and passivity
	Influencing the environment to provide time and space for effective coping and opportunities for choice, decision-making, and action consonant with physical state	Facilitator	*Agency Environment:* Influencing physicians to give needed information to patients and families; introducing organizational innovations to provide for greater participation of patients and families in action and decision-making. Helping staff deal effectively with issues of dependence and independence that create maladaptive exchanges
		Facilitator	*Outer Environment:* Helping families and networks deal with problems of over protectiveness

tive balance between the two positions is more difficult for some people than for others. And the balance may be made more precarious if staff attitudes and expectations favor dependency and passivity of a non-complaining and trusting nature. Some patients who functioned independently may now be vulnerable in the face of severe stress.

The passive dependent position as a response to illness brings gratification to the vulnerable as they yield to the regressive pull toward the comfort of an earlier level of development. They may demonstrate whining, complaining, and demanding behaviors, or they may be docile, conforming, and trusting. Most such patients regain their former level of more or less self-directed functioning upon discharge from the sick role. The social worker's facilitating skills can help reverse the regression even if the illness becomes chronic. However, in both the assessment and the handling of the behaviors, particularly those of the docile, dependent patient, it is of the utmost importance that culturally patterned submissive relationships with authority figures be distinguished from emotional regression.

Much more difficult issues of dependence and independence face two smaller groups of dependent patients or family members. Persons who characteristically are excessively dependent and those who characteristically are fiercely independent often jeopardize their recovery from acute illness or their management of chronic illness. The practice issue lies in helping excessively dependent individuals to release their potentialities for more adaptive functioning. In the case of those who defend against dependency longings, the issue is to help relax the defense so they can begin the long, difficult process of accepting the inescapable dependence imposed by a chronic illness or a disability while maintaining as much autonomy as possible. Since both positions often reflect lifelong patterns of relating to others, the social work task is apt to be difficult, requiring the skills of mobilizing, teaching, enabling, and facilitating as well as much work with the social environment.

THE EXCESSIVELY DEPENDENT CLIENT

Providing support, advice, encouragement, reassurance, and an emphasis on strengths to acutely or chronically ill, excessively dependent persons will help some to move toward more independent functioning, but not others. The latter, often individuals who developed chronic illness in childhood and who perceived their parents as unresponsive to their needs, are usually viewed by staff as difficult to manage. Having little tolerance for anxiety, they seek immediate relief through impulsive behavior. They tend to view others as potential sources of either gratification or danger and act in ways to evoke those responses. Thus they often make staff feel manipulated and divided among themselves. The patient's childlike clinging turns unexpectedly to anger as though staff members are threatening whatever autonomy has been achieved. He constantly seeks approval but expects the worst, thereby inviting the rejection he fears. The incessant demands brought on by psychological need make staff feel helpless and angry, and these patients are frequently referred to the social worker.

A thirty-two year old woman came to the ambulatory care center of a major medical center complaining of headaches, palpitations, and a choking sensation in her throat. She and the nurse agreed that her symptoms were related to stress, and she agreed to see the team social worker. Her symptoms quickly disappeared in their work together.

Her social worker initially fell into the category of being "all good," and when the time came for the worker's first vacation during treatment, the patient found her anger toward the social worker intolerable to express verbally, acknowledge, or experience internally. The patient's presenting symptoms reappeared during the vacation and after meeting with the nurse about them, the patient went into a rage about the nurse's condescending and patronizing notion that the symptoms were stress related. Meanwhile the nurse was totally bewildered by the patient's anger, and wondered whether [social work treatment] was making the patient worse. She became angry at the social worker. It was not until the social worker and nurse talked it out together that it became clear how the patient had split off her anger toward the social worker and transferred it onto the team nurse. An understanding of this phenomenon was essential for the team to continue to care appropriately for the medical and psychosocial needs of this patient. [Lee, 1980]

Such severely maladaptive functioning is called, in psychoanalytic object relations theory, the borderline state, originating in the toddler years when development issues center on autonomy, separation, and individuation. Interpretations of these observable behaviors by other schools of thought (such as the behaviorist, task-centered, or systems views in social work) differ from the psychoanalytic. In the adaptational model presented in this volume, the behavior patterns are viewed as outcomes of exchanges with past *and* present environments, which have eroded the potentialities for adaptive functioning. However, the focus of assessment and intervention is not on the past but on the nature of *present exchanges* with family, work, the health care staff, and others, *within the stressful context of illness or disability*. Intervention is designed to improve the exchanges, in ways described in this chapter, so the individual may achieve more adaptive solutions to his needs, goals, and the stress of illness/disability.

Because of the emotional vulnerability that serious illness or disability creates, the provocative behavior of the excessively dependent patient must be handled as supportively as possible to avoid increasing anxiety, impulsiveness, and self destructiveness. With recognition of the defensive patterns of splitting (people as all good or all bad), insatiable demands (viewed more as entitlements), and anger when demands are not met, the worker must set firm limits (Adler and Buie, 1972). This must be done nonpunitively and within a context of concern for the patient's well-being. Such concern includes recognizing with the patient the stress caused by the illness or disability, avoiding any assault on needed defenses, and being careful not to overstimulate either the patient's anger or his wish for closeness.

Such a support structure focuses on current issues related to the illness and to the patient's current perceptions, experiences, and goals. It is more likely, than either confrontation or a focus on past issues, to move the patient forward on the coping tasks. The strengths, and he usually has many, and a *growth-promoting environment* are the levers of change by which improved reality testing, calmer exchanges with others, task-oriented action, and elevated self-esteem may be brought about. The growth-promoting environment may be achieved by concurrent work with staff, and often with family members, to interpret needs and behaviors. An important aid for the worker, as for the staff, is self-awareness so that one may understand and control the negative feelings and attitudes one can experience toward this patient.

THE EXCESSIVELY INDEPENDENT CLIENT

By contrast the overly independent patient is likely to be severely threatened by a chronic illness or disability that undermines his conception of himself as the self-sufficient caretaker of others. He may exhibit unreasoning anger toward staff or his family or may express anger at himself in self-punishing ways, including depression that is often outside of awareness. (As in all depression, the risk of suicide must be evaluated.)

It is important to help such patients reduce their expectations of themselves, find new interests or rediscover old ones, accept more modest and realistic goals in the light of the illness and experience fulfillment in achieving them, and accept the needed dependence on others.

The losses these patients experience are inexpressibly painful. Thus they need considerable encouragement to talk about them and express their sadness and anger rather than acting out the anger. Illness requires them to give up former self-concepts, life goals, status, and roles and to accept new down-scaled ones, which are perceived by the patient as signs of failure.

Network and group supports can also be helpful in these areas. Work with the family is important, so they may help correct the patient's perception that they will now abandon him as a worthless failure. Family work is especially important when circular feedback loops are present:

> The patient, for example, may have serious concern about his future sexual potency, and out of his concern, conveys the message that he no longer sees his wife as a love object, in this way covering his deeper fear of sexual impotence. Feeling rejected, the wife in turn responds by distancing. The patient then responds to her emotional distancing, which confirms his deeper fear, by depression, retaliation, or other symbolically based defensive maneuvers. [Lane, 1975–1976, p. 196]

It is well to remember that in matters of physical illness and disability, in possible contrast to the treatment of emotional disturbance in mental health settings, issues of excessive independence, dependence, and passivity have to be handled as much as possible by supportive measures and an emphasis on strengths and conflict-free areas of functioning. The skills of mobilizing, teaching, enabling, and facilitating, together with those of mediating and organizing, will all be needed.*

Summary

The four components of coping, the associated tasks for client and worker, and the worker's associated roles actually overlap in client and worker activity. All are directed toward maximal recovery in acute illness or effective management of chronic disease and disability, and the losses they impose. All seek the achievement or restoration of an adaptive person–environment relationship. For the purpose of analysis, coping behaviors were broken down into their component parts. But a coping strategy is also a whole, and in its wholeness it is likely to serve more than one component and sometimes all four all at once. Each component depends to some degree on the others, and each influences the others. The individual responds to stress in an integrated way physiologically, emotionally, and behaviorally.

Similarly the social worker's activities in support of clients' tasks were

---

* Readers interested in pursuing psychotherapeutic matters from other vantage points are referred to Strean (1978, 1979), Turner (1978), and selected issues of the *Clinical Social Work Journal.*

broken down and reassembled into clusters conceived as practice roles. But the worker's activity, like the client's, is also a whole, and the realities of practice are such that the worker moves freely and sometimes imperceptibly from task to task and from role to role. She draws from all the skills at her command in response to her moment-to-moment assessment of what is required. Roles are only imperfect abstractions of practice realities, but they do serve to show the rich diversity of social work tasks and skills. The skills described in this chapter are mediated by the worker's own style as she designs and adopts techniques for carrying them out. This is the creative art of practice.

CHAPTER 7

The Helping Process: Ending Phase

THE ENDING PHASE presents a new range of tasks to clients and workers as they bring their work together to a close. Processes of the ending phase include termination, sometimes accompanied by transfer and/or referral, and evaluation of outcomes. These processes are affected by such organizational factors as the function of the health care setting, its temporal arrangements, and its funding requirements and by the nature of the population served, the helping modality used, and factors in the client–worker relationship.

Terminating the Helping Relationship

The characteristics of the particular field of practice and the particular setting influence not only the processes of the ending phase but their content as well. Two features of health care settings are especially important. One is the imposed termination of discharge, often requiring inter-disciplinary planning for posthospital care. Discharge itself may be influenced by mandated procedures such as utilization review in federally supported services, reimbursement policies of private third-party payors, and the expiration of funding for grant programs. The second feature flows from the nature of illness and injury, so that death and bereavement impose the most poignant ending of all. Social work practice during the ending phase requires special knowledge and skill in helping some patients and families to formulate discharge plans and others to cope with death and bereavement.

Time is an aspect of organizations that affects the ending phase. The

164

way time is structured varies across settings. In acute care settings where client–worker contact is usually brief and all phases of the helping process are telescoped, or in ambulatory settings where contact may be only occasional and irregular, the feelings associated with the ending of a relationship may not be intense. They may not even be aroused. In contrast, in chronic care or long-term ambulatory services, where contact is regular and relatively frequent, the process of termination is likely to be accompanied by strong feelings on the part of clients and social workers.

Time is important not only in terms of duration of contact but also in terms of the tempo of ending. It takes time to deal with the feelings generated. In health care settings it takes time to develop individualized and helpful discharge plans. Time, always a scarce resource in health care settings, must nevertheless be set aside to deal adequately with both tasks. Attention to tempo implies an adequate period of time in advance of the last session for the expression and handling of the feelings aroused, determination of any needed next steps by patient or family after the contact is ended, and evaluation of what has and has not been accomplished in the helping process. Attention to tempo underscores the need for discharge planning to be built into the helping process at the time of admission wherever possible.

The demographic features of the population being served is another organizational factor affecting the ending phase. The sick elderly and very young, and the disabled of all ages, are particularly dependent upon their environments because of impaired or insufficiently developed competence and autonomy imposed by age or degree of disability. Too often members of these populations are socially and emotionally isolated and beset by feelings of helplessness, hopelessness, and despair. While those who are institutionalized in congregate facilities are particularly susceptible to such feelings, many who are residing in the community are also isolated and feel abandoned. Hence the loss of a relationship to a caring and helpful social worker may be painful to the client, evoking grief and its components of anger, self-hate, and sadness. And the social worker may feel guilt at "abandoning" such a client.

It sometimes happens that patients may be abruptly transferred to another unit or to another facility, particularly in settings where team practice does not exist or exists in name only. Such events leave the client and worker totally unprepared for the end of their relationship. Often an organizational factor, but sometimes a reflection of defensive or even unethical practitioner behavior, is the unexpected and unplanned ending that occurs because the worker leaves the setting for another post or is transferred to another division, or a student completes a field internship and the client has not been prepared for these events.

Depending on duration and other factors, feelings connected to the ending of the relationship when present are likely to be more intense in work with an individual than in work with the family. Intrafamilial relationships continue after service is ended, and the potential for intensity in the worker–family relationship is diluted by the one-to-many aspect. In some ways a formed group of patients or relatives may have a more difficult time with termination than a family, because intragroup relationships are ending as well as the individual member's relationship to the social worker. On the other hand, the termination process may be easier not only because of the one-to-many aspect as in the family but also because most groups in health care settings are time-limited so that the ending time is built into the process from the beginning. Indeed, work with individuals and families may be on a similarly planned, time-limited basis. In all such instances the strong feelings associated with separation are less likely to be generated. The time limit is itself a powerful dynamic in maintaining a focus on the tasks to be done, thereby minimizing the arousal of irrational responses to the ending. Even so, there may be a reluctance to relinquish what has been a productive and helpful relationship.

Many groups are structured on an open-membership basis. Members move in and out, often for only one or two sessions. Hartford (1976, p. 70) notes that in one-session groups, a brief period should be saved at the end of the meeting for comments on the process of coming together and ending. In short-term groups at least one session should be reserved for attention to ending. In longer-term groups more time must be allowed.

Relationship factors shaping the ending phase, in addition to those already alluded to, include the symbolic meaning of attachment and separation to the individuals involved and both the irrational and the realistic elements of the particular client–worker relationship. Separation is a ubiquitous feature of human life, and we experience it to varying degrees very early in life. Our later responses to separation are shaped in part by these earlier experiences and in part by continuing experiences with separation and endings over the life course—especially those involving real or perceived loss.

Thus every client and every practitioner have unique responses to the ending of a helping relationship, whether it was dominated by negative, positive, or ambivalent feelings. The responses are influenced by the symbolic meaning attributed to the relationship and to its ending, which is shaped by both emotional and cultural factors as well as past experience. Physical states, age, and even gender also influence the responses to ending. All these factors can generate irrational and realistic, unconscious and conscious feelings such as anxiety, guilt, anger, sadness, resentment, fears centered on dependence or independence, pleasurable anticipation in new beginnings, or satisfaction in achievement.

The importance of professional attention to the ending phase is clear.

The gains made in coping with the psychological and social consequences of illness or disability and the optimal enhancement of self-esteem/identity, competence, autonomy, and relatedness are more likely to be sustained when the ending phase is handled knowledgeably, sensitively, and with recognition that endings are mutually experienced and responded to by both client and social worker. Preparation by the worker therefore involves (1) an empathic review of what responses ending is likely to evoke in the particular client and in the worker, and (2) a consideration of steps required for an adaptive integration of the experience by both participants.

Shulman (1979) has identified the skills of ending as (1) pointing out endings, (2) responding directly to indirect cues, (3) acknowledging the client's ending feelings, (4) sharing the worker's ending feelings, (5) crediting the client, and (6) inviting the client's positive and negative evaluations of the shared work. *Pointing out endings*, at some time before the last session, sets in motion the process of integrating the ending experience. It comes about either as a reminder, if the termination date was set at the beginning, or as a mutual decision by client and worker because goals have been achieved at an optimal level, because nothing further can be achieved, or because of processes beyond the participants' control: medical discharge, worker moves and job changes, and the ending of grant-supported projects. Client responses may include a forgetting of the ending date set earlier, an upsurge of feelings of helplessness, regression to dependent behaviors, an eruption of new problems and needs, or—especially where the relationship was a satisfying and significant one—an avoidance of the topic.

Responding directly to the indirect cues is useful when there are negative feelings. The indirect cues tend to occur most often where the reality of the ending is recognized but is perceived as a form of rejection. The negative feelings of anger or resentment may be directly expressed through hostile comments or questions ("Did they fire you?") or behaviorally through inappropriate or destructive action, missed appointments, or lateness. Some clients may be unaware of their anger and instead experience a depressive sense of unworthiness and guilt for having caused what they perceive as the worker's disappointment in them and subsequent rejection of them.

The worker's skill lies in the ability to accept the direct expression of personally directed anger nondefensively and to encourage direct expression of indirectly expressed feelings. Nondefensiveness means that the worker acknowledges the validity of the client's feelings as an expectable part of the process of ending, thus making it possible for the client to take some control over the process. Nondefensiveness is dependent on a process of empathy similar to that discussed in Chapter 3 with respect to the preengagement preparation in the initial phase. It rests on the capacity both for identification with the client and for separateness and objectivity. The skilled, knowledgeable social worker, in touch with her or his own feelings and responses to endings, can then understand the content and sources of the client's feeling while remaining separate enough to invite and accept their direct expression.

Acknowledging the client's ending feelings and sharing the worker's ending feelings are skills typically used in the phase of sadness. When the expression and acceptance of anger and resentment about ending have occurred, the underlying sadness then appears (recognizing that for some the anger will not be present and for others the sadness will not appear). It is possible now for a mutual acknowledgment of the personal meaning of the relationship to be expressed and a sharing of the regret that it must end.

> People have varying capacities for this kind of expression, and with some, the worker's recognition of their unexpressed feeling may be relief enough. Many clients, of course, will not feel anything as intense as sadness but only a mild regret, perhaps, that the relationship is ending. Hence, the worker must be surefooted in her empathy, guarding against the projection that results in overemphasis and overintensity. At the same time, she must be aware of her own and the client's attempts to cover up the feelings, and to avoid the embarrassment often associated with the expression of positive affect. [Germain and Gitterman, 1980, p. 267]

Shulman (1979, p. 98) observes, "Often workers must risk their own feelings first for the clients to feel free to risk themselves. Both may feel vulnerable, but it is part of the worker's function and a measure of professional skill to be able to take this first, hard step."

Crediting the client and *inviting evaluation* help move the process of termination to a satisfying end. They include (1) recognition of gains and achievements; (2) development of next steps, including plans for client and family to complete any unfinished tasks after termination, transfer to another setting and/or to another worker, or referral to community services; and (3) the final goodbye or disengagement. While these processes are part of discharge planning in a health care setting, they may also be part of the termination process where medical discharge does not require the development of a formal plan. Hence these processes are mentioned here, but they will be reviewed in the section on discharge planning and again in the context of evaluation.

In this final part of ending the work, recalling earlier agreements on goals and tasks provides a starting point for a review of achievements in the work together. Crediting the clients enables them to "own" what has been accomplished in coping with the stress of the illness or disability; helps to consolidate the achieved levels of self-esteem, relatedness, self-directedness, and competence—however modest they may be in an individual situation—and prepares for their continued development. It is equally important that client and worker look together at what was not helpful in the joint efforts, what didn't work, and why it didn't work. This lays the base for ongoing tasks for the client after termination or transfer, and it also supports the professional development of the worker. The client is helped to generalize the experience to other future demands and opportunities, while the worker is helped by the process to generalize to future helping situations what has been learned from this one.

All phases of ending and their associated tasks are as important for collectivities of family and group as they are for individual patients and relatives. Group members need to review and relive their shared experiences over the life of the group and to receive recognition for their individual and collective success in developing ways to cope with the demands of illness and disability. With both individuals and collectivities, it is important that clients experience the ending phase as a new beginning, the fears of which are not brushed away by false reassurance from the worker but are accepted as understandable. The worker expresses both confidence in the new or rediscovered abilities and hope for a successful new beginning.

Evaluation of Service Outcomes

The mutual review of achievements, unfinished tasks, and positive and negative aspects of the helping relationship is necessary but not sufficient. For the continuing evaluation and development of the individual practitioner's effectiveness and the social work department's program effectiveness, more formal procedures are needed. Health care settings of all kinds can and do use problem-oriented recording, which lends itself to quality assurance at the practitioner level (Kane, 1974; Martens and Holmstrup, 1974; Biagi, 1977). Other forms of self-monitoring of practice in use include goal-attainment scaling (Kiresuk and Garwick, 1979), originally designed for mental health services, and single subject designs (Bloom and Block, 1977; Thomas, 1978; Jayaratne and Levy, 1979), and an accountability system for social work based on the combined use of goal-attainment scaling and the problem-oriented record (Spano, Kiresuk, and Lund, 1977). In this section only the problem-oriented record (POR) will be considered.

Originally conceived for the use of physicians, the POR was adopted quickly by nurses and social workers in medical settings. It fits well with the social work emphasis on client participation, mutual contracting and recontracting processes, and continuous mutual evaluation throughout the contact. Interventions are planned, carried out, and assessed in terms of predefined goals mutually agreed upon. The POR format allows for the social worker's emphasis on (1) person–environment transactions and changes in them; (2) problems, needs, or predicaments rather than personality diagnoses or behaviors alone; and (3) accountability to the client and other team members as well as to the institution and the profession. It is also an instrument for quality assurance at the departmental and institutional levels.

The POR has four components: an initial data base, a problem list, assessment and plans for each problem identified, and progress notes on the implementation of plans. The minimum data base, defined in advance for consistency in data gathering, includes physical, psychological, social, and cultural information. Sources of data will include the patient, family, medical and other records, staff, and other significant persons. Once the initial collection of data has been made, a list of problems/needs emerging from the data is drawn up and becomes the first page or index to the record. Each problem/need is numbered, and all subsequent entries are numbered to conform with the problem to which it refers. As problems are resolved, the date of resolution is entered and they are eliminated from the record.

A numbered plan of intervention is developed for each problem. Not every problem may need attention at any given time, so those problems not being dealt with should bear a notation to that effect. The plan might include the collection of more data, intervention, and education of the patient about the illness and its management. Progress notes concerning implementation of the plans are dated and also numbered and titled to correspond with the indexed problem. They are structured in a form that has come to be referred to as S.O.A.P., a useful acronym and reminder: Subjective data relevant to the problem and obtained from the client or others; Objective data based on tests, observation, and verified information; Assessment or conclusions drawn from the added data; and Plan as updated by the changes or additions to the data.

Closing summaries and transfer notes are also related to the indexed problems. Each problem requires an entry regarding its status at the time of discharge or transfer, including recommendations. In the records of those patients requiring social work participation in discharge planning, specificity regarding the plans helps assure the participation of patient and family, as well as interdisciplinary involvement in the planning process. It can also help reveal gaps in resources and the impact of legislative mandates and institutional policies that may substitute mechanically carried out processes for careful, individualized planning.

For the purpose of quality assurance and accountability, peer auditing of randomly selected records can be readily carried out and remedial action instituted at once. The POR does not guarantee quality, because that depends on the knowledge, skill, and ethics of the recorder and the consistency with which the complete format is followed. But it does provide a means for picking up and correcting the deficiencies in data gathering, problem/need definition, assessment, planning, and intervention. An important additional benefit accrues from the fact that for the practitioner and for the social work department, service gaps and problems in patient care, in responses to families' needs, and in external resources and services can be noted—including those emanating from the social work component. Such patterned gaps become important data for justifying efforts to humanize the setting and to introduce innovative programs and procedures. These matters will be taken up further in Chapter 9.

Evaluation can proceed beyond the ending phase as well. For example, individual practitioners in some settings follow up on the consolidation of gains by a telephone call to clients a month or more after discharge or even at intervals, or by a postdischarge questionnaire sent out routinely to all those who have used social work services. More formal program evaluation by the social work department, beyond the scope of this book, frequently requires consultation with researchers if the social work staff lack specialized research skills.

Discharge Planning

In the Suchman (1965) model of illness stages, described in Chapter 3, the fifth and final stage is that of recovery and rehabilitation. One of two outcomes is possible: (1) recovery or rehabilitation in which the patient relinquishes the sick role and resumes normal roles to the degree possible, and (2) the sick role is not relinquishable, and the patient must leave the present setting for another, such as his or her own home with specialized home health care services, a chronic care facility, a rehabilitation setting, or a foster home. In the second outcome the social worker has a critical function to perform in identifying and assessing needs and resources that will make discharge possible.

Discharge planning has had a checkered history in social work practice. When medical social work began at the Massachusetts General Hospital under the aegis of Dr. Richard Cabot, as described in the Preface, its principal function was to help in posthospital planning so that patients could sustain their gains in health. As the years went by, however, medical social workers tended to move away from what were termed concrete services to counseling services. This was in response to the infusion of psychoanalytic concepts and to the striving toward professional status, which many social workers in various fields of practice believed would be best achieved by developing psychotherapeutic skills directed to intrapsychic processes. In many health care settings discharge planning came to be relegated to social workers with less than graduate education, on the assumption that it required less knowledge and skill than did the counseling function. In hospitals the redefinition of the social work function was rarely congruent with the expectations and perceptions of physicians, patients, and hospital administration, who placed greater value on the social worker's help in developing sound discharge plans than on psychologically oriented counseling (Davidson, 1978).

Concern grew in the late 1960s and early 1970s about the costs of hospitalization; it led to the introduction of Professional Standards Review Organizations and Utilization Review structures. These were to aid in cost containment by controlling bed utilization and overstays. The discharge function then became a way of protecting the hospital from having to pay for extra days of care not medically needed. Put another way, the hospital would not be reimbursed under Medicaid and Medicare for the cost of patients held in the hospital beyond their medical need for such care. About this time also nurses began to move into discharge planning, especially in settings where it had been viewed with disfavor by social workers. Ironically, this now became a function highly valued by administration, thereby strengthening the position of the occupational group filling it and threatening the status of social work departments that had relinquished it. Fortunately, they were the exceptional case.*

In many settings the social work departments have moved ahead to redefine the professional components of sound discharge planning and to reclaim the function. The struggle now is more often to resolve the conflict between the institution's need for reimbursement and protection against overstays and the patient's need for service and for careful planning. The discharge planning function is described by the Committee on Discharge Planning of The Society for Hospital Social Work Directors of the American Hospital Association as follows:

> Successful discharge planning is a centralized, coordinated, interdisciplinary process that ensures a plan for continuing care for each patient. It reflects both the patient's and family's internal and external social, emotional, medical and psychological needs and assets. It recognizes that the transition from the hospital is often more threatening than the actual hospitalization and a plan must be developed to both provide for a continuum of care and address the patient's immediate needs following discharge. It is the clinical process by which health care professionals, patients, and families collaborate to ensure that patients have access to services that enable them to regain, maintain, and even improve the level of functioning achieved in the hospital. [Cochrane et al., 1980, p. 3]

---

*Since this chapter was written, the federal government has instituted prospective payments to hospitals serving Medicare patients, effective October 1, 1983 (see Chapter 1, p. 13. This increases the urgency of discharge planning for social work as described here.

The committee later added:

> How patients are discharged from the hospital and the kinds of after-care they receive is the concern of many health care professionals. But, the skills required to help patients and families identify their goals and fully use their own strengths, as well as translate these into realistic, coordinated plans, are basic *social work* skills [Italics in the original]. . . . The discharge planner must provide emotional support to the patient and family, both before and during the transition from the hospital; must assist the family in exploring options for adjusting their finances; must help the patient adjust to a new self-image; must coordinate the community resources that support the transfer from the hospital and that provide post-hospital care; and must refer the family to support and education groups which will continue to assist them. [Cochrane, 1981]

Hospital social work departments have prepared guidelines for identifying patients having potential discharge planning problems, with the aim of early referral to social work for discharge planning. For example, one department set forth the following criteria for early referral:

1. Patients living alone or with spouse with limited social network or no immediate support system.
2. Patients 65 and over whose age, physical limitations or mental status may affect their functional ability.
3. Patients admitted with a diagnosis of catastrophic illness, (e.g. CA, CVA, M.I., progressive renal disease chronic or acute, neurological or neuro/surgical disease such as MS, brain tumor, para or hemiplegia resulting from spinal cord injury) requiring placement or alternate aftercare arrangements and/or major changes in life-style and living facilities.
4. Patients with repeated hospitalizations due to debilitating or chronic illness or questionable home situations necessitating home health care planning and follow-up, (e.g. diabetes, arteriosclerotic heart disease, chronic pulmonary disease, hypertension, children with asthma).
5. Patients in the terminal phase of illness requiring home health follow-up.
6. Patients admitted for surgery where help with post-surgical care is anticipated. (e.g. fistulas, appliances, prostheses, home supervision or instruction).
7. Patients with incapacitating fractures, trauma victims, etc. requiring home care plans or alternate placement.
8. Children with congenital defects or abnormalities such as spina bifida, mongolism, hydrocephalus.
9. Medically or socially "at risk" mothers who may need follow-up care or health aide in the home (e.g. toxemic, unwed, history of psychiatric hospitalization).
10. Suspected situations of child or spouse abuse.
11. Infants admitted for failure to thrive.
12. Children from fragmented or questionable home situations (parents separated, incarcerated, institutionalized).

13. Any patient with a diagnosis suggesting placement in another facility or home health care planning may be indicated.
14. Any patient with a diagnosis suggesting inherent adjustment problems or difficulty in coping that will affect discharge plans.
15. Any patient known to have a history of discharge planning problems. [J. T. Marshall, 1979a]

The same social work department that formulated these criteria also conducted a study of all admissions on a randomly selected weekend (N = 177). One hundred fifty-six of the admitted patients, or 88 percent, met one or more of the criteria, warranting early social work planning. Ninety-eight, or 55 percent, proved to have actual discharge problems. The most frequent problems referred to criteria 2, 3, 4, and 1. By the end of thirty days, eighty-three of the ninety-eight patients had been discharged. Of the fifteen others, five had died and ten were still in the hospital, five of whom had not yet been referred to social work. All five met one or more of the following criteria: 1,2,3,4,5,13, 14, and 15. The situation of these patients was as follows:

Patient A is ninety-nine years old, has no money, and his family is unable to care for him. He will need nursing home placement.
Patient B is a woman with eleven previous admissions who will need home health care.
Patient C is a chronic alcoholic with repeated hospitalizations in need of counseling on health care and home management.
Patient D is a man who will need a rehabilitation facility.
Patient E is a cancer patient who will require nursing home placement.

This study was based on only two days' admissions. The social work department concluded that five patients, every two days, for one year would mean a total of 912 possible discharge delays, which could be avoided through early social work intervention (J. T. Marshall, 1979b). For this hospital, at least, the figures suggest the importance of early referral for discharge planning or, better yet, the importance of screening of all patients by social work at admission or very soon afterward. The figures also underscore the contribution made by social work to the institution's ability to contain costs and to humanizing mandated procedures by careful, time-oriented planning.

Berkman (1977) specifies eight social needs that may be involved in discharge planning: hindrances to discharge of a psychological, social, or legal nature; concrete aids medically recommended such as appliances or transportation; fear of the prognosis on the part of patient or family member; finances; home supports such as homemaker or nursing service; housing; long-term institutional care; and temporary institutional care. The following situations illustrate the social worker's function in meeting discharge-oriented social needs so that discharge can proceed:

HINDRANCE

Mr. Cantrell, age forty-five, proprietor of a small business, had been hospitalized following a myocardial infarction. When he was ready to be discharged, the physician told him to decide whether he wished to go directly home or to a convalescent facility first. When the social worker spoke to Mr. C and to Mrs. C a problem of marital conflict became apparent. Mr. C said he had been seriously thinking of divorce because "I can't let her break my heart." He feels she leans on him too much and can't make personal decisions even though she holds a responsible job. He will give her a few weeks to see if she can change. In her interview Mrs. C complained about her husband's bullying ways. They fight over his work because he feels threatened by those who work for him. He wants them to take responsibility, but when they do, "he becomes furious and takes it out on me by constantly threatening to leave me." She is going to give him about three months to see if he can change. He has never helped with household tasks, but she doesn't mind this if only he would stop bullying her and appreciate what she does for him.

Further exploration revealed Mrs. Cantrell's fears of abandonment and of her husband's becoming dependent on her, thereby wearing her out physically and mentally. While Mr. Cantrell's dependency needs were more disguised, they were now more threatening to him as a consequence of the passivity and dependence his physical status imposed and his wife's demands that he be more giving.

The worker helped the couple to see some of the adaptive tasks that Mr. Cantrell's convalescence would pose for them both. They discussed their needs and expectations of each other and wanted to achieve a greater reciprocity. Recognizing they could not do this alone, they accepted the worker's suggestion of marital counselling. They also decided on Mr. Cantrell's returning directly home, partly for financial reasons but also because of their ambivalent need for each other. A referral to a family agency was arranged, and the Cantrells followed through. When the worker called them several times in the next six weeks, they reported things were going fairly well at home and in their weekly sessions at the agency.

CONCRETE AIDS

Lisa, two and a half years old, was transferred to a university medical center from another hospital, where she had been brought by her parents with a high fever of one day's duration. The diagnosis was meningitis, and Lisa was admitted to the pediatric intensive care unit in a comotose state. She was not expected to live. The social worker met with the parents daily. The family had recently come from a rural state to live with the paternal grandparents in an urbanized area. The father was self-employed in construction, making a very modest living, and they had no health insurance. Within a week Lisa began to improve, and three weeks later she was medically ready for discharge. Because of spasticity in the lower extremities, she needed a roller chair. The worker made the necessary arrangements for this through the Crippled Children's Services and helped the parents make application for state funding to cover the cost of the hospitalization ($13,000).

Following discharge, Lisa was to return to the hospital weekly for physical therapy. Her walking did not improve, and leg braces and orthopedic shoes were prescribed. The worker helped the parents to negotiate the complex systems involved, since by now the first hospital was demanding payment and threatening court action, state funding had been delayed because the worker assigned had left the agency, and authorization for the appliances was not released in a timely fashion. The parents were worn down by worry, frustration, and Lisa's irritability. They responded well to the worker's support.

FEAR OF PROGNOSIS

Mr. Rimsky came to a sectarian hospital's Department of Social Work requesting nursing home care for his aunt, seventy-four, and his uncle, seventy-three. He said they were brother and sister who never married and had always lived together. They needed medical care, had poor vision, were forgetful and required "outside help." Mr. Rimsky helped to arrange for their medical work-ups in the outpatient clinic. The physician recommended immediate cataract surgery. Both patients underwent surgery on both eyes, which was successful, and both recovered rapidly. The social worker met with them regularly during their hospital stay. Both were extremely resistant to short-term or long-term institutional care and insisted on returning to their own apartment. They lived in a low-income housing project in an impoverished high crime area. Mr. Rimsky refused to participate in any discharge plan that permitted his relatives to remain in their own home. He felt it was a mistake not to force them into custodial care. It was clear he feared that he would be expected to look out for them in their very frail condition, and he was not willing to accept the responsibility as he perceived it. He remained unconvinced that they could manage on their own and asked that he not be contacted any further.

With the approval of the physicians, the social worker arranged for homemaker services and visiting nurse service, and the patients were discharged. Since both were in need of continued health care, transportation was arranged so they could attend the outpatient clinic. Because they needed eyedrops three times a day, a neighbor and a member of the congregation of the nearby synagogue were enlisted. The nurse administered the third set of drops. Financially, the patients continued as before with Social Security, Medicaid, and Medicare.

FINANCES

Mr. Bunter, age sixty-four, a migratory, undomiciled black man, was admitted through the emergency room with a possible diagnosis of myocardial infarction, later revised to hiatus hernia and esophagitis. He remained in the hospital one week. The social worker saw him for four interviews. He was an attractive, appealing person, and as soon as he felt better he visited around the floor, making friends, gaining candy and cigarettes. He was illiterate, never married, and worked as an itinerant farm laborer. He was picking corn until the onset of his physical distress. He had his heart set on returning to his home state in the South. Since he would need assistance once he got there and should not be alone, the social worker contacted two friends there, as well as the local Travelers' Aid Society and the local Department of Social Services. Unfortunately, none of the friends could help, and neither agency was willing to assist on the basis of ineligibility and an earlier episode in which he had sold his food stamps to his landlady.

The social worker then tried to help Mr. Bunter recognize the advantage in remaining in the large city where he now was. He could apply for public assistance, a semiprotected living situation could be arranged, and the hospital would continue to provide him with medical care on an outpatient basis. His need for regular checkups at the G.I. Clinic, dental attention, and avoidance of strain from lifting were all stressed. He listened politely but still seemed determined to return to the South if only the hospital would furnish bus fare. He was advised this wasn't possible without a sound and permanent plan for him, but local referrals could be arranged. He accepted this, but on the day of discharge he was observed shaking hands happily and making the rounds of the patients and doctors, and it seemed likely he had managed to develop some income for travel purposes. (Earlier he had so charmed the house staff that they considered instituting a "Back to —— Fund for James" but were dissuaded from doing so when the lack of resources for sustaining him was explained.) Although the intake supervisor at the local Department of Social Services was alerted in connection with the referral, Mr. Bunter never arrived. Efforts to trace him were futile. The worker continued to hope he would turn up so he could receive medical care and the resources for which he is eligible, if not in this city, then in his home town. There the public agency would have to pick up service if Mr. Bunter arrived, even though they had refused to plan for him.

HOME SUPPORTS

The situation of Mrs. Ryan, the sixty-year-old textile worker seriously injured in a hit-run accident, was described in Chapter 3. The social worker anticipated that discharge planning might be difficult for Mrs. Ryan because of her lifelong sense of self-reliance and independence. He saw his tasks as presenting and explaining the options and constraints, and helping her to decide. This also involved consulting with the medical staff about the level of care needed. As it turned out, Mrs. Ryan refused to go to a nursing home when the physicians prescribed it. She saw herself as being able to go back to work "in a few months" (an unrealistic expectation) and insisted on returning to her home. "I'm not going to no nursing home and sit around with old people. I'll be old soon enough. I don't like nursing homes. I know you are concerned about me but I want to go home. The landlord will come down to help me, and I'll be all right."

Mrs. Ryan remained adamant despite the social worker's efforts to have her consider temporary institutional care. He looked into her insurance coverage and found it included home care. He then talked with the physicians, and they agreed that with her strong feelings it might do more harm than good to send her to a nursing home. They did insist she have a live-in aide for two weeks. Mrs. Ryan was pleased and relieved about going home but she balked at the plan for twenty-four-hour care. She said she didn't want anyone in the house all the time, she was used to living alone and didn't need anyone to take care of her.

The worker continued to recognize and accept her independence while clarifying for her that without such care she might prolong the period of uncomfortable helplessness. He also suggested that after all her years of working and independent living she had earned the right to a little help while convalescing. Mrs. Ryan did agree to the plan, and arrangements were made for a live-in aide, visiting nurse service, and physical therapy.

HOUSING

Mr. Mangold, age sixty-nine and divorced, a retired florist, was a patient on the coronary care unit. He also suffered from diabetes and osteoarthritis. He receives social security and had been living in a small hotel. It was not considered wise for Mr. Mangold to return there, because his heart attack had occurred right after he had been attacked by an intruder brandishing a knife. He had no friends or relatives who could locate new quarters for him, so the social work student, who had been seeing him regularly, offered her help in finding another hotel. She visited four hotels near the hospital since Mr. Mangold would need out-patient care; one seemed quite suitable. It was clean and well cared for, and the manager seemed interested and helpful. The worker then took Mr. Mangold to see the hotel, and he agreed it was acceptable. He did feel sorry to leave his former neighborhood. In an effort to engage him in peer contact, the worker described a group of elderly former patients who meet weekly at the hospital with a social worker. This is a social and discussion group whose activities are supported by a small endowment fund. Mr. M was interested, so the group leader visited him and invited him to join. The discharge went well, and the worker continued to be in touch with him: "I gave him adequate time to adapt to our ending. He handled this in his own fashion by expressing the wish that I call from wherever I am, 'just to see how I'm doing.'" He went to the group meetings regularly, was respected for his horticultural knowledge, and made some friends.

LONG-TERM INSTITUTIONAL CARE

Mr. Muncey, age eighty-two, a childless widower and retired professional dancer, had been in the hospital three months following a myocardial infarction. He suffered serious complications and became withdrawn and depressed. The social worker on the coronary care unit saw him three times a week. When his physical condition began to improve, so too did his emotional state. By the time of discharge he was demonstrating a charm and sense of humor that endeared him to the staff. He had been living in a dilapidated hotel. Because his condition was only fair, the physician felt he needed continuous care. Mr. Muncey agreed, "because there is no one there to care for me, and I want to be in a place where there are other people." He did have two friends, a couple in their forties who had known him for many years and visited him frequently in the hospital. They asked that he be placed in the nearby town where they lived so they could continue to visit regularly. With the social worker's help, Mr. Muncey was approved for Medicaid, an appropriate nursing home was found in the desired area, and transportation to the home was arranged. Mr. Muncey looked forward to the move, although when the day approached he felt sad to leave the staff, telling them, "I'll miss you."

Several weeks later the social worker spoke with Mr. Muncey, the nursing home director, and Mr. M's friends. He was in good spirits and was described as communicative and able to walk about without much help.

TEMPORARY INSTITUTIONAL CARE

Ms. Egan, age seventy, unmarried, a retired office worker, was admitted to the hospital with a cardiovascular condition and diabetes. She had multiple leg ulcers, and a below-knee amputation was performed because of gangrene. When it was time for discharge, Ms. Egan was advised by her physician to enter a nursing home because she still needed some further care before she could look after herself at home. She agreed but wished to go to a facility near her relatives. The social worker helped with the medicaid application, and then,

Finding a Medicaid bed was extremely difficult. One home was willing to accept Ms. Egan as a Medicare patient and then would change her later when the Medicare ran out. That raised another problem; Medicare will cover only skilled nursing in a nursing home, but Ms. Egan now needed only the rest. She did have some bed sores, which required skilled nursing. But if they healed in the hospital she would not be eligible for coverage, and I would have to find another home. Yet this one was near her family, which was very important. Then the home called and told me the bed would be given to someone else if I didn't move. When I finally reached her doctor he was vague about her release date. I explained the situation, but he said, "Find her another one," and hung up. I knew Ms. Egan was not receiving acute medical care any longer, so I consulted with the Utilization Review Coordinator. She reviewed the chart and sent notice to the doctor asking for medical evidence to justify the patient's stay in an acute care facility. The next day the doctor called the department and said, "Ms. Egan can leave whenever arrangements can be made." Ms. Egan left by ambulance, very happy to know that she would be near her relatives.

An additional perspective on the exigencies of discharge planning is provided by the following practice experience of a second-year graduate student:

Mr. Murphy's doctor asked me to arrange his transfer to a nursing home. He has been in the hospital six weeks because of emphysema but is becoming weaker and is deteriorating. I said I would talk with the patient and look into the nursing home situation and then get back to her. When I saw Mr. Murphy, I was struck with how very sick he was. He is fifty-two but looked ninety. He had no teeth, little hair, and weighs only 75 pounds. This was his fourteenth hospitalization for emphysema. He had been a stagehand but had been unable to work for seven years. He was never married. His older sister had been taking care of him. She came to the hospital every day to feed him his lunch.

I went up to Mr. Murphy's bed and explained who I was and why I was there. He seemed glad to have someone there and motioned me to sit down. I lowered the rail on the bed and drew close. He tried to speak, but it was a very soft whisper. The only way I could hear him was to lean over his small body with my turned head near his mouth. I tried to catch the words. When I did, I told him that I had heard and understood him. He said something about his sister, and I asked if this was the sister who visited him each day? He panted yes and said someting about how she had suffered so much because of his sickness. I said she must mean a lot to him. He said yes, and she had taken care of him over the past few years. He tried to give me her phone number at work but could not remember it. I asked him if he wanted me to call her, and he said yes, but I could not make out why. Throughout, he had a terrible racking cough. I gave him wads of tissue, and he nodded his head each time as if to thank me. He could breathe best when he was sitting upright, but he kept sliding down on the bed. I frequently put my hands under his armpits and gently pushed him back up. Each time I did this, he put his arms around my shoulders and left them there as I tried to hear what he was saying.

His sister came into the room on her lunch break. She was very warm with her brother, urging him to eat so he could regain his strength. She thanked me for what I could do about arrangements for nursing home care, and I left them together. That night his heart failed, but staff response was quick, and he was resuscitated. He spent the weekend in the Respiratory Care Unit on a respirator. When I went in to the unit Monday morning I was surprised to see him there. He seemed very upset and wanted to talk. He was easier to understand, and he said he wanted to go home, he wanted me to help him go home. At this point I still didn't know that Mr. Murphy had gone into heart failure (and the hospital would not let him die), but I could sense his urgency. I repeated that he wanted to go home and that he wanted me to help him. He was panting and said yes. I asked him what he wanted me to do. He said get him a taxi and take him home. I shook my head and said that both he and I knew I could not do this today for him, that he was very sick. I said that I could help him by listening very closely to what he wanted to tell me. He shook his head, and said he was very thirsty. I asked the nurse and got him some fruit juice. As I helped him drink it, he said, "Bless you, you have no idea . . ."

He then rambled for a bit, and I tried to understand without asking him to repeat. He was talking about either a dream or a memory of a real experience. There were Japanese soldiers attacking him with machine guns, and there were only four hours left. He was panting when he finished this, and holding very hard on to my arm. I felt he was telling me that he fears an overwhelming force is killing him. He is obviously terrified and exhausted. I said he seemed very tired. He said yes, he was tired, which he repeated several times. I said he had so little energy left, and he said yes, yes. He began to relax. I felt he was telling me he was going to die in a few hours. What more could I do than tell him the message was received and that I would try to support him in his weariness rather than help him fight the force?

The nurse came by to say that he would be leaving the RCU soon to go back to his room. He said to me, with a desperate look, that he didn't want to go back there. I said he was tired of struggling any more, and he kept repeating he didn't want to go back to his room. He became quite angry with me and said I had to do something to help him, that I was the only one who understood. I felt very impotent and felt that all I could do is reflect back to him his desperate desire to "go home." I said I would do what I could and that I would be by to see him once he is in his room. The orderlies came to take him upstairs.

I went to see him in his room an hour later. He looked very tired now and was difficult to understand again, this time because of the extreme quietness of his voice. I put down the railing of the bed and sat down close to him, leaning over him and putting my head close to his face. He said he couldn't breathe, and I asked him what he wanted me to do. He said to get his chest pills. I asked the nurse and she said he had some pills for general pain, which she would bring in when she was finished preparing another patient for surgery. I told Mr. Murphy the pills were coming, but he angrily sent me in search of the nurse twice more. The anger soon passed, however, and he asked for water several times. I helped him drink it. He either kept his arms around my shoulders or held onto my hand. He said that the three most important people in his life were his mother, his sister, and his niece. His voice was almost inaudible. So he would know that I had heard him, I repeated the words as I understood them. If I got the sentence correctly, he would say yes. He said he wanted to die. I repeated this, and he said yes. A nurse came in to suction his lungs, and for about ten minutes she worked to do this with some difficulty. Mr. Murphy held on to my hand and was in obvious pain at many points during the procedure. After the nurse left, he said he would never go through that again. I repeated his statement, and he said yes.

I was not afraid at any point here. Mr. M obviously needed to express these thoughts, and my accepting them validated them. It seemed sufficient for him to know I heard his messages. He finally turned his back to me and curled up into a little ball. I sat quietly rubbing his back. Then he would turn toward me for a bit, and I rubbed the other side of his back. Finally he said he thought he would "snooze" for a while. I repeated this, and got up from his bed. I touched his leg, and said I hoped he slept well, and left. There was an all-pervasive calm about him now. I had the feeling he was decathecting from all that was around him, and that this was a strangely beautiful thing to sense. In telling him to sleep well, I was using his symbolic language to say it was OK to die, that I would not try to persuade him to "keep awake" any longer.

The nurses told me later that his sister came to feed him his lunch, but he ate nothing. She stayed with him for an hour, and just after she left, Mr. Murphy died. I wrote his sister that evening, telling her that I had spoken with her brother that morning and he had told me of his concern about all that she was going through on his account. And I said he had told me at the end that he wanted to die. She wrote back a warm letter thanking me and all the staff for caring for Mr. Murphy. She said that while she had hoped he would pull through once more, she felt consoled that he was finally "at rest" and that he had gone quickly.

Death, Dying, and Bereavement

Although Mr. Murphy's physician had asked for the social worker's help in securing nursing home placement, the social worker encountered another kind of ending. Recognizing that the requested service was inappropriate and sensing the imminence of Mr. Murphy's death, she chose to assume another function, that of comforting the dying patient. Death and bereavement may be pervasive experiences in the practice of a social worker in certain health care settings such as acute care facilities and nursing homes.

The widely known work of Kübler-Ross (1969) on the stages of dying—denial, anger, bargaining, depression, and acceptance or resignation—freed many health care practitioners to deal more openly with the dying person so that death could come with optimal dignity, humaneness, and a sense of closure to one's life and affairs. At first it was assumed that open communication as a right made it automatically desirable for every patient and family member. That position has been tempered by the realization, based on clinical experience, that not everyone wants to know the truth, that the positive expectations of some may be dashed by the truth, thereby undermining the power of hope. And denial in some others seems to serve important functions right to the end. The readiness of patient or family member to hear the truth, to want to hear it, and to deal with it must be carefully appraised. (Fisher, 1979) Where information is a need, the social worker is often helpful in persuading the physician to provide it and in helping the individual and family members to deal with it in an adaptive way.

Many health care professionals have come to question the concept of stages in dying, preferring to view the shifts that occur as phasic in nature. This takes more accurate account of the twists and turns, the overlaps, and the going forward and back observable in patients and families as they move through the period of living with dying. Viewed as a life transition, fatal illness presents internal biological changes, physical pain, emotional pain and fears, grief, possible changes in physical setting, sometimes emotional withdrawal of staff and/or family, and difficult medical procedures. Yet the person must cope with the massive stress created by these demands while trying to maintain an optimal level of self-esteem, sense of competence, self-direction, and relatedness as internal resources are dwindling. It is important that environmental resources be enriched in an individualized way and to the greatest degree possible.

Out of concern for providing more humanized environments for the dying and their families, which acute care settings are not organized to provide, the hospice concept was developed in England during the 1960s. In 1967 Dr. Cicely Saunders, a British physician who had earlier been a nurse and a social worker, opened St. Christopher's Hospice near London. The concept was adopted in the United States in the early 1970s and quickly spread around the country.

The hospice concept refers to interdisciplinary care provided to dying persons and their families. It includes both emotional support and control of symptoms such as nausea, weakness, difficulties in breathing, and prevention of pain without sacrificing the patient's alertness. Hospice care may be provided in free-standing facilities, in specially designed inpatient facilities in hospitals, or only at home with no central facility as backup (*HEW Secretary's Task Force on Hospice*, 1978). The development of the hospice movement reflects growing recognition that acute care facilities, geared to treatment for cure or optimal recovery, cannot switch to meeting the needs of dying patients who are beyond cure and recovery and their families.

The emphasis in scientific medicine on relentlessly prolonging life as much as possible by technological means may be contrary to the wish of the dying person. The organizational needs of acute care settings tend to separate the dying patient from needed human contact because of constantly changing staff, limitations on styles and times of visiting, the impact on visitors of life-prolonging equipment, and the separation of the dying patient from other patients in order to protect the latter from shocking experiences. Also, the focus in acute care is more on the illness than on the person; in treatment, pain-relieving drugs are generally administered as needed, that is, *after* pain is experienced (Millet, 1979). Both aspects are contrary to the needs of the dying for emotional support, personalized care, and the control of pain.

Clinical and personal experience has suggested to practitioners of various professions that the two greatest fears of the dying person are the fear of pain and the fear of abandonment, of dying alone. Mr. Murphy's situation is illustrative of the acute care setting's difficulties in dealing adequately with those fears. Fortunately, but accidentally, a compassionate social worker entered into his dying. Many patients would prefer to die at home in familiar surroundings and in the midst of their families. By providing the needed services that will enable such patients and their families to carry out the wish for care at home, the hospice meets an important need. For the patient who can no longer remain at home, for whatever reason, or for the patient for whom home care is not appropriate, hospice inpatient care meets an important need. In both instances the quality of life for the dying person and for the family is enhanced.

Hospice home care may be provided by an already existing home health care agency or by a separate unit of the hospice inpatient service. The home care team makes regularly scheduled visits, but is also on call around the clock. Inpatient hospice care in a hospital is often provided in a redesigned unit that is more like a residential than a medical setting. Patterns of care and stringent regulations that exist elsewhere in the hospital can be relaxed to take into account the shift from curative to palliative functions. Hospice inpatient and home care staffs are especially trained for work with the dying and bereaved.

An example of a free-standing hospice facility is the Connecticut Hospice, Inc., opened in 1980 to provide a continuum of services at the appropriate level of care. Its home care program had begun in 1974, and in that interim period it had served 888 patients and their families. The average duration of home care over the first three years was 3.1 months. In the first six months of the inpatient facility's operation, it admitted 280 patients, ranging in age from eighteen to ninety-three. Of these, 215 patients died after an average stay of $17\frac{1}{2}$ days, and 31 were discharged after an average stay of $19\frac{1}{2}$ days (*Connecticut Hospice Newsletter*, 1981). A bereavement team provides services to the family during and after the patient's terminal illness for both home care and inpatient families. This is an important means of prevention of physical and emotional illness among the bereaved. The forty-four-bed inpatient facility was carefully designed to provide a warm and inviting physical environment that would meet the needs of patients and families and to support the creation of the kind of social environment that makes living while dying possible. The interdisciplinary team caring for the patients includes medicine, nursing, social work, pastoral care, physical therapy, clinical pharmacy, the arts, financial counseling, and trained volunteers.

Millet (1979) points out the potential uniqueness of the social work function and roles. Because the hospice concept is in the early stage of development, the opportunity for innovation and creativity is present. Social work functions can include direct services to home care and inpatient families and patients; bereavement programs; staff support; educational activities with volunteers, staff, and community groups; program coordination and policy development; research; and, as Foster (1979) suggests, legislative and political activity to promote programs and to press for institutional change.

Hospice care is for the person who has a fatal illness and, in the judgment of the treating physician, has a short life expectancy. The majority of admitted patients have cancer; some facilities restrict admission to cancer patients. Even where patients suffering from any incurable illness are eligible for admission, however, most patients admitted have cancer (*HEW Secretary's Task Force*, 1978).

But what of the families of patients for whom there has been little or no warning, for whom death comes suddenly and unexpectedly, perhaps through accident, criminal assault, heart attack, or an illness with a rapid downward course in which there is no real terminal period for anticipatory mourning? In considering the function and roles of the social worker in helping families of such patients, the hospital emergency room will be used as the exemplar setting of catastrophic situations, although these events occur also in surgeries and intensive care units in a variety of services.

In one emergency room treating 32,000 patients in a year, 756 of whom were involved with the ER social worker, there were 23 cases of unexpected deaths, anticipated deaths, and deaths on arrival in the ER (Groner, 1978). Two examples are provided:

A 3-year old girl drowned while in a baby-sitter's pool. The case required continual follow-up with the mother and the sitter and terminated with appropriate counseling referrals in the community. On the day of the death, hospital staff, paramedics, police, parents, neighbors, a minister, and the sitter were contacted. Social work intervention included dealing with the shock of unexpected death, beginning preliminary grief work, and helping the baby-sitter with her guilt feelings.

A cardiac arrest patient was medically treated in the ER but died a few hours later in the Intensive Care Unit. The social worker was involved with the family from the beginning. She assisted family members with news regarding the patient's medical progress in the ER, counseled the wife, daughter, and son-in-law in the grieving process and in viewing the body to help them accept the reality of death, and left our Medical Social Work Department card with family members for continued counseling as needed. [Groner, 1978]

In the ER of another large hospital, which is also a regional trauma center, social workers provide twenty-four-hour staffing. (Holland and Rogich, 1980) They provide a wide range of services, but "the first priority is caring for the family and friends of critically ill and injured patients, including those of patients who die in the emergency room" (p. 12). Two categories of patients have been identified: those who are dead on arrival in the ER or who die in the ER despite the provision of immediate medical care; and those who are in critical condition but who may live several hours or days. The families of those in the first group are likely to experience more stress than those in the second group because of the lack of warning or of time to prepare themselves for the loss. The ER social workers have identified three stages in the initial process of grief: (1) shock, manifested by denial, numbness, guilt, and internal conflict; (2) affective reaction of anger, fear, sadness, or anxiety, internally experienced, or outwardly expressed; and (3) alpha mourning, "the beginning process of mourning, which involves the elementary perception, expression, and acknowledgment of catastrophic loss" (p. 13). With the first category of patient the family members experience shock and affective reaction but are not likely to remain in the ER long enough to experience alpha mourning there. With the second category of patient, the family members may stay in the ER for a longer time, and the social worker may spend from two to eight hours with them. There is more time for a relationship to develop and for the family members or friends to be helped in the initial mourning process. Because medical staff is involved with medical lifesaving procedures, they are not available to respond and care for the members of the patient's network as they arrive in the ER. That becomes the social worker's task.

The ER social work staff in this hospital have developed a protocol to guide their management of the acute grief reactions in the family members of patients of both categories. The protocol is shown in Table 7-1. The social worker needs to be aware that people experience shock and grief in very different ways, and their reactions and outward expressions will vary. During this initial period all reactions should be considered normal, and this should be conveyed to the family. The social worker will need to recognize and deal with somatic symptoms including "(1) rapid, tense speech, (2) shortness of breath or hyperventilation, (3) tension headaches, muscle spasms, and nausea, (4) loss of strength and faintness, (5) restlessness and hyperactivity, (6) hypertension, and (7) confusion and impaired concentration" (p. 13). The worker's functions include repeating and clarifying realistic information about the severity of the patient's condition; serving as liaison between family and medical staff, which helps the family to secure the information they need and helps the physicians and others to understand the family members' responses; and helping to stabilize and manage the feelings.

TABLE 7-1.   Protocol for Emergency Room Social Workers

Step 1. A member of the registration staff notifies the family or a significant other that the patient is at Harborview Medical Center.

Step 2. The triage nurse informs the emergency room social worker that the family is en route to the hospital.

   a. The worker arranges coverage for immediate existing cases in the emergency room by, for example, calling the psychiatrist or other social workers.
   b. The worker observes the condition of the patient and determines the initial assessment by consulting with the emergency room doctor or nurse or with paramedics or police who were at the scene.

Step 3. The social worker or the triage nurse escorts the patient's family or friends to the Family Room when they arrive.

   a. The worker greets the family, explains his or her role, clarifies the sequence of events as they are known to have taken place concerning the patient, and explains the general status of the patient.
   b. The worker discusses when the family can see the patient, depending on his or her condition.

Step 4. If the patient is deceased, the worker first prepares the family by stressing the extreme seriousness of the injury and the patient's poor prospects for recovery.

   a. The worker introduces the physician to the family and assists them in asking appropriate questions.
   b. The worker makes sure the family knows the name of the physician and his or her service, the nature of the precipitating incident, and the patient's condition at the time of death as well as the life-saving procedures that were attempted.
   c. The worker begins to lead the family to work through their grief by allowing them to express their feelings and by giving them verbal permission to express their feelings.

TABLE 7-1.   (cont.)

    d. The worker helps the family to decide whether to view the patient's body and whether to do so now or to delay until the body is transferred to a funeral home.

        (1) The family must carefully decide whether they need to see the patient's body in order to believe the death has occurred; the worker can assist them in making this assessment.

        (2) If the body is viewed in the emergency room, the worker accompanies the family and gives them support.

        (3) In case of an accidental death, the worker helps select a member of the family to talk with the medical examiner, explains the medical examiner's role, and helps the family with the interview.

        (4) The worker remains with the family until the situation has become stabilized and a decision is made about the family's departure from Harborview. The worker also assists with the following: arranges for transportation, if needed by the family; arranges for them to be accompanied by friends or other family, if feasible; makes arrangements for the patient's belongings; questions the family about their further needs and makes appropriate plans; and arranges for follow-up support, including ways that the family can contact someone for counseling later.

Step 5. If the patient is not deceased, the social worker orients the family to the uncertainty of the patient's condition and prepares them for the impact that the illness or death will have on their lives. At the same time, he or she assesses their abilities to cope with the situation.

    a. If the emergency room physician cannot meet with the family immediately, the worker explains why and periodically observes the patient and talks with staff members.

    b. The worker describes and clarifies medical procedures and the status of the patient, several times if necessary, until the physician can meet with the family.

    c. The worker explains the degree of seriousness of the accident or illness and describes the patient's condition as critical, serious, or stable, modifying the description as the condition changes.

    d. The worker acts as liaison in obtaining information from the family, such as the patient's history.

    e. The worker gathers information about other helpful persons available to the family, such as neighbors, ministers, professionals, and relatives.

Step 6. If the patient is dying but is to be transferred to another service, the social worker initiates a referral to the appropriate social worker on the inpatient unit.

    a. After 5:00 P.M. or on weekends, the worker escorts the family to the appropriate unit and maintains intermittent contact with them. In addition, the worker asks staff members on the unit to call the emergency room social worker if problems arise or the patient's condition becomes worse. He or she also introduces the social worker on the next shift in the emergency room to the family and has the worker continue to follow the patient's progress at the change of shift. The patient's relevant history is transmitted to the oncoming emergency room worker.

b. The worker explains the patient's transfer to the family and describes the type of unit to which the patient has been admitted.

c. The worker accompanies the family to the waiting area of the unit and notifies medical staff members of their presence. He or she also identifies for the family the staff member from whom they should seek information.

Source: From Lin Holland and Lee Ellen Rogich, "Dealing with Grief in the Emergency Room." Copyright 1980, National Association of Social Workers, Inc. Reprinted, with permission, from *Health and Social Work*, Vol. 5, No. 2 (May 1980), p. 16, Table 1.

The anguish of family members whose relative has died in an intensive care unit, and the accompanying demands on them and on the social worker who seeks to help them, are similar to what has been described regarding death in the emergency room. In addition it has been observed that "family members experiencing shock and disbelief may need assistance with decision making. Issues such as the choice of funeral home, what to do with the patient's personal effects, or permission for an autopsy may arise" (Williams and Rice, 1977). The same authors note that while medical staff may resort to sedation of extraordinarily upset relatives as a way of dealing with their own helplessness, human support is preferable to the chemical masking of the traumatic reaction, underscoring the important function of the social worker on both counts.

The fundamental difference—for the dying person, the family, and the social worker—between dying over time, as in a lingering incurable illness, and sudden, unexpected death has been captured by Glaser and Strauss (1968) in their conception of dying as a status passage. The course of that passage can be long, as in a chronic incurable illness, and may or may not be punctuated by periods of remission followed by further deterioration. It can be relatively short, as in a rapid downhill course, or it may cover only a few brief hours or days. Each person's dying "trajectory" has its own temporal dimensions of duration and tempo and its own element of certainty/ambiguity. Pattison (1977a) suggests that different trajectories require different coping strategies on the part of patient, family, and the health care professional, and they vary in their evocation of stress. Four sample trajectories are:

1. *Certain death at a known time*, which provides the dying person, his social network, and the social worker and other staff with a relatively specific time frame in which to order their responses. Such situations, while painful, of course, are generally easier to cope with than those in which there is ambiguity.

2. *Certain death at an unknown time*, as in chronic fatal illness where the living-dying interval may continue for several years. Family and patient live constantly with dying and can best be helped with a focus on what is certain, the predictable daily issues of life.

3. *Uncertain death, but a known time when the question will be resolved*, a

trajectory likely to be pervaded by intense emotion on the part of all involved. There is an acute phase of uncertainty as in "waiting for the pathology report after surgery, waiting to see if the organ transplant will work, waiting to see if the severely injured person will survive, waiting to see if the malformed infant will survive (p. 306)," followed by intense reactions when hopes are dashed.

4. *Uncertain death and an unknown time when the question will be resolved,* in Pattison's opinion, appears to be the most problematic trajectory because of the double load of uncertainty. It creates a high level of anxiety that cannot be resolved and may therefore generate maladaptive efforts to deal with it. An example is multiple sclerosis, in which the problems of living with the disease are much more serious for some than any concern with death from the disease, although one-third live less than a normal life span and some individuals die within twenty-four hours of the first attack (Van den Noort, 1977). Another example is the patient maintained on renal dialysis who lives with chronic uncertainty and "with the ever-present possibility of an untimely death" (Beard, 1977). Pattison notes, however, that younger patients at least, with conditions that are now managed by technology such as cardiac pacemakers, may make successful adaptations to chronic uncertainty.

These matters raise the important question of the age and social value of the dying person. Death coming at its expected time at the end of a long life and death coming in infancy, childhood, youth, or young adulthood pose coping tasks of differing orders of difficulty. Typically, the elderly person occupies less critical roles in the family structure, however cherished he may be. The young and middle-age adult is likely to occupy many statuses and roles on which family and network functioning depends. The meaning of the loss to the dying person and to the family is different in these two examples, the coping tasks are different, and the pain of grief may be of differing intensity. Similarly, dying in infancy, childhood, and youth is typically regarded as unfair and inappropriate and is a particulary anguished experience for all involved. In human experience there is a correct time to die and a wrong time to die. Because death is a psychosocial event, whether its time is right or wrong will depend, in part, on the individual's age and roles, the self concept and the conception of death, the nature of the illness, the cultural context (particularly ethnicity and religion), and the presence or absence of supportive human relationships.

For very young children the fear of separation and abandonment is uppermost, so that helping efforts of the social worker must be directed toward helping parents and other caregivers to assuage those fears. Indeed, a movement to provide parents with the option of caring for their dying child at home is gaining ground (Martinson, 1977). The older child has those fears as well as the fear of annihilation or mutilation through painful diagnostic and treatment procedures. Help to a child of this age "calls for careful explanation of the causes of illness, the need for procedures and treatment. The child needs to understand the emotional reactions of parents so that he or she does not feel guilty, does not feel rejected, does not feel unwanted or unloved" (Pattison, 1977b, p. 21).

The school age child, too, fears separation and annihilation. She has intellectual comprehension of death to some extent, but an endless tomorrow stretches ahead for the pleasures of doing and achieving. Dying and death at this age is an interference with the sense of self as dysfunction interferes with growing competence and industry. For parents, caregivers, and the social worker, the child must be helped to do what she is still able to do and to maintain connections with peers. The adolescent, in addition to separation anxiety, annihilation fears, and coping with lost pleasures of activity and possibly friendships, has the added fear of losing his newly acquired sense of identity. "The affirmation, confirmation, and clarification of the adolescent as a unique and real human being may be the most important task in coping with dying at this age" (Pattison, p. 23).

The young adult, embarked on new roles in the world of work and in a newly created family, faces the loss of cherished hopes and plans. This means having to cope with rage, frustration, and disappointment. The adult in the middle years faces these issues too but may also experience guilt about leaving spouse, children, and even parents, as well as concern for how they will manage. Frustration arises from thwarted efforts to achieve in one's work or with one's special talents.

Reference was made earlier to the elderly person, with an implication that her social value may be less, her roles less critical, and her loss to the family less difficult to cope with, since her death comes at the "correct" time. It is important to note, however, that as people live longer lives now, in better health for a longer time, and are more financially independent (in general), dying may entail some of the same issues for the "young-old" as for those in the middle years, including as well the loss of anticipated pleasures and rewards of the retirement years. For the "old-old"—the group past seventy-five years of age, which is growing faster than any other group of the elderly—the issues may be quite different. For some terminally ill "old-old," the acceptance of dying may be a somewhat lighter task if one has led a life of some satisfaction. The task may be onerous for those who look back upon an unhappy or a disappointing past with anger or regret. Three general types of responses have been specified by Peak (1977):

1. Most elderly persons face the prospect of death and handle it by active means within their capacity. They accept dying as part of being old and as part of life itself. Their mastery of its threat implies that they feel in control of their situation, based on a minimal amount of denial. Most

have worked out the acceptance of dying long before the terminal phase, and many have made plans for their death or are ready to do so.

2. A small group of elderly persons appear to block out the idea of death completely. This prevents their making the plans and preparations that might lead to a sense of closure and peace. When such excessive denial is extended to serious illness or disability as well, there is danger that death may be hastened.

3. A still smaller group comprises those elderly who are greatly disturbed by ideas of death. They may become preoccupied with their own bodily functions and turn away from the environment. Some may give up, perceiving themselves as socially dead, that is, ''I'm as good as dead,'' or ''I may as well be dead.'' This response may be precipitated by a terminal diagnosis (Kalish, 1968). Others slip into depression, become extremely agitated, or withdraw into a pseudo-senility, becoming psychologically dead.

For the fatally ill patient, the major tasks are (1) to secure and receive the permission to die from significant others if death is to be peaceful, and then (2) voluntarily to let go of every person and possession held dear, finding completion and freedom. Permission to die is granted in open and honest interaction between the patient and family members or other significant persons in the life space, reflecting their mutual recognition of the reality and of the differing needs of each other. The patient will then be able to die without blaming himself or others; family members and friends display their ability to go on living without blaming the dying person or threatening irremediable anguish. Health care staff grant their own permission by continued devoted care. With permission gained, the individual can let go (Kavanaugh, 1977).

> He can begin to release his hold on life, then gently, with growing decisiveness, unlock the chains that bind his heart to all earthly treasures, to valued persons, and to every possession. He begins with the outer circle of important acquaintances and business associates now rarely seen, extending to close friends and family. . . . Internally, the dying individual agrees to allow the world to go on without him. [Kavanaugh, 1977, p. 418]

Family members must remain involved with the dying person; remain separate from her or him; adapt suitably to role changes; bear the affects of anticipatory grief; come to terms with the reality of impending loss; and say goodbye (Lebow, 1976). These ideas about permission to die are useful guidelines for the social worker seeking to help the dying person and the family. Such work is demonstrated in the concluding segment of the help given to Mr. and Mrs. Kahn. Their situation was introduced in Chapter 4 and further considered in Chapter 6. Mrs. Kahn had accepted the need for open communication with her dying husband. Together she and the social worker enter Mr. Kahn's room. His demeanor is the same as usual, withdrawn and depressed. He stares straight ahead, looks at neither woman, and answers questions in a flat tone. He does answer, however, and his choice of words reveals the feelings:

I asked Mr. Kahn if he could tell us what he's feeling inside. He talked of seeing that he's going nowhere fast despite his doctors' optimism that he's getting better. He adds, "This is my body, and I know how I feel. I don't think I have much time left."

The worker gently asks how this makes him feel, knowing he doesn't have much time left. Such a question legitimizes the feelings and conveys to Mr. Kahn—and also to Mrs. Kahn—that the worker cares enough and is strong enough to bear the pain of Mr. K's reality, both the fact of his dying and the fact of his awareness.

Without affect or facial expression, he answered, "Depressed, very depressed." I asked him what thoughts he is having, and he replied, "I don't feel badly for myself. I had my work and I was fortunate to be successful in my work." I commented he had accomplished good things in his life and that makes it easier for him. He agreed, and added, "But I feel badly for my wife and children—they're the ones I feel sorry for. I don't want to leave them now. They deserve much better than this." Here Mrs. K broke in, sobbing, "Carl, don't say that, please don't say that!" Mr. K did not look at her, and she went on, "You're only fifty-four, you're too young to die. You deserve better than this! I'm scared too. I don't want to lose you. But I need you to tell me what you're feeling. If we share it together, it won't be so bad." Mr. K responded, "Well, what do you think? I'm scared shitless." Mrs. K, still crying, pleaded, "Then share those feelings with me, Carl, I need to share this with you!" Mr. K looked at her helplessly.

Mr. Kahn had, of course, been sharing in his own way. At the intellectual, verbal level he has expressed fear, anger, acceptance, and he is attempting to cope, in what may be his characteristic way, by controlling his emotional expression. In fact, when the worker comments that Mrs. Kahn is reacting to the difference between the words and his demeanor he says he has never been an emotional man, but he's trying to tell what he feels in the best way he can. And Mrs. Kahn, at least, has been able to relinquish her cheerful façade. She expresses her awareness of his dying and her wish to be close, to share his reality as she shares her own. The worker wonders if it upsets him to see his wife crying, and he responds:

"Yes, it upsets me, but what can I do? I can't reach for her." As he said this his hand reached across the bed toward Mrs. K. She then extended hers toward Mr. K, and they held hands. I said, "See, you can reach for each other now." At this, Mrs. K got up from her chair and hugged him. He continued to stare straight ahead without responding except to put one arm around her in a rather passive way. She returned to her chair. Gently, I said, "Mr. K, I've noticed this whole time you've been staring straight ahead, looking at the wall. It seems very painful for you to look at Mrs. Kahn." At this, Mr. K looked up at his wife and their eyes met for the first time. Then his face crumpled and he began to sob. Mrs. K got up and put her arms around him. He put his arms around her, and they held each other. Mrs. K said, "I love you Carl, I love you so much." And he responded, "I love you too." Mrs. K now sat on the bed, and they continued to hold each other. Mr. K said, "I hate to leave you now, you deserve so much better than this — I hate to think of you alone now." Mrs. K said, "Oh Carl, how can you say that? I don't feel that way. It's not the quantity of life that's important. It's the quality, and we've had so much together. We've shared so much together, good times and bad times. We've had our share of fights, but we've shared so much love. And you've given so much to me and the kids. You are such a good man, and everybody loves you and respects you. So don't feel badly for me Carl. I just feel badly for you — you deserve so much better than this." He answered, "No, I've had the best — in you." They began to talk about some memories, almost like a life review. Toward the end of the session, Mrs. K was smiling and relaxed, which was very different from her former cheerful façade, which had not hidden her anxiety.

What was even more encouraging was the way in which Mr. K seemed to mobilize himself. Before, he had seemed totally cut off from the world and indifferent to events involving him. He hadn't wanted his parents or business partner to be told about his dying. Then he seemed no longer to care and left the decision to Mrs. K as though he were already dead. Now, he asked that his partner be brought to the hospital this night. He wanted to straighten out certain financial matters so that Mrs. K will be well provided for. He also asked Mrs. K to bring his brother to the hospital tonight so they can discuss how his parents can be told he is dying.

Clearly, Mr. K has received permission to die from Mrs. K, and he is now freed to take up the tasks of leaving. Mrs. K has been able to give him that permission, because she entered his reality, finally feeling what he is going through and sharing her own experience with him. One senses, particularly as the account of the case proceeds, that she also recognizes her separateness and her own ongoing existence so that she will be ready to integrate the remaining tasks of anticipatory grief and to say goodbye. This worker, actually a first year graduate student, mediated the exchanges between husband and wife, enabling each to reach out to the other in ways they had not previously been able to do. With empathy, skill, and knowledge, she herself became part of the transactional field so that her clients could move into and through the most difficult transition of all, the passage from life to death.

The next day Mr. K's condition grew worse. Mrs. K was finally able to tell her two children, who lived out of the state, and her sister that Mr. K was dying and they should come at once. Two days later the worker met with the daughter and sister in order to provide support to them so that Mrs. K would not be overwhelmed by their feelings and could focus her energies on caring for Mr. K. She had not prepared her daughter and sister for how Mr. K looks, and when they entered the room they did not recognize him and were extremely shocked and upset.

In addition, the daughter was angry at Mrs. K for not sharing the truth earlier. She felt guilty for not coming to her father sooner. The worker accepted the women's feelings and clarified Mrs. K's situation so they could provide some support to her. Later in the day, with Mrs. K present, she met with Mr. K's brother. Not only was this supportive to him, but the interview revealed that he had been negating the seriousness of the illness to Mr. K in the same way Mrs. K had. As Mrs. K and the brother saw in each other their own behaviors and feelings, the worker reports they reached out and gave support to each other in the impending loss. In a still later session that day, the entire family met with the worker and discussed how they should tell Mr. K's parents that he has cancer and is dying. With the support of her sister and daughter, Mrs. K and her brother-in-law did tell the parents and brought them to the hospital that evening:

Mr. K was weak and unable to talk. But whereas before he had avoided eye contact, now he stared into the faces of his family, continually moving his eyes from one person to another. Curiously, he kept looking at his watch, as though counting every minute.

Before I left on Friday, I told Mr. K I was leaving for the weekend and wanted to say goodbye. I said I understood that he was feeling very uncomfortable and could not talk, but I would be back on Monday. However, Mr. Kahn died early Monday morning, so I did not see him again.

The social worker had, however, helped make it possible for Mr. K to say goodbye to his dear ones, blaming no one, and with his own guilt at leaving them stilled. She made it possible for them to say goodbye to him, letting his death become real without blaming him or threatening unconsolable anguish. For each of the family members, accepting the loss and relinquishing the ties will take time as they grieve and eventually come to terms with an environment bereft of Mr. K's presence. In addition, there will be the psychosocial tasks of dealing with new statuses and roles such as widow, childless parent, fatherless child, and the social and financial consequences. For many families this will include the reorganization of family functions, roles, tasks, and relationships, establishing new connections to the social environment, including the world of work or school, and social networks. This social worker was able to continue that work with Mrs. Kahn. In some health care settings the social worker might have to refer her to a community agency for such help or to consider with her the benefits of a mutual aid group such as a widow-to-widow program. (Silverman, 1978; Silverman et al., 1979; Stubblefield, 1977)

Dying, like life itself, is an ecological process of transition involving the interplay of biological, social, cultural, psychological, temporal, and spatial forces. All must be understood as fully as possible if the social worker is to be helpful to the dying person and the family. The emotional demands experienced by the worker, however, can be exceedingly stressful. Coping with them requires continuous development of self-awareness in order to understand one's feelings and responses to dying and bereavement and thus to control them in the service of the client. The feelings may be generated by the sense of one's own mortality and vulnerability, existential rage, anxiety in the face of distressing symptoms present in some terminal conditions, earlier losses now reexperienced, and personal grief in the patient's death (particularly in long-term relationships, or in the case of a child, or for a particularly appealing individual of any age). Without self-awareness, one may either overidentify with the patient or family and be overwhelmed by their grief, or avoid anything more than superficial involvement and minimal helping efforts.

Support systems among staff are crucial aids in coping with the stress and developing self-awareness. These systems are often found on such services as ERs, ICUs, oncology, burn units, and hospices and among the members of the social work department. The social worker needs the support and consultation of colleagues if she is to continue being supportive to patients and families, escaping avoidance or overidentification, and maintaining compassionate caring. Indeed, it is frequently the social worker on the team or the service who facilitates the development of such support systems.

Summary

This chapter has considered the skills required in ending the work with individuals, families, and groups. Organizational, relationship, and temporal variables and the reason for ending influence the character of the termination process and the clients' and worker's responses to it.

In all terminations the social work tasks are instrumental (making plans and carrying them out), expressive (handling the feelings aroused by the ending), and evaluative (determining the effectiveness of the work together). Skill in facilitating an appropriate referral and ensuring the connection may be the only instrumental task in some instances. But in many more, the social worker is involved extensively in interprofessional discharge planning. Skill is required in acknowledging and dealing with the feelings surrounding the ending of the relationship. Eliciting and accepting them, where present, help ensure that achievements will be sustained and the potentiality for further growth preserved.

Evaluation of the work together reinforces the client's sense of accomplishment, the acceptance of a new self-image and new life goals if those were issues, and the courage to face and carry out continuing tasks pertaining to chronic illness or disability. For the worker, such informal evaluation yields clues for further development of practice skills as well as providing preliminary data for more formal follow-up studies of effectiveness.

The ending phase draws on the principles and skills of all the social work roles examined in Chapter 6. Like the initial and ongoing phases, it may also draw on the skills of collaborative practice to be considered in the next chapter.

CHAPTER 8

Collaborative Practice in Health Care: The Social Work Function

COLLABORATION IN THE PROVISION OF HEALTH CARE by members of two or more professional disciplines is not new. Doctors and nurses have collaborated from the beginnings of formalized nursing care. Social workers were originally brought into the Massachusetts General Hospital in 1905 by Dr. Richard Cabot to work collaboratively with the physicians by meliorating social conditions that interfered with treatment. The assumption was that the physician did not have the time, knowledge, or interest to do so.

A team concept of collaboration appeared following World War II, arising out of concern for the care of disabled veterans. During the 1950s the Vocational Rehabilitation Act and amendments to the Social Security Act on behalf of the disabled led to the development of the rehabilitation team, coordinated by the physiatrist (specialist in physical medicine). Recognition of the contributions that could be made by several disciplines working together was present, but principles for such collaboration had not yet been developed. Such teams had to rely on trial-and-error methods of collaborating in a work group directed by a physician. In the 1960s the influential ideas of Maxwell Jones on the therapeutic milieu led to further interest in interprofessional collaboration. Meetings of patients and professionals as a therapeutic community in psychiatric institutions were designed to encourage self-management and system change by the patients.

The community mental health movement also strengthened the team concept. Collaborative practice in mental health settings, however, often

198

led to role blurring, even role fusion, and to ambiguity of function and task, which actually weaken collaborative practice. The patient is deprived of the distinctive therapeutic contributions that can be made by each of the collaborating disciplines.

Collaborative practice in medical care continued to spread throughout the 1960s and 1970s among institutional settings and into the community. Several forces underlay this trend. These included the rise in health care costs, growing interest in holistic ideas about the individual and environment in matters of health and disease, and the growth of neighborhood health centers and other community-based services. Recognition grew among administrators and staffs that health care and medical treatment were becoming more and more complex with the rapid pace of social change. Coordination and comprehensiveness of care became the watchwords. The trend is continuing in the 1980s, marked by growing interest in interdisciplinary education for interdisciplinary practice in health care and the development of principles for team development, team management, and evaluation of team effectiveness.

The distinguishing features of contemporary collaboration in health care are the rationale for its use, the nature of the collaborative relationships, the number of disciplines represented on many health teams, and the emphasis on a systematic, knowledge-based approach to collaborative practice. As health care, and even medical treatment, move more and more toward an adaptational view of health and illness, the knowledge and skill required for comprehensive quality care exceed the capacity of any one individual or any one discipline. This is especially clear in the case of the elderly, the chronically ill, and the disabled, and in family-based primary care, in which multiple health and social services are called into play.

Collaboration may be defined as a cooperative process of exchange involving communication, planning, and action on the part of two or more disciplines (or, in some instances, on the part of two or more individuals from the same discipline). Its purpose is to achieve specific goals and tasks related to health care that cannot be achieved, or achieved as well, by one discipline (or individual) alone.

Collaboration may be informal or formal. When it is informal, the process may consist of occasional or irregular conferring between social worker and physician, social worker and nurse, or social worker and other health professional, initiated by one or the other participant in response to a patient's need or in the interest of more effective, higher-quality patient care. Informal collaboration may also be carried out by written reports on program development and outcomes or other occasional information transmitted by one discipline to others.

When it is formal, collaboration is characterized by a structure in which two or more disciplines communicate in a planned or regular way as through chart entries, nurse–social worker cardex rounds, and medical rounds in which the participants might include house staff, medical students, the chief of service, social worker, nurses, and an occasional attending physician. In ambulatory settings formalized conferring may take place through a staff meeting or a patient care conference for all those involved directly or indirectly in the patient's care. Consulting, like conferring, may be informal but is more often formalized. It is also more structured than conferring.

The most structured type of formal collaboration is the team. It comprises two or more disciplines as an organized system that exists through time, although the patient and individual members may change. Teams range from a simple structure (nurse and social worker meeting regularly to review the cardex in order to identify patients with psychosocial needs or those presenting management problems) to very complex structures involving as many disciplines and individuals as the particular patient population requires for quality comprehensive care. Health care teams may have members from several different agencies, as in hospital-based child abuse teams or geriatric teams that comprise representatives of community agencies providing services to the client population.

The Collaborative Process

Five progressive stages in collaboration among two or more disciplines can be identified: role separation; overestimation and disappointment; realistic appraisal; accommodation; and integration (adapted from Schoenberg, 1975).

ROLE SEPARATION

In the first stage, each discipline tends to operate according to its accustomed function and role. The commitment to collaboration remains at the abstract or theoretical level, with professional boundaries sharply maintained. Role separation serves to contain anxiety and competitiveness, which are manifest but not verbalized, as in the following example:

The nurse clinician and social worker on a renal treatment team had similar professional interests and goals related to the psychosocial impact of illness on patients and families. They found themselves in frequent conflict about role expectations. Because they themselves did not understand each other's functions and roles, other team members—and even patients—saw them as interchangeable figures. This further increased their role conflict and turf struggles. These, in turn, created strained relations and confusions within the team itself, as both the social worker and nurse clinician sought alignments and support from other members. [Lowe and Herranen, 1978]

OVERESTIMATION AND DISAPPOINTMENT

As members of each discipline recognize the complexities in achieving the shared goals of their collaboration, they turn to one another for answers. But they overestimate the knowledge and skill of the other(s) and at the same time oversimplify the complexity of the tasks needed to achieve the goals. For example:

An ambulatory but terminally ill patient whose cancer of the colon rendered him incontinent of feces was resistive to using disposable diapers. The situation was further complicated by his long history of mental illness, which made working and communicating with him quite difficult. Therefore, when discharge planning to a nursing home was begun, a process was set in motion for the social worker to search for a terminal care facility. The unfeasibility of the plan was soon apparent due to the reluctance of any community resource to accept the patient in his "socially unacceptable" condition. Reassessment clearly indicated the need for further planning. While in prior team meetings sharing of expertise took place, each team member saw the problem of the patient as falling within the realm of another's expertise. Therefore the social worker took initiative in convening a formal meeting through which a conscious decision was made to prepare the patient more adequately prior to his discharge. [Mailick and Jordan, 1977, p. 450]

In this example each team member is operating in a specialized professional function, his or her own base of knowledge and competence. Even though meeting as a team, the members had not yet integrated their professional perspectives into a holistic understanding of the patient's needs and the environmental context of care. Such lingering role separation, added to the oversimplification of the complex clinical tasks involved in the achievement of the goal (in this instance a sound discharge plan), can lead to disappointment, anger, and the persistence of rigid disciplinary roles. But in this example the team faced and dealt with the patient's totality, thereby reaching toward a more integrated level of collaboration. On the initiative of the social worker the inappropriate action was corrected, and the team's development was enhanced.

REALISTIC APPRAISAL

Gradually, as each discipline becomes aware of how the other(s) can contribute to achieving the shared goals, realistic appreciation grows. Less effort is exerted in establishing superiority of one discipline over the other, while more is directed to challenging stereotyped thinking and behavior. Professional boundaries tend to become less rigid. An example of this process is reported by a resident physician in an inner-city family medical center operated by a family medicine residency training program (Phillips, 1977). The center was staffed by two faculty physicians, eleven resident physicians, two LPNs, three clerks, an RN, a pharmacist, a medical technologist, and a receptionist. A graduate social worker with two years' experience in another health setting joined the staff.

After she had been chosen by the staff, but before she started to work, attitudes of all staff toward social work membership on a patient care team were surveyed by questionnaire. Four months after she started work, staff attitudes were again surveyed. Attitude change was significant along a few dimensions in the later questionnaire. The social worker was viewed as more competent and more passive by all staff. Physicians rated social work as more difficult than they had in the first questionnaire, while other staff rated it less difficult. Physicians' mean estimate of the patients who could be helped by a social worker in this practice dropped significantly from 35 percent in the preexperience period to 23 percent in the postexperience period. For the total staff, the drop was from 38.8 percent to 31.4 percent (not significant). Many other scores were in a similar direction, although they failed to reach a level of significance. As compared with the preexperience, for example, in the postexperience period the social worker was seen as more of an individual worker than a team worker, less valuable, less theoretical, and doing less difficult work.

Generalizations from such a small data base at one setting cannot be made. But at least in this setting the knowledge and skill of the social worker may have been overestimated beforehand and the complexity of social work was oversimplified afterward. The overall ratings are all above the midpoint of each scale. One can therefore assume that, after more than only four months' experience with a social work member of the team, the appraisal of the social work function and role will become more realistic and will reach toward the next stage.

ACCOMMODATION

Progress toward integrative collaboration is now apparent. Explanations of phenomena by each participant tend to be complementary. Differences are recognized and verbalized, and satisfying accommodations are attained. For example:

A fourteen-year-old girl in the seventh grade was referred by her rural school to the children's evaluation team at the state university's school of medicine because of increased learning difficulties during the year. She suffers from multiple physical handicaps and a bilateral hearing loss that followed upon meningitis at age three. Other team members saw the need only for physical and psychological testing. But the team's social worker learned in a home visit that the father, age sixty, and the mother fifty-six, were having severe marital difficulties. The father has been in and out of the home seven times in the past year, living intermittently with a young woman, and tension was high in the home. The mother reported that the child had always been a loner but had also become obese and increasingly morose in recent months. The social worker reported to the team that the marital situation was likely to block their work on the child's health problems and the family's cooperation with psychological testing and special educational services. They then agreed with the social worker's plan to help the parents accept a referral for marital counseling.

INTEGRATION OF ROLES

In a collaborating group of two or more that reaches the integration stage, the collaborative process has moved away from fragmented thinking about the patient and context, based on disciplinary specialization, to a holistic or systemic view of patient-environment relationships bearing on health and illness. As each professional learns from the others, the social worker might, for example, consider matters of nutrition in her work with the patient and family, and the nutritionist might be alert to environmental and psychological factors in the patient's inability to follow a dietary regimen.

Actual interchangeability of roles, or role blurring, while it still occurs in mental health settings, is less likely to occur in acute physical care settings, where specialized knowledge, functions, and skills are essential. Some role blurring may occur to a degree in chronic physical care settings, home health care, and geriatric care, but not to the point of interchangeability. Indeed, the so-called blurring is better described as overlapping of roles. When actual role blurring does occur, it creates ambiguity and confusion for patients and families and generates conflict within the collaborating group.

While the knowledge base, perceptions, and conceptions of the participants are expanded at this stage, tasks in any given situation are assigned on the basis of which discipline has the specialized knowledge and competence to achieve them. In some instances that person may carry out tasks of another discipline as well, using the other participants as consultants. Decisions for such crossovers are usually made on the basis of the patient's trust in, or strong relationship with, a particular team member.

On reaching the stage of integration, the two or more collaborating persons have now achieved a nonthreatening, open climate for the exchange of views about diagnosis, treatment planning, discharge, and other shared goals and tasks. Where overlapping of roles occurs, task allocation is more easily negotiated and more readily accepted. By now the participants have acquired understanding of, respect for, and comfort with the values, philosophy, education, knowledge, and skill of the other participating disciplines. Having reached this stage, the participants are assumed to be providing patient care at higher and higher levels of quality.

The collaborative process itself will be described in the following sections, with further distinctions made between such forms as conferring, cooperating, consulting, and teaming.

Collaborative Practice: Conferring, Cooperating, and Consulting

Conferring is one of the most common collaborative processes in health care. The social worker and nurse in an extended care facility confer about the meaning of a resident's sudden regression in behavior, and they exchange views about the probable cause and ideas of how to help him return to his prior level of functioning. Conferring assumes a reciprocity between colleagues. It requires reciprocal respect and trust so that observations are exchanged, views are freely expressed and compared, and each is free to agree or disagree. Ideally, greater clarity about a need or problem is achieved, and feasible solutions are developed, to be carried out mutually or singly as appropriate. In a rehabilitation service, for example, the social worker and the spouse of a stroke patient soon to be discharged may confer with the speech, physical, and occupational therapists in order to assess the home's physical environment, plans for ongoing care at home, arrangements for needed services, and availability of respite for family members.

Conferring can be a group effort as well when more than two professionals are involved, together with patient and family, as in the example just mentioned, or when persons from other agencies such as the school, a child welfare agency, or a rape counseling center meet with the health organization's staff members. Such a group is not a team. They are coming together only to confer on a case for planning purposes. Each participant remains autonomous. Someone—often the health care social worker—has called the meeting with an explicit agenda that includes an exchange of views about objectives for the patient's care and division of responsibilities and tasks to be carried out by each participant, including, perhaps, the patient and family members.

Still another type of conferring takes place when the social worker confers with the chief of service in an arthritis clinic, and then with medical and nursing staffs, about her interest in offering a group for patients and their spouses or partners. She shares her ideas about the needs that could be served and the impact of such a group on the clinic and elicits the ideas of the others. If she hears no objections or meets objections satisfactorily, she moves foward with the plan and keeps the conferees informed of the program's development and its outcomes. Such information may be communicated by written reports or informally in face-to-face contacts, depending on the norms of the setting.

Even within a structured team informal conferring may have a place, as indicated in the previous section. Out of these various avenues to conferring may also come a process of *cooperating*. The large group brought together for an exchange of ideas through a case conference may agree to cooperate on a particular issue with a patient or family. They are still not a team but will work in symmetrical ways to resolve a particular issue or to help the patient work on a particular task. One member may be designated as coordinator to monitor the process and to reassemble the conferees should it falter or should the original agreement have to be changed.

Consulting, more formal and more structured, involves less reciprocal exchange than conferring. In this process the consultee usually seeks out the consultant as someone believed to have the knowledge and skill to provide needed advice or guidance in a matter related to health, illness, or disability. Whereas in conferring the participants put their heads together and compare notes and exchange views, in consulting one participant is the seeker of information or advice and the other is the provider. But like conferring, the consultee is free to act on the advice or information or to ignore it. Unlike team process, in which decisions are made by the leader (multidisciplinary) or consensus (interdisciplinary) and all members are expected to work on the agreed-upon tasks and goals, consultation is an advisory process.

In home health care, for example, the social worker may not be able to see every patient with psychosocial needs, but he serves as consultant to the nurse in helping her to help the patient with some of the social and psychological consequences of the illness or disability. One nurse in an urban home health agency consulted with the social worker about how to handle the stressful interaction between a seriously limited MS patient and her sixteen-year-old son who was drinking heavily. In an adolescent health center the social worker consulted with the center's law student about what might be done to counter the refusal of the backup hospital to admit a teenage patient. In a geriatric facility the administrator consulted with the social worker about how best to plan with the patients for a move to the institution's new location.

Occasionally a potential consultant may reach out to a potential consultee to offer specialized knowledge or skill. The parents of an eight-year-old boy with diabetes told their physician in an HMO that he was refusing to go to school. David said he didn't like his teacher, and his classmates teased him about his need for snacks during the day. With the permission of David and his parents, the social worker visited the teacher. He found that she knew little about diabetes, was fearful about the child's falling into a coma, tended to restrict his activity unnecessarily, and singled him out for her special attention. When the social worker, after accepting her fears and feelings as understandable, offered to answer any questions she might have, the teacher eagerly accepted. The worker answered her questions, provided some information about causation and treatment regimens, and suggested several alternate ways she might wish to consider in helping improve the interactions between David and his classmates. At the teacher's request he agreed to make a follow-up visit in two weeks to review with her how things were going and what else might be needed so that David would be happier at school.

Consultation is carried on only until the problem or concern of the consultee has been resolved. Not infrequently, however, a successful consultation may develop into a group process. In this example, the school might have had a number of chronically ill or disabled students, and the principal, following the teacher's suggestion, might then have asked the consultant to provide one or two group sessions on childhood disability for all teachers in that school.

Because consultation is a formal process, certain practice principles have been specified for effectively carrying out the role of social work consultant (Collins, Pancoast, and Dunn, 1977). For example, in most consulting the consultant's relationship is with the consultee, not with the persons with whom the consultee is working. Nevertheless, the consultation is client-focused, as in the case of David, or program-focused, as when a social worker is asked to work with nurses in her health organization to help them prepare for leading patient groups. Even in that instance, however, the social worker's professional interest is centered on the potential group members.

Whether the social worker is acting as consultant to an individual or group in her own health care organization or in another agency, it is important that she learn as much about the consultee and the particular setting as possible. In the more structured kinds of consultation, it is also desirable that consultant and consultee discuss their expectations of the process with each other in order to be clear about their objectives, respective roles, and so on. In the case of an outside agency, it is also important that the same clarity and contracting be achieved with the administrator as well, including issues of confidentiality regarding the consultee's statements.

Once the consultant has decided she has the needed competence to provide the requested consultation, has learned all she can about the consultee and setting, and has clarified the process with the consultee, the consultation formally begins. Occasionally it becomes clear that the consultee is really seeking supervision, therapy, or even a substitute to take over a troubling situation; it is important that the consultant not assume these roles. Instead, she must convey willingness and ability to help the consultee with the clinical tasks through a mutual process of problem-solving.

The first step is asking the consultee for specific data related to the problem or predicament, what has previously been done about it, and how is it like or different from the consultee's usual array of problematic situations. Collins and associates (1977) suggest that it is usually best to avoid rushing in with a solution, especially since the questions asked may alone help the consultee to understand the situation better, think about it differently, and come up with his own solution. It may also be wise to suggest a second session to continue the discussion; the consultant can explain that in the meantime she will consider the data in the light of her experience with similar situations. In other words, it is important to avoid establishing an image of herself as a superior expert with instant answers to a situation that the consultee has found difficult, perhaps over a period of time.

When the consultant is ready to present several alternative ideas— even in the initial session, if that is to be the only one—it is wise to present them as possibilities only. It is important to avoid any suggestion that the consultant's view is the right one. Presenting the consultee with several ideas increases his own cognitive and decision-making powers and hence his competence in his own profession. This is the ultimate goal of social work consultation.

Consultation should be terminated—at least on a particular problem —as soon as the consultee has decided on a tentative course of action and feels secure enough to proceed. It is helpful if the time limit can be set at the outset and referred to before the final session. In the last session (generally most consultations do not go beyond three sessions), a review of the consultation and its positive and/or negative effects on the client or program can help the consultee see how he has added to the knowledge and skill that he already had.

These principles of consultation are especially pertinent to a significant area of social work consultation, nursing homes. Federal regulations and sometimes state licensing require that social work services be provided to patients in long-term facilities if they are to be eligible for Medicaid reimbursement.* Depending on size, commitment to quality patient care, level of care (skilled nursing care, intermediate care), and other factors, some facilities have qualified social workers on their full-time or part-time staffs. Most nursing homes, however, designate a staff member, who may be a nurse or clerical person, to provide such services and retain a fully qualified professional social worker as consultant. Most such consultants only consult with the social work designee on specific cases. Some consult with nursing and other staffs in programmatic areas such as work with dying patients, with families, and the like. But rela-

*These regulations are being threatened with elimination. At the time of this writing social workers are engaged in politically oriented activities to ensure their retention.

tively few consult with administrators on organizational and management issues such as admissions procedures, staff development, or administration–patient relationships.

In a study of 28 consultants and 49 designees in Arkansas (where consultants number 42 and designees 232) the average consultant is female, thirty-five to forty years of age, with the MSW degree, ten years' paid experience as a social worker, and less than five years' experience as a consultant (Mercer and Garner, 1981). She maintains a full-time job or is retired, although one-third worked full time as consultants to long-term facilities. The average consultant has taken one or more courses or workshops on social work consultation. She has worked for less than two years at the facility where she is currently providing consultation. Most have worked for one to four facilities, but some consult with more than ten.

Among the purposes of their consultations with designees, the consultants identified the following in descending order of frequency:

1. To teach or demonstrate social work techniques
2. To review the designee's work
3. To assist with problems relating to residents, the staff, or the community
4. To provide ongoing evaluation and support (Mercer and Garner, 1981, p. 7)

Other purposes included direct work with patients and families and promoting higher-quality care.

Mercer and Garner concluded that these consultants seemed to function more as case supervisors, perhaps because most (60 percent) perceived the staff person designated for social work, and not the administrator or the facility itself, as the consultee. Their view of function was therefore limited to direct services rather than expanding to include programmatic, administrative, and organizational foci. Not one consultant in this sample sought to develop professional social work services within the facility. The authors indict this supervisory model of consultation for falling short of the aims for an integrative and comprehensive activity. Consultants, they suggest

> . . . have special access to the facility and the opportunity to influence not only the provision of social services but the entire system of long-term care. To assume a role of professional leadership in this situation, the consultant must be prepared with the knowledge, skills, and attitudes appropriate to administrative and managerial functions as well as to casework. Clearly, guidelines regarding the goals and objectives of consultation and the qualifications of consultants must be developed, standardized, and maintained. To do less would be to negate the professional responsibilities to those institutionalized elderly who call a facility home. [Mercer and Garner, 1981, p. 13]

While it is true that supervision of the designee is an inappropriate model of consultation, influencing the entire system of long-term care is probably more pertinent to the advocacy function at legislative levels than to the consultative function. As such, it will be considered in the Epilogue. Nevertheless, a skillful consultant to designees who recognizes that the facility is the proper consultee may work, as Mercer and Garner suggest, to engage the administrator's interest in and agreement to mutual work on administrative, managerial, and programmatic ways to improve services. An example of such organizational influencing is given in Chapter 9.

The provision of consultation to the administrator is appropriate only if he has asked for the consultant's knowledge and skill in achieving a particular goal or has accepted the consultant's offer of such collaborative work. It is important to remember that the consultant is in the facility usually only because the law requires her presence. Moreover, most nursing homes are operated for profit; most administrators have little or no knowledge of social work and tend to think that any staff person is fully capable of doing whatever needs to be done in the realm of social services. For these reasons the social work consultant is apt to be viewed by administration and staff with suspicion if not outright hostility. In their eyes, she is an unneeded, expensive commodity.

It is therefore important that in entering the nursing home the consultant seek to establish with all staff a climate of trust, respect, and mutual concern for the patient care. Acceptance is likely to be attained through affirming the facility's strengths and relating improved services where possible to reduced costs and increased contentment of patients and, hence, of staff.

Collaborative Practice: Teaming

The word "team" has several dictionary meanings. It denotes two or more draft animals harnessed to something heavy such as a plow or vehicle, which connotes cooperation. It is also used to denote a number of associated persons vying against another such group in a match or game, which connotes competition. But it is used in health care, and in mental health and industry as well, to denote a group of persons organized to work together, which connotes "the integration of differentiated functions" (Pepper, 1976). Teams may be categorized as multidisciplinary or interdisciplinary, depending on their structure and functions.

Multidisciplinary teams have a longer history than interdisciplinary teams and are probably still the more prevalent form. They are hierarchical in nature, with leadership and control vested in the physician because of her medical expertise and her legal responsibility for the patient's care. Members are chosen for their specializations as needed for the team to perform its function. Such a structure is found in ICU teams, surgical teams, and others where clinical tasks are relatively predictable and uniform across patient situations and technology is a salient feature in care. Typically such teams are maintained over time with the same disciplines and even the same individuals. The collaborative process is marked by the coordinated activities of experts, with the physician clearly in charge. A genetic counseling team, for example, is multidisciplinary. It is composed of all those professionals who contribute information upon which a diagnosis is made (Burns, 1976). It is led by a physician trained in medical genetics and may include a cytogeneticist, a biochemist, a nurse, and a social worker with special training in genetics or a genetic adviser with a master's degree. Each member has a specialized function to perform. The social worker may be the person who collects the family history and provides the data (family pedigree) that may clarify the mode of inheritance. She may also help the family to manage the feelings aroused by the diagnosis and to make necessary reproductive decisions as well as planning for the needs of the afflicted child already born.

It is the physician, however, who conducts the physical examination, considers the information gathered by the other team members, and makes the diagnosis. The physician does the initial counseling with the family regarding the diagnosis and the medical and genetic implications. Usually the social worker is present at that session. She may then stay on to give the individual or family needed help in coping with the stressful situation, to answer questions, and to help them understand the genetic data and probabilistic information. For example:

Tina, a six-month-old baby girl, was referred to the birth defects clinic of the medical center by a private pediatrician for evaluation of delayed motor development and poor visual function. The purpose of the evaluation was, (1) What is wrong with Tina and prognosis for her? (2) What are risks for future children? The genetic social worker visited the parents at home for a preclinic interview. She secured the baby's prenatal and postnatal history and family pedigree (no consanguinity, no indication of hereditary problems). Tina is a first child, born after an uneventful full-term pregnancy. Fetal vigor had been weak. Delivery was essentially normal except that the baby was blue and had a weak cry. Oxygen was administered, and the baby pinked up quickly. Both parents are twenty-six years of age, intelligent, and well educated. The father is in a PhD program, and the mother has one more year in a graduate professional school.

They have been concerned about the baby's development and are watching her progress closely. She cannot roll over or sit unsupported, and head control is poor. The baby's hearing and emotional responsiveness appear normal to the parents. They have told their friends and parents about the baby's slow development and are receiving lots of support from their parents, who live in the area. They are hoping that Tina has only some problem in motor coordination but have some awareness that that could not account for the visual problem: lack of eye contact, failure to track objects, nystagmus, and ptosis of the right eye. The worker discussed briefly the possibilities of an infant stimulation program and planned to give them more information following the clinic session.

A week later Tina was given a genetic and dysmorphology evaluation at the clinic. "The findings do not recall a specific dysmorphic syndrome but suggest some problem during formation of the brain." This was shared with the parents, and the doctor explained that no specific prognosis could be given. He recommended neurological follow-up at three-month intervals, reevaluation at the genetic clinic at one year, and participation in an infant stimulation program. Since no specific diagnosis could be established, the parents were given a recurrence risk of 5 percent (5 out of 100). [This is an empiric number derived from clinical data and based upon the exclusion of known genetic and environmental factors.]

The parents' grief and sense of loss and the coping tasks they will face in the light of an unknown etiology and an uncertain risk factor and in planning for Tina indicated to the social worker the desirability of a follow-up session. Three weeks later she made a home visit (mother only) for further discussion of the diagnosis and plans for Tina. Mrs. Curry said she and her husband were trying to remain hopeful and not looking too far ahead, especially since the pediatric neurologist had questioned the certainty of Tina's having a "primary brain malformation." She seemed aware that Tina may have serious difficulties in the future but was concentrating on the development and progress Tina was slowly achieving.

Attempts to begin in the infant stimulation program at the regional MR center had been delayed because of "administrative tie-ups" at the center. Mrs. Curry expressed a strong desire to learn about activities she could be doing with Tina. She had been putting great effort into providing stimulation to Tina but felt somewhat at a loss as to how much and what kinds of activities would be best.

The family's future plans were in a state of flux. Mr. Curry was finishing his graduate work and was now considering postdoctoral positions here and in other parts of the country. Mrs. Curry had a strong desire to complete her third year of professional school. She was therefore eager to begin the infant program so that she could determine if her participation would be needed in the coming year. The parents were not planning to have another child for at least another couple of years. Mrs. Curry said her husband felt the 5 percent risk figure was quite high, although she felt uncertain and probably wanted a second child more than he did. In any case, she felt they would want to see how Tina would be doing in a few years and try to make a decision at that time. This interval between children had been in their original plans for a family.

The worker had some concern about the difference between the parents in their perceptions of the risk factor; the differential burden on the mother, who has had to drop out of school; and the immediate and long-term impact on the marriage of these issues. She therefore suggested further follow-up visits and also offered to contact the regional center in order to expedite placement in the infant stimulation program. Her area of expertise on this multidisciplinary team is clearly in the psychosocial implications of genetic disease for child and family.

In certain settings, especially those providing institutional or community-based long-term care, an integrated structure or *interdisciplinary team* is a growing phenomenon.

> Interdisciplinary is defined here to mean a process where the solution of problems or completion of tasks requires the interdependent talents of different people. If I can do the task or solve the problem alone, then my actions are not interdisciplinary. If a task can be divided into two parts and you and I can solve our parts alone, the process is multidisciplinary. If you and I need to work on a task together but are each using the same skills, then the task is monodisciplinary, and two people can just get the job done faster. But, if you and I must work together, each contributing different skills to the task and our individual skills are both needed to complete the task, then we are interdependent and interdisciplinary! [Marion, 1980]

The aim of the interdisciplinary team is to integrate, not simply to coordinate the concepts, methods, and data of diverse disciplines in order to provide better health care for the individual, family, community, or population. Instead of an illness-focused approach, the interdisciplinary team reflects a biopsychosocial-cultural approach. It rests on a total person-in-environment conception that is congruent with an adaptational model of health and disease. In contrast to the multidisciplinary team, it is less crisis-oriented, less bound by time constraints, and in less need of direction from one individual. Also the application of a high level of technology is less salient. (Mailick and Jordan, 1977). Clinical tasks are less uniform and predictable, so rigid specialization of function yields to an interdependence of functions and tasks and shared decision-making. The active participation of the patient and/or family in the collaborative process is encouraged. In other words the team is organized around patient needs and clinical tasks rather than specialized function, and it is therefore nonhierarchical in structure. For example, in a rural home health agency, the patient care team meets twice a week. Nurses, physical therapists, occupational therapists, and the social worker attend. ''Collectively, we put our heads together . . . and attempt to look at the whole person. We look at needs, define problems, develop strategies, and delegate responsibilities. We are flexible enough to work through a member of the team most trusted by a patient without violating the integrity of our specific roles'' (Heald, 1982).

The membership of the team is determined by the nature of the needs of the population to be served. Hence in an occupational health clinic, the team comprises an occupational medicine physician, an attorney, an epidemiologist, and a social worker (Shanker, 1983). A community-based holistic health care center for youth, which provides integrated, comprehensive health, mental health, and social services to a disadvantaged adolescent population, uses several kinds of team structures drawn from a professional staff of thirteen disciplines, including medical specialties, nursing, social work, health education, nutrition, psychology, health administration, law, and vocational rehabilitation. Treatment teams develop as the adolescent's needs change or become more apparent so are not structurally fixed. They include all staff who have relevant contact with the client and are coordinated by the youth's primary counselor or practitioner. In addition, structured health care teams include a physician, nurse, counselor, health educator, nutritionist, social worker, and medical assistant. These teams meet formally at the end of each day to review the problems of the youth seen that day and to discuss assessment, treatment, formulation of health goals, and directions for the future (Glover, 1979).

While this is an unusually comprehensive program, a primary care team is apt to have almost as complex a structure. It may include several kinds of physicians (family practitioner, internist, pediatrician, obstetrician), social workers (community specialist, family specialist, and mental health specialist), and nurses (staff nurse, nurse clinician, and public health nurse). In addition, physical, occupational, and speech therapists, clinical nutritionists, a dentist, a clinical pharmacist, and even a social scientist such as a clinical anthropologist may serve on the team regularly or as needed according to the tasks in a given situation or on behalf of a particular population or community.

Interdisciplinary teams are not limited to personnel in a given setting. In certain situations, they comprise representatives from several agencies as well as health care staff in a team effort to integrate services, knowledge, and skill on behalf of a population of clients and families over time. Going beyond conferring or cooperating on a single issue, this is an interdisciplinary, interagency team, not merely a group of autonomous agency representatives. Often it is the health care worker who chairs such a team and who coordinates its activities.

For example, a hospital-based child abuse team includes members from the hospital's medical, nursing, and social work staffs and representatives from child protective agencies as well as from such agencies involved in specific family situations as the VNA or family violence centers. On one such team the pediatric social worker serves as coordinator. Her functions include chairing the meetings; managing team activities such as proper follow-up of plans and actions; maintaining statistics to be used in evaluating the program; liaison activities with hospital staff such as educating medical students, residents, and nurses about the dynamics of child abuse and neglect; liason with community agencies; processing requests for evaluation and initiating referrals; and helping other hospitals develop similar child abuse teams. In addition to these coordinating functions, she performs clinical tasks related to team goals, including psychosocial assessments of referred children and their families, brief treatment, preventive services for families in situations of medical and social risk, giving court testimony, and participating in community education programs to develop public awareness of child abuse.

The Social Worker's Functions

The functions of the social worker in multidisciplinary and interdisciplinary teams will vary across types of health organizations and kinds of settings. They may include any of the functions, roles, and tasks discussed in Chapter 6, as required by the team's goals and plans. They may include coordinating functions like those just described in the child abuse team. They may include emotional support to the team itself in helping members to manage the stress generated by such services as hospice care, neonatal intensive care units, and oncology services.

Indeed, all staff groups and teams are subject to the same processes as other formed groups. They go through analogous stages of development, shifts in statuses and roles, and critically stressful events in group life. They also experience maladaptive interpersonal processes that interfere with their moving through these transitions or dealing effectively with environmental issues. A social worker, alert to the ways in which these processes affect the team's tasks in providing good patient care, may facilitate the team's work on its maladaptive patterns that impede goal achievement. The following example is taken from a renal dialysis unit:

During a regular meeting of the nursing staff, social worker, and consulting psychiatrist, held for discussion of problematic patient situations, a nurse reported she was having difficulty in treating a particular patient. She had been dating him for several months and had recently terminated the relationship. She was finding it difficult to provide nursing care for him, and the feelings he had over the ending of their relationship were creating stress for her. There is no formal policy on staff–patient relationships of this nature, and the nurses did not feel it was an ethical issue since nurses in any hospital date former patients. But as we discussed the special dependency problems that dialysis patients confront, they did agree that the unit is different from other settings, dating could have a negative impact on patient care, and the nephrologist would probably discharge a nurse for dating a patient. It was considered an isolated incident, and the discussion moved on.

A few days later, however, another nurse told me in confidence that she is dating another patient. Some of the same issues discussed in the meeting were in her mind. She is ambivalent about the relationship, feeling guilty about the effects on the patient of terminating it and fearful of losing her job. With her permission and my assurance of confidentiality, I conferred with the head nurse and the psychiatrist about the desirability of a formal statement concerning patient-staff relationships. We agreed that such a statement might help the nurse to offer a reason to the patient for ending their relationship as well as giving all the nurses a basis on which to handle patients' invitations. We also decided that the psychiatrist would bring the matter to the medical director of the unit on a physician-to-physician basis. Although we anticipated that the nephrologist might ask for the names of the two nurses, the psychiatrist agreed to maintain the confidentiality of both reports.

The medical director later inquired of me about the need for the policy. I connected it to patient care and to the stress generated for nurses in the absence of formal guidelines. Although he continued to question the necessity, he did issue a statement regarding staff-patient relationships outside the professional setting. On the whole, the nurses' response was positive, their trust in me increased because of the protection of confidentiality, and several nurses asked me for referrals to ouside resources for help with difficult personal problems.

At times functions customarily thought of as social work responsibilities may have been fulfilled by other discipines in the absence of a social work member on the team; they are not easily relinquished when a social worker is then added. For example, social work had not been utilized on the research floor of a large cancer hospital, although it was present on all other services. Nursing staff had been accustomed to providing emotional support to families as well as to patients, and to engaging in discharge planning as needed. These were draining demands on nurses in light of their heavy nursing duties with an extremely ill patient population. Yet when a social worker was appointed to the service at the request of its chief and became a member of the multidisciplinary team, nurses resisted her assumption of functions related to psychosocial support to patients and families and to discharge planning. She was an experienced practitioner and had anticipated this response, at least to some degree. She therefore maintained a low-key approach initially, supporting the nurses in their efforts. As active resistance diminished and acceptance of her presence grew, she gradually offered to take a more direct role in difficult patient or family situations. Ultimately she established herself as a competent specialist and fully functioning member of the team.

Teamwork

Effective teamwork emerges out of three levels of interaction: the team as a group, as a team, and as an organization. Members must attend to all three:

Any health team is probably operating at all three "levels" at any moment in time. That is, there are group issues to be resolved, decisions to be made about roles and tasks, and negotiations to be conducted with administration. Furthermore, there may be a crisis brewing in one area, e.g., a deadline for a grant proposal, when the team's energy is focused on another area, e.g. doctor-nurse conflict. Is it really any surprise that team members feel the way they do at times? [Edinberg and Baldwin, 1980, p. 20]

TEAM AS GROUP

Social workers often have an advantage over other team members, because their education and practice usually includes knowledge of and experience with small groups. They understand, for example, the complementarity between the need to focus on the group's task and the need to focus on internal maintenance of the team itself. The team's relationship and communication patterns affect and are affected by both instrumental and maintenance needs. They may lead to such processes as scapegoating or coalitions. They will affect the form and substance of the norms that the members set for behavior, handling conflict, and other issues.

Kane (1975) has suggested that teams may also reflect the same successive stages of development manifested by small social work groups: (1) ambivalence about involvement with one another and the leader; (2) struggle with issues of autonomy, power, and control in defining relationships; (3) a new level of intimacy, involvement, and comfort with one another; (4) differentiation and interdependence of formal roles for achievement of group goals; and (5) termination and evaluation (Garland et al., 1965). These stages ought not to be viewed as rigidly set. Some teams may experience regression to an earlier stage in response to some event, such as member turnover; other teams may not experience one or more stages at all, skipping over the first and second stages, for example, or remaining stuck at the first stage.

To be an effective member of a team, one must have knowledge of small-group theory and skill in the areas of group dynamics, processes, and developmental aspects. Because of their experience, social workers are often able to help team members develop these skills, putting them in touch with what is going on (process) and enabling them to see obstacles to the work and how to deal with them.

TEAM AS TEAM

The major difference between a group and the team is the nature of the demands placed on a team. "Teams are characterized by deadlines, by work loads, by the need for predictable output, by the need for making decisions and establishing priorities, and by having to satisfy external constituencies, such as students, patients, and administration" (Edinberg and Baldwin, 1980, p. 17). Rubin and his colleagues (1975) have suggested a model of task accomplishment based on a hierarchy: goals ("What?"), roles ("Who?"), procedures ("How?"), and interpersonal relations. The *goals* relate specifically to patients' needs. Because the needs are interdependent, so too are the goals and tasks. The effectiveness of the team derives, in part, from the clarity and specificity with which it sets goals and the degree of agreement and commitment to the goals among the team members. Clinical tasks to meet the needs and achieve the goals are allocated on the basis of *role*. The tasks are translated into professional functions, so members' clear understanding of the functions of the various disciplines on the team enables the team to decide who is the most capable of carrying out which tasks. Role expectations must be clear to avoid role conflict, blurring, or ambiguity.

At the next hierarchical level are the *procedures* and processes that the team develops for its work. They pertain to both the instrumental (task) and maintenance functions referred to earlier. Norms and procedures must be developed around communication, decision-making, planning, conflict management, information sharing, and leadership. They must be accepted by all members. If goals, roles, and procedures have been clearly established, then it is less likely that *interpersonal relations* will interfere with task accomplishment.

Usually interpersonal difficulties in a team are less the result of personality problems and more the consequence of ambiguous goals, unclear role expectations, or dysfunctional decision-making, and other procedures. Actually the issue of interpersonal relationships is complicated inasmuch as goal conflicts, role conflicts, and procedural issues manifest themselves in interpersonal relationships, so in that sense interpersonal relations are present throughout the hierarchical levels.

It should be noted here that the multidisciplinary and interdisciplinary teams as analyzed are actually ideal types or models. In the real life of health care practice, few teams could be classified as pure examples. Comparatively, however, teams may be distinguished on a continuum with respect to their goals, roles, procedures, and interpersonal relations. At one end is the surgical team, having the goal of a successful, life-preserving surgical procedure (high level of technology) and little inclusion of psychosocial factors in goal-setting; requiring strict specialization of roles based on professional function; and with the surgeon clearly in charge of decision-making, requiring little or no attention to interpersonal relations. At the other end of the continuum is a community-based primary care team characterized by the inclusion of psychosocial factors along with the biological in goal-setting; roles assigned on the basis of tasks, including overlapping; shared decision-making; and ongoing attention to team process and interpersonal relations. Also, it is far more likely that patient and family members will be included as team members on those teams falling toward the interdisciplinary end of the continuum.

TEAM AS ORGANIZATION

Health care teams operate within larger organizational environments. Depending on its own complexity an organizational environment may comprise multiple professional, technical, management, maintenance, and clerical staffs, as well as patients, trainees, visitors, and others. A team may have direct exchanges or indirect relationships with many of these organizational components as it seeks to secure resources of time, space, information, and energy. Who is to negotiate them and how it is to be done may be critical questions for some teams to address.

BARRIERS TO TEAMWORK

The hierarchical aspect suggests that problems in teamwork should first be examined for goal-related issues. If the source is not there, then role-related issues need to be examined next. If the source is not there, then procedure-related issues should be examined. If the team has worked through its goals, roles, and procedural issues and still finds barriers to the work, the problem may indeed be interpersonal, such as a value conflict or a personality conflict that has to be resolved.

Interference with the team's effectiveness may arise because goals are unclear or because not all team members agree with the goals or the priorities among them. Different people have different goals and different priorities, which must be elicited and discussed. Sometimes there is a discrepancy between manifest and latent goals, as when members' conscious or unconscious goals are oriented to power and status rather than to team objectives.

Problems are generated if role expectations are unclear, leading to ambiguity so that members are uncertain about who is to do what. Lack of clarity can also lead to role conflict, as in the following example of conflict between the self-expectations of the social workers and the expectations of other team members concerning the social work role on a newly formed primary care team:

[W]hile the social workers saw their role to be clinicians, the physicians and nurses at first expected them to be involved almost exclusively in arranging for such concrete services as transportation, nursing home placements, finances, support service at home, and housing. The social workers had a choice at this point—they could fight, they could quit, they could be co-opted. What they decided, of fundamental importance at that point in the program, was to build an alliance. In the service of this endeavor, they felt they must first prove their competency in those terms that were expected and that would initially be regarded as most useful by other providers. So they concentrated on demonstrating their expertise in arranging for concrete services.

Once we thus established a basic level of trust and credibility, we were able then to move into expanding the nature of their work on the team. During this phase, as in the beginning, we chose to make ourselves very visible to team members. Rather than simply being available on a referral basis, we undertook a more vigorous stance. We spent many hours in the medical clinic interacting with staff, reviewing charts, involving ourselves in decisions about patients, and talking with patients. We listened, questioned, discussed, and offered a willingness to share the burden of managing difficult patients. [S. Lee, 1980]

Lee gives an example in which a nurse was confused and upset by a patient and accepted the social worker's offer to meet with her and the patient. She reports that their joint participation in the interview and discussion afterward helped the nurse understand a psychotic presentation and how her own feeling of helplessness can be a diagnostic tool.

Such experiences led to team members' recognition of the importance of psychosocial knowledge and understanding in planning and carrying out treatment. Social workers, instead of only being asked to find a nursing home for a patient, were also identified as the professional particularly equipped to assist in assessing and intervening within a broader psychosocial realm. This was a fairly dramatic change in role expectations.

Dysfunctional decision-making is another barrier to effective team work. It is experienced by the individual team member in the following ways:

When some people try to participate in a discussion of job issues they often get cut off or their suggestions seem to die. People only seem to pay attention to some team members and not others. Some people seem to do most of the talking while others don't participate very much.

When we sit down to discuss something I usually walk away wondering what we just did and what is supposed to happen next. If, as a result of a discussion, I am assigned to do something, I often do not agree with the tasks assigned me. It seems like the same problems keep coming up for discussion even though we thought we had worked them through already. [Rubin et al., 1975, p. 35]

In the first instance not everyone participates, so the team is deprived of valuable ideas and the quality of decisions suffers. Teams must make active efforts to ensure the participation of all members.

In the second instance, not everyone understands the decision, and therefore those who do not are not committed to it.

> One reason why people do not participate is that they do not understand the discussion. If this is true, it is very unlikely that they will be able to carry out their part of the decision. Further, if someone does not participate in a decision, it is less likely that he will be committed to implementing the decision. The result is that many decisions do not get carried out. [Rubin et al., 1975, p. 47]

Ideally, decision-making in an interdisciplinary team is by consensus. But there are dangers in consensual decision-making as well, and these can lead to problems in team effectiveness. Consensual decision-making may result in a leveling down rather than a leveling up of responsible decision-making (Rae-Grant and Marcuse, 1968). A process of "groupthink" may take over: Group loyalty supersedes individual thinking because the latter might lead to conflict, thereby upsetting the team members' comfort (Janis, 1971). Lowe and Herranen (1978, p. 328) refer to collective indecision or pseudoconsensus, which serves to maintain the team's equilibrium and to avoid open conflict. But it actually leads instead to covert anger, low productivity, scapegoating, and the absence of a norm of accountability.

Some of these outcomes appear to be related to norms governing decision-making, such as "In making a decision silence means consent"; "We don't disagree with the doctors"; "Conflict is unacceptable—it's best to let sleeping dogs lie" (Rubin and Beckhard, 1972). Rubin and colleagues (1975) point to four styles of conflict management: smoothing it over (avoidance); forcing a solution (exertion of power); compromise (this can be good if it does not occur too early in the process, closing out more innovative solutions); and confrontation (open discussion of the conflict, analysis of causes, and problem-solving). In order to manage conflict successfully so that the tasks can proceed, members have to move beyond rhetoric and share and explore their own personal objectives. Clearly, norms regarding decision-making and other procedures must be discussed rather than remaining unspoken, covert, and even unrecognized.

Interpersonal barriers to teamwork can arise from issues of difference among participants such as professional status, gender, age, education, race and ethnicity, and social class. These problems are especially likely to arise in health care settings, not only because of the diversity of professional disciplines on the team but because of the traditional dominance of the physician.

The profession of medicine is the oldest of all the professions and has served as the model for others. It is steeped in tradition and resistant to change. In addition, physicians enjoy the highest or close to the highest social prestige in American society. In common with shamans and medicine men and women in other cultures, they are viewed with awe and deference as having almost magical powers, although this has started to change in recent years. Social work, on the other hand, is a relatively new occupation still struggling for full professional status.

Because of their specialized, exclusive knowledge, their legal responsibility for the patients' care, and their social prestige, physicians are granted supreme authority in matters of acute illness and disease. In addition, medical education enculturates its students to the sense of authority. This becomes generalized to health care and chronic illness, for which authority and dominance are less appropriate. As the medical model yields to a holistic view of patient-in-environment, the exclusivity of the physician's knowledge and his authority begin to break down. But, with few exceptions, little in contemporary medical education prepares the physician to move beyond the expert role in biomedical matters to the expert role in emotional, social, and cultural matters bearing on health and illness.

Interpersonal conflict can be generated if the physician member of the collaborative group is unreceptive to nonbiomedical information, viewing it as irrelevant, or if he fails to give it recognition or actually downgrades the knowledge and skill required in handling the psychosocial factors in illness. Group cohesiveness and a positive group climate are undermined if mutual trust, respect, and acceptance are not present. Even on what is purported to be an interdisciplinary team in long-term care a physician may still view the other health professions, including social work, as merely ancillary to medical treatment.* He or she may then take on a directive, prescriptive, authoritarian stance inappropriate to the nature of the clinical tasks, and conflict ensues. To counter such trends, both social workers and nurses are developing more assertiveness, clarifying their functions, roles, and tasks in ways that will enhance the sense of professional identity, competence, and interdependence.

Members of all the health professions are socialized by their respective professional educations to particular value orientations, ideologies, language and terminology, perspectives on human beings and their environments, client–practitioner relationships, and types of continuing education (Huntington, 1981). This suggests that the social work profession is not blameless in matters of communication and interpersonal rela-

---

*Rita Black (1983) has observed that with the growing prevalence of chronic disease and the increasing proportion of the elderly in the population, the need for community-based social services also increases. And while these patients' need for medical services continues, such services may well be on the *ancillary* level (usually accorded to social work services in health care), while the social services may emerge at the level of primary service!

tions. For example, very few social workers are provided with a base of biomedical knowledge and terminology in their professional education, despite the fact that issues of health and disease extend into every field of practice and are not limited to health care alone. This is a significant barrier to communication in the health care field—perhaps even more of a barrier than that generated by the lack of psychosocial knowledge and terminology among other health professionals, often a cause for complaint by social workers.

Occasionally social workers assume a role of serving as social conscience for the team, presuming that only social work values and ethics display a caring orientation to patient's and family's needs. Such an error is understandably resented by other disciplines and is apt to "spoil" interpersonal relationships, blocking any effective contribution the social worker might make.

Similarly, the social work value of confidentiality may need reexamination in a team context. When a social worker says to team members, "I don't have the patient's permission to tell you that," the statement may be construed by other team members as a power play—information is power. Or it can lead to the setting of clear and overt group norms regarding the use of information: All team members will tell all patients and families that whatever is told to an individual team member has to be shared with the team. The team's information, however, is confidential to the team.

In general, social workers hold liberal, socially oriented ideologies while physicians, at least the older ones, hold more conservative and elitist ideologies (Huntington, 1981, p. 170). Physicians are also oriented to "doing" more than to "problem-solving," whereas the emphasis is reversed among social workers. For most physicians the patient is, or should be, a passive recipient of care. The social work client, although actually the same person, is encouraged and supported to be self-determining. These differences are potential sources of interpersonal conflict.

The issue of self-determination is interesting when considered in a collaborative context. The social worker is apt to be more reluctant than other health professionals to impose a point of view and will more likely rely on skillful questions to move people toward a desired level of understanding or decision (Karkalitz, 1980, p. 29). The assumption is that then the others will be committed to the understanding or the decision. One wonders if this is what leads some observers to comment on the alleged passivity of social workers as team members, as in the report of a family practice team cited earlier in this chapter.

In this connection, however, Huntington (1981, p. 20) notes that demands in the literature for greater social work autonomy in health settings that are dominated by the powerful profession of medicine, and efforts to develop political skills for gaining power and influence in medical settings, are made by male social workers in health care despite the greater number of women in the field. Is there a reason for this in the demographic composition of the various health care professions?

There are still differences in gender, social class, income, education, and race among the health care professions, particularly between medicine and all of the others. While changes in gender and social class composition are taking place, the process is slow. Hence the medical profession is still largely male, white, well-educated, economically affluent, and middle- or upper-class in origin. By contrast, social work, nursing, occupational therapy, physical therapy, and nutrition are largely female, with baccalaureate degrees and fewer with master's degrees. Many, such as nurses' aides, have only high school or technical training, earn modest incomes, and are women of color. Even among nurses and social workers holding advanced degrees, most are at the master's rather than the doctoral level.

By contrast, many physicians, after receiving their doctoral degrees and then completing internships, pursue further postgraduate specialized (residency) training. It is not surprising that they might view those with less education as having less knowledge and no right to differ. Nor is it surprising that many of those women might agree. Would they struggle for autonomy and power to the same degree that their male counterparts would, or would their struggles be as acceptable to the male physicians and administrators? Probably not, at least in many institutions.

Added to the differences in gender, education, and race are likely age differences. These may generate the potential for interpersonal tensions, for example, between a male physician of middle age or older and a female social worker who may be young or in early middle age (Hunting-ton, 1981, p. 156).

Finally, physicians for the most part are still socialized to solo practice, while social workers for the most part are socialized to agency-based practice. This makes for differing orientations to time inasmuch as fee-for-service places a premium on time for the physician. Also, social workers have been socialized into supervised practice beyond the terminal degree, although this is changing somewhat. But it can be a source of irritation to other team members, raising issues of team management if the social worker cannot make independent decisions. Moreover, the emphasis on supervision contributes to the perception of the social worker as less than an autonomous professional and does nothing to enhance her status.

These and other interpersonal barriers to effective teamwork are obviously difficult to counter—perhaps more so than tensions due to personality conflicts. They have their roots in earlier educational experiences and traditions, in the competitive struggle among groups in the occupational structure of our society, and in the nature of discrimination based on gender, age, class, and color. Kertesz (1980) suggests that just as the team must maintain permeability of its boundaries with the environment, individual team members must also maintain openness to the input of other members:

> Professional permeability allows team members of one discipline to be receptive to input from team members of other disciplines in areas which involve their own professional decisions and actions. Intellectual permeability encourages the sharing of knowledge and data bases, perspectives and preferences, and more importantly, gives equal creditability to the input of all the disciplines. Personal permeability allows for self-disclosure and personal sharing that leads to better understanding and responsiveness among team members [Kertesz, 1980, p. 25.]

While this suggestion is more horatory than descriptive, it does return us to the emphasis on the team's internal processes and the need for open communication and conflict management to support the task function. Task and maintenance functions are indeed complementary.

Summary

The process of collaboration is ubiquitous in health care. Social work practice in health care is therefore characterized by conferring, cooperating, and consulting with colleagues of one's own and other disciplines. It is also marked by team practice in many health care settings. All forms of collaboration require particular knowledge, skills, and attitudes in working with others to meet patients' needs, solve problems, and carry out clinical tasks. Marion and Angermeyer (1980) see these attributes extending into four domains: self, other, context, and interrelationships. The domain of "self" refers to competencies and self-awareness; the domain of "other" refers to what must be know about colleagues and about those whom one serves; the domain of "context" refers to what must be known about the work environment; and "interrelationships" refers to how people interact, solve problems, change structures, and deliver health care. Each domain has its distinctive knowledge, skills, and attitudes. Together, these form a matrix, as shown in Table 8–1.

For the social worker these matrix elements require a comfortable professional identification that includes a realistic sense of professional competence, confidence, and pride in being a social worker; a readiness for professional autonomy in participating in decision-making and accountability for outcomes; a capacity for relatedness involving nonjudgmental

TABLE 8-1. Matrix Model of Knowledge, Skill, and Attitudes Required for Effective Collaboration

DOMAIN	KNOWLEDGE	SKILL	ATTITUDE
Self			
A. Possesses and is able to project a clear self-image.	A.1. Aware of impact of self-image on situations and the relationships of situations to self-concept in terms of: (1) assertiveness level; (2) defensiveness level; (3) confidence level; (4) interaction style; and (5) expectations.	A.2. Able to interpret self-image in terms of coming from within or from others and whether accurate or imagined. Able to maintain a positive self-image most of the time. Able to distinguish between times when self-image is threatened by another person or a group. Able to respond appropriately to situations when self-image is actually threatened by self or others, reaffirming positive self-image.	A.3. Is willing to use feedback and introspect to modify self-image.
B. Possesses and is able to project a clear professional identity.	B.1. Has mastered and continues to develop in the essential knowledge areas of own profession.	B.2. Has mastered and continues to develop in the essential skill areas of own profession. Can explain roles, duties, and responsibilities of own profession.	B.3. Feels capable and able to accept responsibility in own professional role. Is willing to change conception of roles, duties, and responsibilities of own profession based on new information.

(continued)

225

TABLE 8–1. (cont.)

DOMAIN	KNOWLEDGE	SKILL	ATTITUDE
Other			
A. Is willing and able to learn what others (providers and clients) can do and cannot do in different situations.	A.1. Recognized when, what, and why he/she needs to learn about the capabilities of another.	A.2. Able to seek appropriate information about capabilities of others.	A.3. Is willing to change his/her impression of others based on new information.
B. Is willing and able to accept and include others (providers and clients) as appropriate to the situation.	B.1. Knows how and where to obtain information from appropriate sources about other's capabilities and limitations.	B.2. Distinguishes between strengths and weaknesses of another on an individual basis rather than from a stereotyped image. Analyzes information received as to its accuracy and forms an impression which may then be used.	B.3. Is willing to accept another as a person, with certain capabilities and limitations. Is willing to accept another in their role as a professional or client with certain capabilities and limitations. Is willing to accept in another the capabilities overlapping with one's own and the unique capabilities of another. Is open in including or not including another based on knowledge of capabilities and limitations.
Context			
Is willing and able to analyze the system (environment/setting) in which interrelationships between self and others	1. Is knowledgeable about systems theory; the goals, components, and interrelationships between the components in systems of concern (personal settings, client set-	2. Is able to identify, define and analyze goals (the reasons why self and others are in a given setting). Is able to identify, define, analyze the system components and	3. Is able to approach each setting with flexibility and openness. Is willing to modify behavior to be consistent with the situation. Is willing to modify the setting to facilitate

226

tings, immediate work settings, health systems, community systems, from local to international.

Interrelationships

Is willing and able to utilize communication, confrontation, small group, and management skills to work with others in solving problems.

1. Is knowledgeable about how people communicate with each other and how to solve communications problems when they occur. Is knowledgeable of trust building techniques and other methods of providing support to others. Is knowledgeable of the concept of social distance. Is knowledgeable of the dynamics of the small group. Is knowledgeable of management concepts. Is knowledgeable of problem solving and decision making process. Is knowledgeable of ethical decision making concepts. Is knowledgeable of change theory.

interrelationships between components in a given setting as they might impact on self and others.

2. Is able to facilitate communication with others and can solve communications problems. Can articulate and advocate the viewpoints of others. Is able to deal with frustrations and assess risk elements of communicating with others. Can work with others to establish feelings of trust and belonging; clarify power/authority issues; and define goals and procedures; while determining and maintaining an appropriate social distance. Can exhibit appropriate behaviors in a small group (Task Oriented Behaviors and Maintenance Oriented Behaviors). Can plan, or-

interrelationships between self and others.

3. Is willing to open and maintain communication with others. Is willing to understand another's point of view, values, and feelings without being judgmental. Is willing to build trusting relationships and to engage in and resolve conflicts. Is willing to take risks in communicating with others and in decision making. Feels comfortable when selecting close or distant relationships with others depending on the situation. Is willing to work alone, with another, and with groups as necessary in accomplishing goals. Is willing to work on task and maintenance ori-

(continued)

TABLE 8–1. (*cont.*)

SKILL	ATTITUDE
ganize, staff, motivate, implement, and evaluate in order to accomplish goals. Can contribute to problem solving and decision making processes. Can contribute to ethical decision making processes. Can develop and implement activities to produce changes in organizations.	ented functions to most efficiently achieve the goals. Is willing to assume leadership and accept the leadership of others, depending on the situation. Is willing to become involved in ethical issues. Is willing to both initiate and accept change.

SOURCE: Developed by Rodger Marion and Katie Angermeyer in *Prospectus for Change* 5 (September–October 1980): 6–7, published by the Center for Interdisciplinary Education in Allied Health, University of Kentucky, Lexington. Used with permission.

and facilitating attitudes, communication skills, and empathic responsiveness and respect for colleague concerns, interests, and viewpoints; and clarity about the social work function in health care. As Karkalitz (1980, p. 34) put it:

[L]et me urge you to make visible your competence by the conceptualization and demonstration of your own clinical skills. At the same time, validate and make use of other disciplines' clinical skills. Move from the need to negotiate general issues of role, to attention to the clinical needs of the particular patient and the family as the basis for role negotiation. Be assertive about your competency and informed about the competency of others, in negotiating for the needs of the particular patient. The outcome will not only be good health care for the consumer, but a stimulating collaborative work environment for all members of the health team.

CHAPTER 9

Innovation and Change in Health Care Organizations

As INDICATED IN CHAPTER 3, the health care organization can help to maintain the competence of patients and families or can undermine it. It can support or diminish their self-esteem, sustain or dismantle their self-directedness, and enhance or stifle their capacity for human relatedness. The health organization has an equally compelling influence on the social worker's professional competence, professional identity and self-esteem, professional autonomy, and professional relationships with clients, colleagues, and other staff members. Some organizations may impose unreasonable constraints on the practitioner's ability to respond flexibly and effectively to clients' needs, and others may furnish opportunities to provide increasingly effective services. Over time many organizations provide a mixture of constraints and opportunities. In any case, the professional must recognize the health organization as a salient element throughout the helping process.

Earlier chapters examined the roles of enabler, facilitator, teacher, coach, mobilizer, mediator, organizer, collaborator, consultant, and team member in face-to-face practice. This chapter will consider the roles of innovator and advocate for organizational change.

Innovation and the Social Work Role of Innovator

Zaltman and associates (1973, p. 10), define innovation as "any idea, practice, or material artifact perceived to be new by the relevant unit of
230

adoption.'' The following example refers to a pediatric service in a hospital serving a low-income population:

Many of the children admitted have no further contact with their parents until discharge. Often the child is unprepared for hospitalization and has had no experience with medical procedures. Therefore, these children feel a more than usual sense of abandonment, fear of separation from home, and anxiety in the strange environment of the hospital. Since the attention of the medical and nursing staff is claimed by the physical and medical needs of the children, the social work staff decided to organize a program of organized play therapy as a means of facilitating their recovery. . . . We visited two major hospitals to study their play therapy programs and the Director of Child Life Activity at one of them became a consultant to our program. [Menezes, 1980]

A play therapy program on a hospital's pediatric service was not a new invention, but for this hospital it was an innovation, and an important and successful one.

For the purpose of analysis, it is worthwhile to distinguish innovation from organizational change although both are designed to humanize institutions. Innovation is often carried out autonomously by a social work department, a team, or a work group when such a unit has recognized a gap in the service it provides. If the solution does not affect others in a negative or otherwise significant way, including the organization's key decision makers, nor require resources beyond what is available to the unit, the innovative service, program, or procedure is instituted. In contrast to what is here conceived as planned organizational change, innovation leaves power, status, regulations, values, and vested interests largely unaltered. Consensus is assumed at the outset.

Social work skills in innovation include encouraging all members of the unit to participate in evaluating the service gap in the light of new or newly recognized client needs; joint problem-solving; developing a feasible solution based on assessment of resources required, such as time, space, funds, and staffing; and planning collaboratively for the implementation of the innovative solution, often on a demonstration basis. For example, innovation took place on an obstetrical service where the social worker was concerned that attending physicians were uninterested in social work service for their private patients. At her behest the social work supervisor enlisted the participation of the nursing supervisor in calling a meeting of both nursing and social work staffs. The stated purpose was to explore common problems, concerns, new ideas, and channels of communication around service delivery and patient care. The problem was defined as inadequate services to patients socially or emotionally at risk. Excerpts from the minutes follow:

At present there is an effective informal system of communication on a one-to-one basis between the social worker and the charge nurse, who will call regarding a particular patient. Because of brief stays, prompt identification of potential problems is especially important on the service. It was generally agreed that more opportunity for interdisciplinary team meetings on a regular and frequent basis could be valuable. Besides improving the quality of patient service and facilitating our own collaboration, combining forces in meetings of this kind (including postpartum, nursery, and labor and delivery) might strengthen our mutual impact on the system so that patient care is recognized as a comprehensive interdisciplinary effort. If the meetings were in the early morning, obstetricians who make early morning rounds could be encouraged to come in and discuss their patients. If the group identified an "at risk" patient in need of help or having special problems, the doctor could be alerted that his patient had been identified at "Patient Care Rounds" as someone who should be referred for social work service or other intervention. Problems would be picked up more quickly and prevented or alleviated earlier in the patient's stay. Convincing a reluctant physician of the need for nonmedical help as part of the total plan of care for mother and/or child would no longer be the responsibility of one or two concerned staff but would have the backing of the interdisciplinary health care team.

The group agreed that Patient Care Rounds on OB will be instituted on a trial basis twice weekly at 8 A.M., beginning next Tuesday. Follow-up discussion will be held with the two supervisors in six weeks to evaluate effectiveness of this approach to the problem.

By its very nature, however, innovation can evoke resistance among those involved. Change may represent a threat to one's values, commitments, ideologies, personal and professional interests and preferences, and comfort in doing the accustomed. Resistance may also be related to four elements of the innovation: who brings the change; the kind of changes involved; the procedures in initiating and implementing the change; and the organization's climate. For example, if the innovation is brought in by an outsider, resistance will be higher than if the participants feel it is their own. Also, resistance is likely to be less if the top decision-makers give their whole-hearted approval (Zaltman et al., 1973). Resistance will also be less if participants see the change as reducing rather than increasing their present work loads or tensions; if it is congruent with existing values and ideals; if it offers a new experience that interests the participants; and if the participants feel their autonomy and their security are not threatened. It follows that if the innovation can be presented in ways that fit these criteria, resistance may not be aroused or, if present, may be disarmed.

A Family Medicine Office provided in a low-income community by a school of medicine invited the participation of social work students after the office had been in place three years. The invitation was extended by the physician who administered the office and the physician in charge of the training of family practice residents. Social work faculty discussion and planning concerning the roles and functions of the social worker were carried out with these two individuals and not with the office staff, nurses, or residents. This error led to considerable discomfort for the first student. Clerical staff feared their work loads would increase. The nurses were concerned about the shortage of space for seeing patients, fearing that if social workers were also to see patients, it would break the patient flow. The greatest resistance, understandably, came from the residents, despite the attention given in family medicine to psychosocial components of disease and disability. Retrospectively, it was clear that the residents saw no need for social work; indeed, they believed it would deprive them of important learning in the psychosocial realm. In short, it was a new experience that did not interest them, was not congruent with the way things had been done since they had been there, and threatened their autonomy and security. No referrals were forthcoming. Fortunately, the student was creative in working with the problem and with the residents and other staff. But much time and energy were lost that could have been prevented at the outset by eliciting and handling feedback from staff and residents.

With respect to the procedures used in initiating and implementing an innovation, resistance is likely to be less if those involved have participated in the identification and assessment of the service gap, agree about it, and recognize its importance. For example, Sommer (1970) tells of a geriatric facility in which the chairs for some fifty women in the day room stood in straight lines around the walls, with several rows back to back in the center. Around each of the several columns were four chairs, each facing in a different direction. The administrator was concerned about the lack of social interaction, especially since the room had been newly decorated with new flooring, curtains, and chairs in a variety of colors. He could not understand why the listlessness of the residents persisted, why they stared blankly up at the lights, down at the floor, or straight ahead. "They were like strangers sitting in a train station waiting for a train that never came" (p. 27).

The consultant recognized that the arrangement of chairs made it impossible for the women to talk together without twisting to face ninety degrees to the side, which can be difficult if not downright painful. He introduced small tables and grouped the chairs around the tables to induce conversation and interaction.

On the morning when the ladies first discovered the change there were spontaneous comments such as. . . "This is a nice table, but I don't want to eat all day." "Is this my chair now?". . . The maintenance and food service employees complained loudly that the tables and chairs cluttered their route through the ward. Several of the nurses remarked that the tables made the room look "junky." An occupational therapist inquired whether we were getting ready to "hold a party." [Sommer, 1970, p. 33]

The women themselves proceeded to move their chairs back against the walls at every opportunity. Two, in particular, served as self-appointed monitors, restoring order to the day room's chairs the first thing every morning. The movement of chairs back to the walls continued for some time. Sommer refers to findings from later studies that indicate people do like to sit with their backs to the walls and other tangible barriers, partly for comfort and security, and partly to be in a position that permits wide scanning of the environment.

The example illuminates the operation of informal norms and customs in a work group. Maintenance and nursing staffs opposed the innovation because it was easier for maintenance personnel to push a broom down a large room uncluttered with small tables and chairs randomly placed; it was easier for nurses to keep track of residents, their condition, and their actions if they were sitting in straight rows—around the edges of the room—so that the nurses would have an unobstructed view. Custom was a forceful regulator, providing rules of task performance that interfered with receptivity to change. Nevertheless, it is possible that resistance might have been minimized by encouraging staff and residents to participate in assessing their shared environment—its positive and negative qualities with respect to their needs and interests—and by planning together for agreed-upon changes.

Organizational Change and the Social Work Role of Advocate

In contrast to innovation, organizational change efforts are more complex. They comprise politically oriented skills that are designed to influence the organization to change a structure, policy, or procedure that is not responsive to client needs, coping tasks, or cultural patterns (or, for that matter, to staff needs). They are more complex because they rub up against formal rules and regulations that may have become rigid over time and serve organizational needs rather than the goal of patient care; hierarchical authority and decision making that create issues of power and control; and status variables that become linked with vested interests and preferences (Hage and Aiken, 1970).

In the following example, formal rules and regulations have led to the unintended neglect of the social and psychological needs of clients:

A problem arose because of a hospital's rule that bars children under fourteen from the hospital and its grounds. A forty-three-year-old father of two young sons, ages eight and ten, had been hospitalized two months ago for a severe stroke that left him unable to dress himself, write, and speak, and probably permanently incapacitated for work. He was understandably depressed and additionally saddened because he could not see his children. Having already lost touch with the boys for two months, Mr. Collins feared that his handicap meant the permanent loss of his relationship with them. Both he and his wife feared that Mr. Collins's homecoming in a wheelchair would be a sudden and frightening shock to the boys. In addition, both children were becoming more anxious with gastric upsets and sleeping problems and were crying to see their father. The worker and the Collinses decided to meet together with the ward physician to ask his support in obtaining special permission from the chief of staff for the children to come into the hospital for family sessions.

I think the three of us were surprised by our quick success. Our persuasiveness and the norm of professional reciprocity were perhaps the reasons. For example, Mrs. Collins's emotional appeal was followed by my own logical argument directed to the doctor's professional concern. It made sense to him that a patient fearful about returning home may not be highly motivated to exert every effort to reach his maximum potential. Because the doctor had been questioning the patient's slow progress, he could now see it was in his professional interest to provide an opportunity for Mr. Collins to be with his children. Moreover, I had just finished working on a difficult situation with this same physician and had been able to provide him with important information. I think it was advantageous to Mr. Collins's need that the doctor may have felt obliged to "return" the favor.

Although this example is concerned with advocacy on behalf of a single client, it does illustrate the significance of informal influence derived from the competence and interpersonal skills of the worker and the useful exchange of professional favors. Social workers, having relatively low status in the formal structure of some health organizations, do not always recognize that they may attain considerable influence either in the organization at large or in particular subsystems that operate across disciplines.

When Yale–New Haven Hospital constructed its regional intensive care unit for gravely ill newborn some years ago, the chief social worker for the ob/gyn and perinatal units—on her own initiative—participated in creating a physical and social setting for the unit that would support the coping efforts of parents and of staff. Sleeping facilities were provided on the unit for parents coming from a distance. Policies and procedures were developed permitting parents to care for their infants during visits and to telephone the unit day or night for information about their infants' condition. The social worker succeeded in having the social work office located directly across the corridor from the elevators, thereby making the service immediately visible and easily accessible to parents coming to the unit. She also arranged to have a large glass window placed in the social work office wall that faces into the unit, so that young siblings can watch their parents care for the sick baby.

The worker's successful innovations in the unit can be attributed, with some confidence, to the influence she acquired from her consistent demonstration of competence in face-to-face practice, her organizational skills, and her assertive but nonabrasive participation and leadership on the neonatal team—all observable by the decision-makers in the administrative and medical hierarchies. Furthermore, the Yale–New Haven Hospital social work staff was asked at a later time by hospital administration to help plan and carry out a program to ease the burden and upset on all staff as the hospital moved to a new building. The department completed a set of recommendations emphasizing preparation, participation, and anticipatory guidance on the move for all departments and staffs. The report to administration (Breslin, 1982) concluded:

> The essential principle that should guide any effort to assist staff in coping with the move is to engage all levels of employees in communication having to do with feelings, planning the move, problems encountered, and ways of coping with difficulties encountered prior to and after the move.

In April 1981 an ad hoc committee on the move was formed by administration with the vice president as chair. The principle cited above was adopted as the basic operating principle guiding activities associated with the move. A subcommittee on the social/emotional impact of the move on staffs was formed, with the now chief social worker and the director of religious ministries as cochairs. Representatives from social work, nursing, the planning office, management, engineering, and employee relations formed the core of the subcommittee. The group met regularly, reporting their recommendations to the ad hoc committee. In addition, the chief social worker served on the ad hoc committee, which helped reinforce the social work department's position enunciated in the basic operating principle.

The move took place in May 1982. Staff participation in the year-long process produced interesting approaches. For example:

> One "floor" gave a farewell party to their "floor." They took photographs of staff, patients, and significant areas and made them into a large framed collage, which now hangs in their new location in the new building.

A particularly valuable aspect of the planning process was the continuous open communication with staff on every aspect of construction:

> Each "floor" was involved with the architect and the planning staff in the development and the design of space. Not every one got what she or he wanted, all is not perfect, suggestions were not always carried out, but the opportunities to be involved did exist. The settling down period continued after the move. We're getting to feel comfortable with the "newness," and it is all becoming familiar and "homey." We are now in the process of evaluating spatial areas that don't work too well and making recommendations for change." [Breslin, 1983]

Not only are informal influence and formal power illustrated in this example, but one can assume with good reason that the status of social work in the hospital was further enhanced. Advocacy for organizational change in support of the institution's avowed goals and quality care, *and* directed to administrative concerns, helps ensure the value of social work services in the perception of powerful decision-makers. While the foregoing example demonstrates the validity of this point, it is noteworthy that successful organizational change can sometimes be achieved also by recasting change goals into terms that will be congruent with the formal goals and informal preferences of the critical decision-makers, thereby reducing potential resistance.

Respect for the worker's specialized information and commitment to clients is also a significant source of influence. And influence is a form of social capital needed in a change effort.

For example, when the federal Supplemental Security program (SSI) was introduced in the early 1970s, its complexities were difficult for both clients and practitioners to work with. In some locales serious problems developed as a result of long delays in determining eligibility, delays in checks after some individuals were transferred from public assistance—often without being notified—and some were found ineligible because their disabilities did not meet SSI requirements. Also, many people had trouble securing needed services from homemaker, housing, food, and other programs.

A social worker in a large medical center, deeply concerned about the rights and needs of her clients, set about systematically to secure, master, and codify information about the regulations and administration of the new program and to develop relationships with local employees within it. With the approval and continued active support of the Director of the hospital's Department of Social Work, and in a very short while, she was able to arrange for representatives of SSI and the local Department of Social Services (DSS) to come to the hospital once a week to process the 14-page applications of the patients. Training sessions were held for the social work staff on the intricacies of the program—led by this social worker. Training kits with instructions on filling out the forms were distributed to staff, so that patients' applications could be filled out in advance, and SSI personnel could then merely check and verify the material, etc. The worker also set up a SSI Monitoring Committee in the Department, and forms were distributed to all social work staff for recording emergencies and long-term problems created for patients by the new program. The information was used in advocacy efforts to improve the local administration of SSI and to obtain changes in some regulations. [Garin, 1974]

In effect, this social worker became the "house expert" on SSI, and because its problems affected many patients throughout the large medical center, her prestige increased among all staffs—medicine, nursing, social work, and others. She earned respect and esteem for her ability to gather, master, and disseminate important but complex information and for her skill in influencing two large impersonal organizations (SSI and DSS) to respond to the needs of the hospital's patients (and, indirectly, of all applicants and recipients).

The Change Process*

In a now classic paper William Schwartz (1961) asserted that social workers have a professional obligation to raise private troubles to public issues. By this he meant that advocating on behalf of a single client is desirable and necessary but not sufficient. Most practitioners are comfortable and skilled in advocating at the case level in their clients' individual predicaments involving the organization. They work energetically to secure resources and entitlements, bending a rule here, invoking a favor there, on behalf of a particular individual, family, or group. But the practitioner's further responsibility is to undertake an innovation or an organizational change effort on behalf of all clients suffering from the same service gap or oppressive or merely dysfunctional rule, practice, or behavior. The social worker who helped the Collins family secure permission for the sons to come to the hospital for family sessions did not remain satisfied with having a rule bent for a single client. She moved to advocate change on behalf of all patients experiencing the same service problem:

The Chief of Staff approved a letter written jointly by the ward physician and me, and all the Collinses are now being seen together. At least for a little while each week, Mr. Collins is again a father to his sons, and he is even beginning to look forward to returning home. But what of the other patients in the hospital who continue to have their sense of competence, relatedness, self-directedness, and self-esteem eroded by this rule? I have not forgotten them. My objective is to have the rule changed, not only for Mr. Collins but for all patients who are similarly affected. My immediate goal is to establish a family lounge somewhere in the hospital so that the stress of hospitalization may be reduced for patients having young children and for their families.

Weissman (1973) suggests that many social workers begin their professional careers with the view that rationality, personal commitment, open communication, and adherence to client-centered values provide the impetus for organizations to change. They assume, for example, that organizational change is achieved on the following model: The practitioner suggests a change at a staff meeting; the executive appoints a com-

* This section draws, in part, from Germain and Gitterman (1980) and Germain (forthcoming a).

mittee to study the matter; the committee reports back to staff; staff suggests modifications; a vote of approval is taken; and the change is adopted. Time span: one week. This belief leads to unrealistic attempts to introduce change followed by disillusionment and then by cynicism about "bucking the system."

Because of human nature it is always easier to locate program gaps and service problems in other people's agencies and to advocate on behalf of one's client with the welfare department, the housing authority, the school, or the child welfare agency. It is much harder, however, to do something about service problems in one's own agency, especially a health care organization in which social work is not the host discipline. Beyond human nature, more compelling reasons for hesitancy in one's own organization are job security, self-concept, professionalism, and issues of power.

What, then, is involved in influencing the health care organization to increase its responsiveness to the rights and needs of patients and familes? The answer lies partly in alertness to the negative influence exerted by the organization's operations on clients' experience of stress and coping efforts, partly in the worker's acquisition of new kinds of skills as advocate, and partly in the application of basic social work processes to organizational intervention.

ORGANIZATIONAL ENVIRONMENTS

Saegert (1976) has identified six stress-inducing qualities in *physical* settings. These are useful in examining the health care organization.

1. Environments can be physically threatening, as in the presence of frightening machines, sights, and sounds in ICUs. In neonatal ICUs social work and nursing staffs frequently decorate the unit with stuffed animals, mobiles, and pictures, and apply bright colors as ways to soften the impact of the setting on parents. Innovations in many hospitals now encourage teenage expectant mothers to visit the obstetrical service in advance to correct misconceptions and reduce fears of the unknown.

2. Environments can present overloads of stimuli and information beyond what the patient or family can process. Loud, unpredictable, or prolonged noise; unpleasant sights, sounds, and smells; distressing sights of other patients' medical crises or dying; and having to make decisions in emergency situations or in abrupt discharge without sufficient time and space for deliberation can all tax coping capacities.

3. Environments may not be suitable for particular persons, as when a young, severely physically impaired but otherwise competent individual is confined to a nursing home where most of the patients are elderly senile patients. In a large medical center, abortion clients who may be as far into pregnancy as twenty-four weeks await various screening pro-

cedures and medical examinations in the same area where prenatal and family planning patients are also treated. Lively discussions around conflict-free pregnancies are in sharp contrast with the silent withdrawal of women who are seeking to end their pregnancies. And abortion procedures are performed on the maternity inpatient floor, so that abortion patients and families share waiting room space with postpartum and antepartum patients and their families. The newborn nursery is also on this floor.

4. Physical settings may contribute to stress by conveying certain kinds of messages to those within them. The environment may communicate to the patient and family how little they are valued by the society and larger culture—and even how little the staff who serve and care for them may be valued (for example, nursing home aides must perform some of the most unpleasant tasks in health care at the lowest wages, and with little social respect and little or no gratification).

In some facilities for the elderly residents are assigned to dining tables with inflexible disregard for personal likes and dislikes. In a very large facility the first step in conserving energy was to shut down one of the elevators. This increased the waiting time and led to overcrowding and even occasional accidents in the rush. In a lying-in hospital,

> [t]he 'fathers' room" is adjacent to the recovery room—unattended and suggestive that the father is regarded as the least important person in the process. By its sparseness of furnishing, its physical isolation, and its small size, this room seemed to communicate symbolically the idea that the fathers are unnecessary and functionally peripheral. [Rosengren and DeVault, 1970, p. 446]

5. Some physical settings may be overly demanding because of the amount of energy and coping resources required in transacting with them. This is clear in some institutional settings for the elderly and for the physically handicapped, although for the latter new federal regulations are slowly leading to improvement. It may also be seen in some ERs, where high physical barriers are set up so that waiting families have no access to the process of care for their gravely ill or injured member. In one such setting the social worker was instrumental in physical changes that made it possible for a family member to move through the treatment process with the patient, and every step was explained.

In another example,

> A hospital nursery reports on its physical environment: [W]e had a baby expire from a heart condition who had been with us for 3 months since birth. At no time did we consider the feelings of the parents, although not a day went by that both parents did not come to the nursery to see their baby from the outside window. When the baby died, the mother asked to hold him. This she did, sitting, rocking and crying. She made the statement that this was the first time she had touched it. [Barnett, 1975]

6. Insufficient sensory, cognitive, and social stimuli may characterize some physical settings. The stereotyped environments of some nursing homes offer no variations in colors and textures and no easily accessible clocks and calendars. Some have regulations against bringing one's own treasured objects into what is likely to be the final dwelling place. Other nursing homes make no effort to control pilfering, which has the same effect.

Such physical attributes of health care settings may add to patients' and families' stress and undermine efforts to cope with the stress of illness and disability. Some dysfunctional aspects come about because architects and planners view the physical environment only as a container in which medical events are played out. No attention is paid to the psychosocial experiences people have in the playing out of those events. How physical settings are designed and how space and time are allocated often reflect professional status and power and staff or organizational convenience rather than patients' coping tasks. Social workers, by seizing opportunities to participate in the planning process, can help shape physical environments so they support coping tasks, even though they can never be totally stress-free. More frequently, however, they will be able to introduce innovations or changes to modify existing dysfunctional physical aspects.

With respect to the *social* environment, Howard and Strauss (1975) specify some conditions that are necessary for humanized organizations in health care:

1. Respect for the inherent worth, uniqueness, and holistic self of the individual (and social workers would add respect for cultural differences)
2. Provisions for freedom of action (including options for regimens and life-styles where possible), greater symmetry in staff–patient relationships, and shared information and decision-making to the extent consistent with physical and psychological factors
3. Empathic communication with patients and families and positive regard, as opposed to assuming a feeling stance of neutrality in relationships with those served

These qualities of the social environment in a health care organization are consistent with social work's own value system. Social workers are acutely sensitive to their violation by agency policies, procedures, practices, or staff behaviors. Violations occur when people are treated as things: as objects rather than subjects; as machines or extensions of tubes, respirators, and signaling devices; as guinea pigs for experimentation; as problems instead of whole persons with interrelated or conflicting needs and problems; as lesser people devalued because of culture, age, gender, poverty, sexual orientation, or impairment; or as isolates because of long confinement and hopeless prognoses, especially in the case of geriatric patients. Dehumanizing or "thinging" can be seen in the experience of Mrs. Miller, an eighty-seven-year-old resident in a large geriatric facility:

She is legally blind and from the beginning of her care in the home she was confused and agitated. She presented management problems to the floor staff by shouting, "Help me, I'm blind," when there was no immediate need for particular help, arguing with residents and staff, and trying to get out of bed at night. She had been admitted to a new wing, so the staff was stressed anyway by the fact that all residents were new admissions and staff had not worked together before. To help manage Mrs. Miller, the psychiatrist prescribed 25 mg of thorazine twice a day and 100 mg at night. The staff tied her in her chair to prevent her from walking around, put her to bed right after the evening meal, and avoided relating to her beyond what was essential for her care and feeding. She was left to sit in her room, was not encouraged to participate in activities or to relate on any level with other residents.

A circular feedback system had been established in which Mrs. Miller—confused, depressed, and agitated—becomes more so because she is drugged, restrained, and isolated. The staff can then point to this behavior as requiring continuation of this treatment. Staff needs took precedence over quality patient care, and "thinging" in the management of a needy but very difficult resident increased the behavior it was designed to control.

The ill or disabled are least able to influence their physical settings and social environments. This underscores the importance of health care social workers' alertness to the organization's psychosocial impact and their readiness to consider change efforts when the impact is detrimental. Success in such activities depends, in part, on the acquisition of skills that are different from the helping or therapeutic skills considered in earlier chapters (Brager and Holloway, 1978; Weissman, 1973; Weissman, Epstein, and Savage-Abramovitz, 1984; Patti and Resnick, 1972; Resnick and Patti, 1980; Wax, 1971). However, such helping skills as empathic communication and supportive measures, for example, must often be brought to bear in organizational innovation and change.

SKILLS AND PROCESSES

The success of the change effort also rests on basic social work phases and processes that parallel those involved in working with clients. Phases in the change effort are preinitiation or beginning phase; initiation or ongoing phase; and implementation/institutionalization or ending phase. Parallel processes include problem definition, data gathering, assessment, goal setting, and planning in the pre-initiation phase of preparation, entry, and engagement; action in the initiation phase; and evaluation in the implementation phase.

Preinitiation Phase. Preparation starts with the recognition of a service problem for one or more of one's own clients—patient, family, or group. If it affects only one client, then the problem may lend itself to an individual solution not requiring organizational change. A student social worker in a nursing home, writes:

The only wish of a new resident as she adapts to her new environment is to have the use of her sewing machine. It requires the installation of a grounded plug and the repair of the cord in order to meet hospital standards. Service personnel had not "heard" her repeated requests, and she was feeling discouraged. Together, we attempted to solve the problem. She wrote a note on a work order form and the head nurse agreed to sign it. Still nothing happened. I then retraced the circuitous routes, which can only be described as "buck passing." The person in charge of electrical matters, for example, refused even to talk with me—he had "too many more pressing problems." Eventually I ended up with the director of environmental services for the nursing home. Although it had taken an undue amount of time, we did get the plug installed and the cord fixed, and the resident felt good about her own involvement in achieving her own goal.

The student wonders, appropriately, if staff social workers even have the time for this kind of work that can help make life in a nursing home more bearable.

In many organizational problems one should assume that the problem or the service problem probably affects other patients and families being served by the health organization. The assumption, however, must be validated. Documenting the prevalence of the problem may be accomplished by observations, examination of charts, reports by clients, patient satisfaction studies, and exchanges with other staff about their practice experiences in the area of concern. A log of one's own experiences of patients' similar problems over a specific period can be a useful validating device.

Once the prevalence of the problem has been established, it must be cast into organizational rather than personality terms. Defining a problem as an "arrogant doctor" or a "hostile nurse" is not helpful in developing a solution. It is always conceivable that we have ourselves evoked the arrogance or the hostility. But more than that, changing personality characteristics *per se* is not a feasible solution to a service gap or dysfunctional procedure or organizational behaviors. Experience suggests that defining problems and framing their solutions in organizational terms lead to higher rates of successful innovations and change.

Such a problem definition requires assessment of the statuses and roles of doctor, nurse, social worker, client, and others involved, and of the ways that the organization or a subsystem shapes the perceptions, expectations, and behaviors of the role occupants. Hence assessment must also include an organizational analysis of both the formal and informal structures and the nature of the organization's external environment.

Assessment of a long-standing problem is often aided by considering its latent functions (Merton, 1957). Manifest functions (policies, procedures, structures, programs) sometimes have unplanned and unrecognized consequences that are latent functions. When such consequences are dysfunctional for patients and families they may be serving not the avowed goal of quality patient care but latent goals of organizational growth, power, political influence or staff interests, preferences, or comfort. Examining the history of the service problem and why nothing has been done about it before may produce insights concerning the latent functions being served by its continuing existence. These in turn yield clues about potential resistance to change and where it is likely to appear. It is, of course, important to remember that not all objections to change are resistance. They may be reality-based and important features that have been overlooked by the advocate. It is when opposition is protecting the person from the consequences of change (in this instance, eliminating latent functions), that it is motivated by resistance (Zander, 1978).

Assessment, then, focuses on the meaning the change may have for the various participants, since change comes about by influencing people in their organizational roles. The values, preferences, interests, and ideologies of the decision-makers and of those who will be affected by the change will guide their responses to the proposed change. Components of assessment are usually conceived as prochange and antichange forces. Weighing their relative power and salience can help the practitioner determine if change is feasible—that is, whether the balance between the two groups of forces favors change. Assessment also prepares the way for selecting a change goal or solution to the organizational problem. Possible alternative solutions, possible ways to achieve each, and possible negative consequences must be considered in order to determine which if any is the most feasible solution. When a feasible goal has been selected, then tentative plans for attaining it must be considered. The assessment is basic to the development of measures to support prochange forces and to bypass or neutralize antichange forces throughout the change process.

Zaltman and associates (1973) suggest that [organizational change] may be introduced into five interrelated contexts: in *services* performed as when the social work department in a city hospital center inaugurated a Summer Day Camp Program for regressed elderly patients, many of whom suffered from Alzheimer's disease (J. Lee, 1981); in *processes* such as a change in a nursing home's admission procedures; in the organization's *structure*, such as the introduction of interdisciplinary teams in an agency serving the developmentally disabled; in *people*, such as staff training in team development; and in *policy*, such as a change in visiting regulations to permit children to visit their parents. Social workers may initiate and implement changes in all five contexts.

For example, over a period of five years, units of students placed in different homes for the aged owned and operated by the Metropolitan Toronto Department of Social Services achieved significant organizational changes (Singer and Wells, 1981). They introduced and carried out a new *service* to families in individual, family, and group sessions in institutions where no services to relatives had previously been provided. Concerned about the primitive admissions *process*, the students "developed a preadmissions program, working with applicants and their families to prepare them for the placement, including visits to see the facility and the services available."

The students initiated and implemented a team approach to resident needs that was a *structural* innovation. Previously the charge nurses worked in shifts and switched from floor to floor, so that plans and relationships lacked continuity. The students recommended that one charge nurse be responsible for each floor as a way to strengthen interdisciplinary collaboration. At first the nursing staff resisted the idea, but the following year's students took a different approach, and the nurses agreed to test the proposal. They found it to be a more satisfactory way of operating, and the model was adopted and maintained. *People-focused* change was achieved in the way nurses handled issues of residents' deaths. The subject had been taboo, and staff would not reply to residents' questions about another resident's illness. They saw this secretiveness as protecting the residents from being upset. The students initiated a series of interdisciplinary meetings on understanding and skill in dealing with the subject of death. These had an impact in helping staff to be more open, and the content has become part of ongoing staff training. Through student efforts social work consultation to volunteers became part of administration *policy*, and through a student-initiated program linking community and residents a policy of outreach to the community was developed. Singer and Wells show that the students' successes were the result of sound organizational assessment and the use of many advocacy skills described in the balance of this chapter.

As a consequence of assessment, or even further into the preinitiation stage, it may turn out that none of the alternative goals or solutions is feasible. They may require the approval of too many levels or too many subsystems, they may violate the preferences of too many powerful or influential decision-makers, or they may call for greater resources than the practitioner—or even the organization—can muster. Like innovations, change goals that can be implemented on a limited basis, are reversible, or can be couched in such a way as to reflect present values and practices have a greater chance of being achieved. Without a feasible solution the practitioner is wise to refrain from a change effort.

Still within the preinitiation phase, the next step is *entry*, in which the worker seeks to create organizational receptiveness to change. Brager and Holloway (1978) suggest three methods: practitioner positioning to maximize resources for influencing; inducement and management of tension; and structural positioning. The first was described earlier in terms of the worker's influence gained through professional and personal attributes and through possession of knowledge and expertise pertinent to the service problem, all of which lend legitimacy to the worker's efforts.

Tension among staff is usually necessary if change is to take place. It must be felt strongly enough so that people will experience the proposed solution with relief, perceiving it as a way out of their discomfort (Dalton, 1973). If anxiety about the service gap or problem is absent, the worker may need to generate it by making the problem visible through invoking professional norms and commitments. Professional "guilt" about the problem can be mobilized by pointing to the discrepancy between the organization's or subsystem's avowed goals and the realities of the service, or between professional values and those realities. Where tension is antecedent to the change effort, the worker may have to guide it in the direction of the change goal. Of course, too much tension or stress may immobilize the change effort.

Structural positioning refers to decisions about where the problem and the proposed solution should be presented within the organization (a department? rounds? a floor or service?) and to whom they should be presented (a critical individual? the team? a committee?). Such decisions should take into account the composition of the group to be addressed, especially in terms of likely antichange and prochange forces, and its legitimacy to deal with the identified problem. Occasionally it is useful to consider whether a new ad hoc committee might be a more supportive forum.

The following account of the preinitiation phase is from the case of Mr. and Mrs. Collins. The problem was identified as the rule against children under ten visiting a parent who is hospitalized. The feasible solution selected was the establishment of a family lounge somewhere in this 1,000-bed hospital:

Achieving the goal will not be easy. The antichange forces are many. Space is scarce, and patients waiting to see their doctors in the clinics often overflow into the lobby. When an office in the hospital becomes available, many departments compete for the vacancy. It is likely the Department of Building Management will resist allocation of space to a family lounge. Medical staff and administration may fear that children will transmit disease to patients, thereby interfering with the hospital's treatment goals. The Security Department of the hospital may resist because if children are allowed into the hospital, they may feel their security job will be more difficult. The financial office may resist because with children permitted in the building, insurance rates might be raised for the hospital.

The hospital's structure generates antichange forces. It is highly centralized, and at the top is the Hospital Director. Below him are the Assistant Director, who administers support services (supply, security, finance, building management), and the Physician-in-Chief, who administers professional services (surgery, medicine, nursing, psychology, social work and the rest). The two men have the authority to make independent decisions in their respective areas, but when a decision on policy affecting both areas is required, as in my change goal, it is made by the Director.

The hospital is a highly formalized structure, and the rule against children's visits is defined in no uncertain terms. I believe the Chief of Social Work Service may be a neutral force. She supports the idea, but because she has only recently been appointed to her post she may not want to enter into open disagreement with administration. She is also hoping for approval to take over space vacated by residents who were moved to other quarters and probably will not want to jeopardize that plan.

Supportive forces for the change are strong. The commitment to quality care is present among all staff. If I can make the problem of children's visiting more visible, I believe professional staff will become concerned. My social work colleagues agree that change is needed. When I have spoken informally to them, they have agreed that the present policy is unjust and negates what we know about the importance of the family. We are unable to see a family together even when our professional judgment calls for such an approach. Social work staff have informal influence derived from their competence, with many physicians actively seeking consultation from us on patients' psychosocial needs. I will try to capitalize on that. Through informal contacts I have discovered that several of the Hospital Director's staff, who are in positions of authority and influence, are likely to favor the change effort. Among them is the Chief of Medicine, who is respected by the Physician-in-Chief. Many nurses have been concerned about low patient morale, and so too have the hospital clergy, so I believe they will support the change effort. And, finally, the Assistant Director of Social Work Service, who was recently elected chair of the Utilization Review Committee, has been supportive in my informal conversations with her about the extent of the problem.

I talked with the Chief of Pathology. He feels allowing children into the hospital presents no greater danger to either child or parent than is presented by visiting adults or by staff coming and going. In his opinion the present regulation is a vestige of the polio scare some decades back, when children under fourteen were considered most susceptible and hence a potential source of infection to patients.

Now that the polio danger no longer exists, he believes the regulation can be removed. When I mentioned the need for a family lounge, he indicated his willingness to support such a proposal.

I talked with several psychologists and interested them in the problem, and the possible solution of a lounge seemed achievable to them. One of them agreed to approach the Chief of Psychiatry, with whom he is close, and to enlist his interest and support.

I met with the Chief of Volunteer Services, who works with the several voluntary organizations associated with the hospital. She is sure they will be happy to provide volunteers to serve as patient escorts. In this way patients having medical approval can be brought to the lounge to visit with their children. I am also securing data from Spring Valley Hospital (part of our regional system) concerning their experience with allowing children's visiting.

With the approval of our department's director, I secured the agreement of all social workers to collect needed data: the number of patients on their services—of those who do not go home on weekend passes—with children and grandchildren whom they are unable to see because of the regulation.

The worker also had a fallback solution if space turned out to be an insurmountable barrier. If needed, she would suggest that one of the clinics, which empty by 4:30 week-days and are free all weekend, can be used temporarily as a family lounge. The rationale for the goal is not entirely clear, but it may have been that the worker felt a change in the formal regulation itself was less likely to be achieved than the more modest and reversible goal of a family visiting area. Such a goal can also be viewed as the first step in a process of incremental change designed to remove or modify the regulation. She continues:

Because there is now rather extensive recognition of the problem and concern about it across services and disciplines, and the feasibility of the solution seems clear, I will go forward with initiating the change effort. I believe the proforces can be strengthened and anticipated resistance can be neutralized.

Initiation Phase. When the tasks of the preinitiation phase are competed, the practitioner must plan and carry out the activities needed to bring about the change or innovation. The assessment will have revealed who must be influenced and how this might be done. One of the decisions to be made is whether the worker is the best person to make the change effort. If she lacks sufficient power, prestige, and legitimacy, she may not be able to gain the support of those not actively seeking the change or to disarm the resistance of those actively opposing it. With respect to the family lounge:

Initiating the change can best be carried out by the Assistant Director of Social Work Service. The Utilization Review Committee is said to be the most powerful committee now functioning in the hospital. Its members are the chiefs of all medical and surgical services and of social work, nursing, and psychology. So my Assistant Director occupies a powerful status as chair. She has agreed to place the problem of children's visits on the agenda for consideration of a committee recommendation to the Hospital Director. Emphasis will be placed on the provision of quality patient care, because this is the Hospital Director's formally stated goal for the committee. Lowered patient morale, inability of spouses to visit because of lack of supervision for their children, and the barrier to family unit counseling on the stress of illness or disability will all be in the foreground of the presentation. The data from Spring Valley Hospital and from the social work staff will also be used.

A range of measures for influencing is available. Selection is based on assessment and the principle of parsimony. In general, this means beginning with the measure that requires the least amount of effort and resources and proceeding toward less parsimonious ones as needed. *Collaborative* measures are used when it is likely the decision-makers will agree with the goal. They include joint exploration and problem-solving, program demonstration, information sharing, consideration of alternatives, and friendly persuasion. Opportunities for the use of collaborative approaches are probably more plentiful than practitioners may realize, particularly as they become more adept in defining problems and proposed solutions in ways that are congruent with organizational needs and concerns as well as with patients' needs.*

For example, on a cardiology floor the social worker was interested in providing group services for cardiac patients to help more patients deal with the stress of their hospitalization and the implications of their illness. She received the enthusiastic approval of the chief of cardiology and met with the nursing service to explain the plan, what to expect, what the objectives are, and the like. The nursing supervisor and charge nurse welcomed the plan, and the staff nurses followed suit as their ideas and feedback were encouraged. The only barrier seemed to be one identified by the chief of service. He stated that the private physicians might object to their patients' inclusion in the groups. In response to the social worker's request he agreed to introduce the proposed innovation at a meeting of the medical staff.

---

*Brager and Holloway (1978) describe two additional approaches, the campaign and contest modes of intervention. *Campaign* measures include "hard" persuasion, political maneuvering, bargaining and negotiation, and mild coercion. Social work experience with this more adversarial approach in health care organizations as host settings is sketchy, hence the approach is beyond the scope of this chapter. Interested readers are referred to pages 132–33 of the authors' work. *Contest* measures are still more coercive and, as the authors point out, are rarely used in efforts to change one's own organization (pp. 133–34).

The following is excerpted from the minutes:

Dr. Selkirk introduced the subject of patient groups on the cardiology service as a demonstration project using a treatment method that had been tried and found helpful in other hospitals. It was being presented today for the consideration of the private physicians since their patients would be involved. Two points at which cardiac patients experience anxiety are when they are transferred from the CCU to ongoing care and when they are ready for discharge home. Groups can be helpful to the patients in dealing with these fears and with the implications of their illness. Group members, with the help of the social worker, can aid one another in adaptation to the illness and improve their readiness to resume their usual social roles.

Many questions were raised by the private physicians present and responded to by the social worker with reinforcing comments by Dr. Selkirk. Discussion was encouraged among the group, and then Dr. Selkirk brought the meeting to a close.

Since there were no strong objections, it was agreed by all present that the private physicians consented to the start of a cardiac group on the floor.

Implementation and Institutionalization Phase. Once the proposed change has been adopted, the change is then implemented. Resistances previously handled may emerge again, or objections not previously raised may be raised now. Even those who supported the change goal may now find that its effects on them are unwelcome, or by now their commitment may have worn thin. The tasks of implementing include continued attention to these phenomena, allaying stress, providing support and information, and sustaining motivation. If obstacles arise or ''bugs'' appear in the process, they too must be handled.

In health care settings unanticipated obstacles may appear because innovations in such complex organizations so often involve coordination or collaboration across disciplines. On the coronary service, for example, the successful implementation of the group program will depend on several factors. One is how well the social worker will coordinate meeting times with periods when patients are free from diagnostic or therapeutic procedures and when the designated room for the sessions is not in use. Another factor is how wholeheartedly the nurses will support the patients' attendance and how much supportive ''permission'' the attending physicians will actually give to their patients to participate in the group. If someone other than the social work innovator were to be the group leader, an additional factor would be that leader's continued interest and willingness to take on the responsibility, what allowances had been made in his work load, and so on.

In a meeting with the chief of service, the chief of medical residents, the nursing supervisor, and the charge nurse, the social worker proposed that an open-ended group be started at once with all wheelchair and ambulatory myocardial infarct patients, perhaps adding congestive heart failure patients later. She also suggested that she would screen out any patients who might be too disturbed to participate in the group. The others concurred, and agreement was reached that the group would meet two days a week for an hour and a half in the early afternoon, as the nurses felt this would minimize conflict with scheduled tests, and other procedures. The nursing supervisor wondered about patients who refused to attend, and the worker suggested they be encouraged to attend on the grounds that this is a regular program for cardiac patients. She suggested ways for nurses to describe the group to patients if they should ask.

Anticipating later concerns of the staff nurses, the social worker said that sometimes upsetting material might be discussed in the group and that the patients might look upset or even cry. She would handle this whenever it did happen, would let the charge nurse know about it immediately, and would also enter a note in the patient's chart. She expressed her interest in meeting with all the nurses and aides to orient them to the group. The nursing supervisor then asked her to meet with all three shifts. She readily agreed, and together they planned the content and schedule for the three meetings with the nurses. And so the group was begun, all the more smoothly for the immediate attention given to anticipated difficulties and continuing attention to any that arose as the weeks went on.

After about six months the program was expanded by providing a group service to the spouses of all coronary patients. An interdisciplinary mini task force was formed to consider the comprehensive care of all cardiac patients on the service, including the assignment of a social worker to the CCU and its waiting room for relatives and the inclusion of congestive heart failure patients in the group program. It was clear that the change was no longer considered a change but was now perceived as "the way things are on the service," and the worker knew the change had been institutionalized.

Before that point had been reached, however, the change was continually evaluated to make sure it was meeting its goal and, if any negative outcomes appeared, what needed to be done about them. Accordingly, ongoing assessment of the group experience was made, including common themes, the nature of members' participation, frequent questions, and the nature of client feedback on the group programs. Periodic written reports were sent to all staff and private physicians. These served also to sustain general commitment to the program so that what had originally been proposed as a reversible demonstration became standardized practice.

The skills of the innovator and advocate roles are summarized in Table 9–1.

ISSUES

Throughout the processes of innovation or organizational change the practitioner must be aware of her or his own motives, values, beliefs, and attitudes toward the organization. This helps ensure one's taking action based on objective assessment of the needs of those served and of the organization's functioning, and not on the basis of personal issues regarding authority, turf, anger at administration or colleagues, and the like. Effort to maintain self-awareness also permits the practitioner to "hear" the content of objections to the change voiced by those opposing it. Sometimes such content points to important potential negative consequences of the change that might not otherwise be considered.

TABLE 9-1.   The Skills of the Innovator and Advocate Roles in Filling Service Gaps and Increasing the Responsiveness of the Organization to the Coping Tasks of Clients

SOCIAL WORKER'S PRACTICE TASK	SOCIAL WORK ROLE	SOCIAL WORK SKILLS
Fill service gaps; develop new services in response to new or newly recognized needs and rights	Innovator	Engaging the participation of staff (and sometimes clients) in assessing their shared environment with respect to the needs and interests of clients (and sometimes staff needs); assessing feasibility of an innovative solution to a service gap or an unfilled need; assessing need for and availability of needed resources; planning collaboratively for the new program, service, procedure, or physical arrangements; providing support and encouragement to the participants in the process
Influence the organization, where needed, to be more responsive to the needs, coping tasks, and cultural patterns of those it serves	Advocate	Documenting the service problem; organizational analysis; developing a feasible solution; garnering influence; developing alliances; skills in joint problem-solving, collaborative program demonstration, persuasion, bargaining, and negotiation, observing the principle of parsimony

Furthermore, change for change's sake is not the objective of innovation or planned change; not all desired change is necessarily desirable. Change in harmful or dysfunctional policies and procedures and innovations to fill service gaps are the objectives. Such change goals raise the question of values. The practitioner proposing change is responding to a personal and professional idea of desirable change. The fact the idea is based on personal and professional values and preferences lends further support to the need for self-awareness—as much in planned change as in face-to-face practice with clients. Professional values and ethics must pervade the process. Workers must hold themselves accountable for negative consequences of change or innovation. "The only risks that are permissable are risks to themselves, or the risks that clients and colleagues understand and have agreed to share together" (Brager and Holloway, 1978, p. 28).

Thus a major issue for the social worker engaged in a change effort is what, if any, should be the role of clients in the process, depending on the nature and extent of illness or disability. Potential benefits of client participation in successful change efforts are enhanced competence, elevated self-esteem, increased relatedness to others, and accretions to the sense of self-directedness. Potential disadvantages for clients participating in a failed change effort lie in the negative impact on the same four attributes. But in addition, for many clients—especially those in long-term care, the severely handicapped, and the aged—the risk of retaliation may be present. In nursing homes and geriatric facilities, for example, residents often hesitate to bring complaints and requests for changes to staff or administration out of realistic or unrealistic fears of making things even worse. Social workers who have helped form resident councils or who have led patient groups know there are professional means for reducing this risk and engaging the members in productive action to improve the shared environment.

Still, risk is always present, and where clients are invited to participate it is essential that full particulars of what is involved, the likelihood of success or failure, and the possible positive and negative consequences be completely explained. Clients will then be able to make a fully informed decision about participating or not.

Participation can be indirect or direct. An example of indirect participation involves the parents of patients on an inpatient pediatric oncology service who were invited to meet one evening a month with the social worker and a nurse. After several meetings, the parents voiced their concerns about aspects of patient care. These ranged from nutrition (menus and food inappropriate for children, snacks not available on the floor); the absence of activities for the children in the evening and on weekends; and lack of Sunday papers for older children to problems with the billing system and a request for a physician to talk with them about the state of the art in cancer treatment.

A physician came to the next meeting and discussed developments in cancer research and treatment and answered parents' questions. Included in the letter reminding parents of the next meeting was a full report on the status of their concerns and requests expressed two months earlier. Some new solutions were reported as now in place (for example, changes in the dietary program and availability of Sunday papers). Progress on others was described, including having volunteers available to continue the Child Life Program on the weekends and evenings. Names of individuals to contact in person or by telephone about billing questions and other administrative procedures were included, along with their locations and extensions.

What is striking about this example is the accountability to clients shown by the social worker and nurse. A short time later they also developed a brochure containing this and much other information of interest to parents. Included were the names, locations, and telephone extensions of *all* staff members with a brief description of their function and role on the unit. The draft was approved (and added to) by parents as well as by staff. These various steps not only helped raise the morale of parents as they confronted the life-threatening illness of their children but built the sense of competence as the parents together indirectly effected changes in their children's environment.

An example of direct participation in a change process by another group of parents is found in an outpatient clinic for children with developmental disabilities. The clinic provided stimulation programs and diagnostic, referral, and medical services to the children, and individual and group counseling services to the parents. It was operating at a substantial financial deficit and was placed on notice of closing by the hospital director.

The small staff mobilized itself around the problem of saving the clinic and the goal of changing the decision to close it. Acting as a unit, the clinic team (pediatrician, social worker, public health nurse, speech therapist, and developmental worker) made a careful assessment of pro-change and antichange forces. From this strategies were designed and then divided among the team members. Proposals for new policies and procedures were developed to strengthen existing services, fill service gaps, and expand the client population to include youths up to age twenty-one in order to increase revenues. Two grant applications were submitted, one to the city and one to a federal agency. Flyers were sent to area agencies describing the clinic's services and inviting referrals. These initial steps won a modest but useful extension of time to establish the viability of the clinic.

What is noteworthy in this example is that the assessment had also revealed that parents of the children being served were a powerful pro-change force. The social worker and two students who provided group services to the parents immediately assumed the task of involving interested parents in the effort to reverse the decision if it was therapeutically possible and appropriate. They planned to convey to the parents that the clinic had been put on notice of closing but that staff was attempting to change that decision. If their efforts failed, arrangements would be made to locate other services for the children.

This was grievous news to the parents, evoking first a denial that such a step could ever be taken, followed by considerable anger, despair, and feelings of abandonment and helplessness. The workers accepted these feelings, and over the next two sessions the mothers moved beyond the initial responses to questions about what could be done. Together they decided to write letters to the board of trustees and to circulate petitions to all the past and present clinic parents. The workers helped them see that they needn't limit their efforts to clinic parents alone, and eventually four thousand cards were sent out to community agencies, organized groups, local politicians, and individuals. The mothers became effective in making their need for the clinic known throughout the community, and many people brought pressure on the hospital to retain the clinic. Their efforts formed a human interest story that was picked up by community media in a way that led to greater community awareness of the developmentally disabled child and his family and the value of the clinic to the community, which encouraged more people to make use of its services.

The clinic survived. One unplanned but positive consequence was the formation of a parents' council in the clinic, which helped in the ongoing development of services, including a community outreach program.

Summary

This chapter has presented the social work concepts, principles, values, and ethics involved in introducing an innovation or a planned change into a health care organization. Such activity is regarded as part of the practitioner's responsibility to all whom the organization serves as a significant way to protect patients and families from added stress and to increase the responsiveness of the organization to their needs. The presentation of organizational change was limited to some of the interventions appropriate to a collaborative approach in which it is assumed that goal consensus exists or that goals can be reframed in terms that will bypass or disarm resistance anticipated from a critical decision-maker.

The interventions are equally applicable where organizational structures, policies, procedures, or behaviors interfere with responsive, accountable social work practice or create undue stress for social work staff. In any health care setting social work staff seek to create a service environment in which patients' and families' competence, self-esteem, relatedness, and self-directedness are preserved and enhanced to the greatest degree possible. That is viewed as the best way to support the patients' and families' efforts to cope with the stressful psychological and social consequences of illness, disability, and loss. The social work staff is more likely to succeed in creating such a *service* environment if in turn the organization or the social work department provides a *work* environment that nurtures professional competence; professional identity and pride in being a social worker; professional relatedness to clients, colleagues, and collaborators; and professional autonomy or self-directedness for the social work function. It is not unreasonable to assume that the nature of the work environment will influence the kind of service environment that social work staff will be able to create for their clients.

Where the work environment stifles the professional development of the social work staff, the concepts and principles set forth in this chapter can be brought to bear on solving that problem through innovation or change. The preinitiation, initiation, implementation/institutional phases, and the processes of problem definition, organizational assessment of prochange and antichange forces, goal selection, planning, action, and evaluation all apply to the work environment. When successful, the process of change is very likely to have a beneficial effect on the service environment as well.

Epilogue

Flourishing in an Uncertain Future

AN AUTHOR, according to Winston Churchill, never really finishes a book; she simply stops writing. That moment has come, except for a look at the opportunities and challenges that lie ahead for social work in health care practice.

Opportunities for Clinical Services

Social work is struggling to fulfill its traditional commitments while shaping new practices, services, and programs to meet new needs and social conditions in a world of accelerating social change. An expectable task for any profession, it is a particularly demanding one for social work as it confronts constraining and often hostile political and economic forces. Nevertheless, the social work literature in health care abounds with examples of innovative programs introduced by social workers in the past several years and reports of social work participation in new programs ushered in by advances in medical technology. In addition to those illustrated in this volume, chronic pain clinics now have social workers as essential members of the health care team (Roy, 1981, 1982; Golden and Steiner, 1981), and social workers are involved in stress management approaches used with seriously ill patients (Graham, Howkins, and Blau, 1983). Social workers are moving into dental and craniofacial anomalies clinics as consultants and teachers of psychosocial-cultural content to dental students and hygienists and as service providers to patients. The assumption is that dental patients often suffer problems in living that interfere with their use of dental care just as medical patients do, and that

257

dental students have to learn how to use social services and community resources when in private practice just as medical students do.

The need for health and social services for the elderly is increasing as the population continues to age, including long-term institutional care, community care, hospice services, and home health care (Kirschner and Rosengarten, 1982; Kirschner, 1979). Social workers are important members of the team in all these programs.

New objectives for independent living for the handicapped and chronically ill require more social services, inasmuch as the management of psychosocial needs often predominates over medical management, at least at certain stages of the illness. These populations will probably grow proportionately as acute illness comes more and more under control, and they may grow absolutely as more infants born with genetic disorders, congenital defects, and birth injuries survive. This means an increase in perinatal services and a growing need for genetic counseling in which social workers can play significant roles (Schild and Black, forthcoming).

The rise in teenage pregnancy increases the need for special services to mothers and infants at social and medical risk as well as to mothers of any age deemed at risk of child abuse. Both health and social services are required. One-stop health and social services to adolescents, including programs for both male and female teens, oriented to the prevention of unwanted pregnancies, is a promising area of health care development for social work.

The presence of many refugee populations, with their special health needs yet with limited access to health care because of language and cultural barriers, requires innovative health care arrangements in which social workers will be an important part of the service—especially professionally trained compatriot social workers.

Services to the Health Organization

A program development that is geared not only to patient need but to the wellbeing of the health organization is a critical task for social work in the immediate future (Rosenberg and Weissman, 1981, p. 15). Such services and programs, of which discharge planning is the exemplar, will help ensure the viability of social work in the health care organization. Already, some social work departments are providing employee counseling services geared to substance abuse, preretirement counseling, planning for the care of elderly parents, and group services to the institution's women employees who return to work after maternity leave, to help with the difficult transition from worker to worker–mother (Lowe and Walther, 1981).

Staff stress (burn-out) extracts emotional and physical costs from staff. But it also increases personnel costs of absenteeism, high turnover, and poor service to clients. Social workers can serve as facilitators of staff groups in difficult settings such as ICUs, dialysis and transplant units, burn units, pediatric oncology, and so on. Such groups provide peer support in dealing with work issues and have an educational focus on how to manage or prevent work-related stress. They serve the goal of quality patient care as well as staff needs and organizational needs.

The social work department of a children's hospital developed a seminar program for teachers and school nurses involved with school children who return to school after hospitalization for cancer (Ross and Scarvalone, 1982). The children's return to school was facilitated, and the teachers were helped to understand the children's special needs as well as needs they share with all children. Such a service to a school system, which can cover other chronic illness, benefits the patients and the social work department. But it also enhances the organization's image in the community.

Social workers' cross-cultural knowledge and experience are useful to hospital administration in matters involving special populations or general community expectations and perceptions. For example, a large private voluntary hospital purchased slum housing surrounding the hospital in order to put up new apartments for staff. Understandably this outraged the poor residents about to be displaced, most of whom were Hispanics, and evoked a public protest from the Hispanic community. The hospital's social work department offered its services to the administration and board of trustees to mediate in the critical situation that ensued. From that experience the hospital came to recognize its social work department as a resource in community affairs and is very likely to value its ongoing participation in hospital–community relations.

Service to the Community

Community work is both an opportunity for service and a demand to be met by the health care social worker. A detailed analysis of such work is beyond the scope of this book, but in general the tasks, roles, and skills described in Chapters 5 through 9 are applicable to work with community groups in helping them identify their health needs, utilize resources, plan for filling service gaps, and advocate at organizational and political levels in matters of health promotion and illness prevention (Germain, forthcoming b).

The health care social worker may serve as resource person to citizen groups in the village, town, county, or state who are working on problems of teenage pregnancy, child abuse and family violence, alcoholism and drug abuse, or services to the elderly or to mothers and infants, or on problems of transportation, housing, access to quality health care, and the like. He may use the local media to increase public awareness of health care needs, social needs, and means for meeting them. He may work with professionals in his own health setting and in other community services to identify gaps in services that bear on health and on related social needs and to plan for program development and funding sources with community residents, self-help groups, and others.

For example, a social worker in private practice became chairperson of the family service division of a newly organized local chapter of the Committee to Combat Huntington's Disease (E. Miller, 1976). She and a staff of volunteers began with a case load of twenty-five families who had contacted the national organization requesting services. At the same time they publicized the agency in the newspaper, radio, and TV; contacted neurologists to encourage referrals; and distributed brochures. Eighty-five more families were added to the case load. Training was provided to the volunteers, and they offered referral services (legal, medical, social), counseling, and social outings. Two years later, influenced by the chapter's activities and pressure, a local hospital developed a clinic program for families of Huntington's Disease patients, including medical, social work, and psychological services. The chapter continued its referral function.

In another example, two social workers, in an agency serving Hispanic clients, were concerned about the needs of Puerto Rican deaf children and their parents. One worker was Puerto Rican and the other Anglo and Spanish-speaking. Both had been trained in work with the Latino deaf and knew the problems were severe with no specialized services available. The children were located through the school system, as the first group of deaf pupils admitted to the system after the passage of P.L. 94–142 (implemented in 1978). The children were learning English sign and lip reading,but most parents were monolingual Spanish and were unable to communicate with their children,so the children were isolated from their own families and from their school peers.

Each of the parents (all mothers) were contacted and invited to a group meeting. The mothers were relieved to know there were others like themselves, facing similar worries and concerns about their children. They decided to meet regularly as a group. With the help and guidance of the social workers, the backing of the agency, and the emotional and social support of their own mutual aid system, the group gradually moved into an action orientation. They advocated with the school system and obtained bilingual, bicultural education for their children and work-study programs for the older ones, and with the health care system for achieving better coordination of services.

Building on the profession's knowledge, experience, and skill in family life education should ease social workers' movement into community health promotion and illness prevention. Additional skills will be required to help community groups to identify their needs and interests, participate in program planning, and even to provide services. Epidemiological skills will be needed for identifying individuals and groups in at-risk situations. In planning programs, however, value conflicts and issues of paternalism must be given careful attention. Health care social workers have important and distinctive knowledge of a preventive and health promoting nature that they can and should impart to the public and that can also be used to educate the public about the health care needs of neglected groups in our society. But such activity will require the acquisition of skills in using radio, TV, and various forms of printed news organs (Brawley and Martinez-Brawley, 1982).

Politically Oriented Activity

Most at-risk situations reflect poor social policy, service gaps, and the oppression of powerless groups. This means that health care social workers face the demand to move forward into legislative advocacy and other forms of politically oriented activity on behalf of those whom they serve and in support of social work services. True prevention and promotion of wellness demands that social workers, in concert with other disciplines and citizen groups, work to reduce the technological pollution of physical environments that affect the health of all people in our society; the social pollutions of poor housing, poor education, and poor health care in urban and rural life; and the cultural pollutions of injustice on the basis of race and ethnicity, gender, age, sexual orientation, and species.

Many social workers in health care are already involved in work with legislative bodies and political decision-makers at local, state, and federal levels. Successful efforts require special knowledge and skills, including coalition-building, media skills, lobbying skills, and testifying skills (Mahaffey and Hanks, 1982). The health care issues are many: quality, equity, and access to health care as well as the social issues directly affecting health as described above.

For example, until March 18, 1980, Wyoming was the only state to lack the Special Supplemental Nutrition Program for Women, Infants, and Children (WIC). On that date Wyoming's governor signed a state budget bill that included a provision for the WIC program. This followed two years of steady political activity by a coalition of concerned organizations, chaired by the president of the state's NASW chapter (*NASW News*, 1980). A petition drive, intensive lobbying, persistence in the face of many setbacks, and arousing public opinion through the media—helped by a statement by the governor that WIC causes ''heart problems of fat babies''—led to the successful outcome.

In Boston, the director of social work and the administrator of Massachusetts General Hospital were concerned about the needs of elderly persons in the hospital who were unwilling to consider nursing home placement yet unable to maintain themselves in the community even with home health care. So they developed a novel "extended-family" care program, borrowed from child welfare and psychiatric settings. Massachusetts Medicaid regulations accept such programs. But a bill was needed in the state legislature so that the State Department of Public Welfare could institute a pilot program. The two persons involved, together with representatives from other areas of the hospital, worked closely with legislators, explaining, persuading, influencing, and pressing to make sure the bill was passed and signed. Now five such programs exist in the state, administered by a home health agency, a rehabilitation facility, and a family agency. The programs are cost-effective, and the elderly participants enjoy an improved quality of life (*Practice Digest*, 1981).

In a rural Colorado town several residents formed a nonprofit community-based planning agency for social and health services. With a board of twenty volunteers chaired by a social worker, they rallied social, political, and economic interests in support of needed policies and programs at the town and county levels. These included the construction of a nursing facility, a publicly operated ambulance service, two vans to transport the elderly and handicapped, and the addition of a home health aide to the health department. Political activity included speaking to community groups, the City Council, and the hospital's board; lobbying with the County Commission (three elected members); arranging public forums; running articles in the local newspaper; and bringing in state officials to discuss funding availability and procedures (*Practice Digest*, 1979).

Research Opportunities

Successful political activity depends in part on careful research into the issues, including demographic statistics, evidence of need, impact of programs elsewhere, and so on. In addition, however, future research must include further work on screening procedures. Expansion of this effort in many institutional and ambulatory settings is needed if social work is to achieve desired professional autonomy and provide services to high-risk patients early enough to be effective. Both aims ultimately will serve organizational as well as patient and departmental needs. Testing the effectiveness, costs, and efficiency of social work services is a continuing demand. It is accomplished through more client satisfaction studies; more sophisticated designs (Mullen, 1983); cost-benefit studies

(Nason and Delbanco, 1976); and measurement of productivity (Coulton and Butler, 1981).

Another opportunity in research lies in the area of basic research. Already, for example, Coulton (1979) has studied the person–environment fit among patients in a chronic care facility; Wetzel (1980) has applied her research model of person–environment fit and depression (Wetzel, 1978) to the study of depression among nursing home residents; and Ewalt and Honeyfield (1981) studied VA domiciliary residents' preferences for remaining in the institution or returning to the community. Many of their findings clarified the nature of person–environment fit for that group, but one unexpected finding in particular has implications for policy and programming in all health care institutional settings. Of those preferring to remain in the domiciliary, one-third expressed a wish for opportunities to be of service to others.

Lister (1980) and Mullany and her colleagues (1974) studied role expectations of social workers and other health professionals with findings that bear on collaborative and team practice and service gaps, and that underscore the need for clarity and specificity in describing social work functions. Since informal support systems serve as buffers against stress and help strengthen coping, they form another important area of social work research in health care (Patterson, et al., 1972; Patterson, Brennan, and Memmott, 1983; Pancoast and Chapman, 1980; Farquharson, 1978). In addition, Coulton (1980) has identified other areas of needed basic research in social work and health care.

Finally, practitioners must make sure their practice is informed by the latest research findings. This task, and those related to acquisition of new knowledge and skills needed for moving into new areas of service, may be accomplished through professional reading and participation in staff seminars, institutes, and continuing education programs. All will help support professional competence, esteem, relatedness, and autonomy in a future that is about to begin.

Glossary of Medical Terms Used in the Text*

Aneurysm: A sac or bubble formed by the dilatation (stretching beyond normal dimensions) of the wall of an artery, a vein, or the heart.

Angina pectoris: A paroxysmal chest pain, with a feeling of suffocation and impending death, due, most often, to anoxia (oxygen deficiency) of the myocardium (middle muscular layer of the heart wall) and precipitated by effort or excitement.

Aphasia: Defect or loss of the power of expression by speech, writing, or signs, or of comprehending spoken or written language, due to injury or disease of the brain centers.

Asbestosis: A form of lung disease caused by inhaling fibers of asbestos and marked by interstitial fibrosis (fibrous degeneration) of the lung, varying in extent from minor involvement of the basal areas to extensive scarring; associated with bronchogenic carcinoma.

Atherosclerotic cardiovascular disease: An extremely common form of arteriosclerosis in which deposits are formed within the heart and blood vessels. Arteriosclerosis is a group of diseases characterized by thickening and loss of elasticity of arterial walls.

Alzheimer's disease: A form of senile dementia, the cause of which is unknown. On autopsy, the brains of Alzheimer's disease patients are characterized by clumped and distorted fibers in the nerve cells. Patients gradually become forgetful and then confused and irritable. They may wander at night, become incontinent, lose the ability to speak, and require total care. The disease usually occurs in persons over sixty-five but can occur in the forties and fifties.

Cerebral Palsy: A persisting qualitative motor disorder appearing before the

---

*Most definitions are taken from or adapted from *Dorland's Illustrated Medical Dictionary*, 26th edition (Philadelphia: W. B. Saunders, 1981). Used with permission.

age of three years, due to a nonprogressive damage to the brain. The damage may be caused by injury during birth, hemorrhage, lack of oxygen before birth, meningitis, viral infection, or faulty development. Condition is characterized by defects in sensory perception (balance), muscular incoordination, speech disturbances, and involuntary writhing movements; in some persons intelligence may be impaired.

Cleft lip, cleft palate: A cleft is a fissure or elongated opening, especially one occurring in the embryo or derived from a failure of parts to fuse during embryonic development. Facial clefts are clefts between the embryonic processes that normally unite to form the face. Failure of such union, depending on its site, causes such developmental defects as cleft lip, cleft palate, and so on.

Colitis: Inflammation of the colon (the large intestine).

Congestive heart failure: Clinical syndrome due to heart disease and characterized by breathlessness and abnormal sodium and water retention, resulting in edema. The congestion may occur in the lungs, in the peripheral circulation, or in both, depending on whether the heart failure is right-sided, left-sided, or general.

Coronary thrombosis: Development of an obstructive thrombus in a coronary artery, often causing sudden death or a myocardial infarction. A thrombus is an aggregation of blood factors, frequently causing obstruction in a blood vessel at the point of its formation.

Cystic fibrosis: A genetic disorder that appears usually in early childhood. It is marked by deficiency of pancreatic enzymes, respiratory symptoms, and excessive loss of chlorides in the sweat. Because of the production of thick, viscid mucous by the bronchi, cystic fibrosis patients are highly susceptible to pneumonia.

Dalmane: The trade name of a hypnotic drug.

Degenerative joint disease: Osteoarthritis; rheumatism in which the joints are inflamed.

Developmental disability: A substantial handicap having its onset before the age of eighteen years and of indefinite duration, and attributable to mental retardation, autism (when found to be closely related to and requiring treatments similar to that of mental retardation), cerebral palsy, epilepsy, or other neuropathy.

Diabetes mellitus: A metabolic disorder in which the ability to oxidize carbohydrates is more or less completely lost, usually due to faulty pancreatic activity and consequent disturbance of normal insulin mechanism. This produces excessive sugar in the blood and urine, excessive excretion of urine, giving symptoms of thirst, hunger, emaciation, and weakness. Imperfect combustion of fats with resulting acidosis can lead to shortness of breath, ketonuria, and finally coma. It is frequently associated with progressive disease of the small vessels, particularly affecting the eye (diabetic retinopathy) and kidney, and atherosclerosis.

Diabetic Ketoacidosis: Abnormal increase of ketone bodies (acetoacetic acid, acetone, beta-hydroxybutyric acid), in the blood and urine.

Dysmorphology: A branch of biology that deals with the abnormalities in form and structure of organisms, for example, congenital malformations in a particular individual, an organ, or a part.

Emphysema: A condition of the lung characterized by increase beyond normal in the size of air spaces distal to the terminal bronchioles (minute thin-walled branches of a bronchial tube), either from dilatation (stretching) of the alveoli (air cells of the lungs) or from destruction of their walls.

Enteritis: Inflammation of the intestine, applied chiefly to inflammation of the small intestine.

Episiotomy: Surgical incision into the perineum and vagina for obstetrical purposes.

Esophagitis: Inflammation of the esophagus.

Hematology: The study of the blood and blood-forming organs.

Hiatus hernia: Protrusion of any structure through the esophageal hiatus (gap) of the diaphragm.

Huntington's disease, Huntington's chorea: A rare genetic disorder characterized by chronic progressive chorea (ceaseless occurrence of rapid, highly complex, jerky, involuntary movements) and mental deterioration terminating in dementia. The age of onset is variable but usually occurs in the fourth decade of life. Death usually follows within fifteen years.

Insulin: A fuel-regulating hormone formed in the pancreas and secreted into the blood in response to a rise in concentration of glucose in the blood and also to a rise in amino acid concentration. Essential for the metabolism of carbohydrates, as a manufactured solution it is used in the treatment of diabetes mellitus.

Intravenous hyperalimentation: The intravenous administration of the total nutrient requirements of the patient with gastrointestinal dysfunction.

Juvenile-onset diabetes: Severe diabetes mellitis, usually having an abrupt onset before the age of twenty-five and tending to be difficult to control and unstable ("brittle"); plasma insulin is often deficient and ketoacidosis occurs frequently; oral hypoglycemics and diet are almost never effective, daily injections of insulin being required in almost all patients.

Leukemia: A progressive, malignant disease of the blood-forming organs, characterized by distorted proliferation and development of white blood cells (corpuscles) and their precursors in the blood and bone marrow.

Meningitis: Inflammation of the meninges (the three membranes that envelop the brain and spinal cord), frequently caused by bacterial or viral infection.

Multiple sclerosis: A disease in which there are patches of demyelination throughout the neural tissue of the central nervous system. Typically, the symptoms are weakness, incoordination, paresthesia (sensation of pricking, tingling, or creeping on the skin), speech disturbances, and visual problems. The course of the disease is usually prolonged, with remissions and relapses over a period of many years. The etiology is unknown. (Demyelination refers to the destruction, removal, or loss of the myelin sheath of a nerve or nerves. Myelin is a soft material that acts as an electrical insulator, speeding the conduction of nerve impulses.)

Muscular dystrophy: A group of genetically determined, painless, degenerative myopathies (diseases of the muscles) characterized by weakness and atrophy of muscle without involvement of the nervous system.

Myelogenous leukemia: Leukemia arising from myeloid (bone marrow) tissue in which white blood corpuscles having lobed nuclei, and their precursors, predominate.

Myocardial infarction: Gross necrosis (localized death of living tissue) of the myocardium (middle muscular layer of the heart wall) as a result of interruption of the blood supply to the area, as in coronary thrombosis.

Nystagmus: Rapid, involuntary oscillations of the eyeballs.

Osteoarthritis: Noninflammatory degenerative joint disease occurring chiefly in older persons, characterized by degeneration of the articular (joint) cartilage, hypertrophy of the bone, and changes in the lubricating fluid secreted by a membrane of a joint, bursa, or tendon sheath. It is accompanied by pain and stiffness, particularly after prolonged activity. Also called degenerative joint disease.

Paraplegia: Paralysis of the legs and lower part of the body.

Perinatal: Pertaining to or occurring in the period shortly before and after birth; variously defined as beginning with completion of the twentieth to twenty-eighth week of gestation and ending seven to twenty-eight days after birth.

Ptosis: Drooping of upper eyelid.

Quadriplegia: Paralysis of all four limbs.

Renal dialysis: Usually called hemodialysis. A technique of removing waste materials or poisons from the blood of patients whose kidneys have ceased to function. "A stream of blood taken from an artery is circulated through the dialyzer [artificial kidney] on one side of a semipermeable membrane, while a solution of similar electrolytic composition to the patient's blood circulates on the other side. Water and waste products from the patient's blood filter through the membrane whose pores are too small to allow passage of blood cells and proteins. The purified blood is then returned to the patient's body through a vein."*

Renal disease: Disease of the kidneys.

Rheumatoid arthritis: A chronic systemic disease primarily of the joints, marked by inflammatory changes and by atrophy and diminished density of the bones; in late stages, deformity and fixation of the joints. Cause is unknown.

Sickle cell anemia: A genetic disorder occurring mainly in blacks and less frequently in south Mediterranean peoples, characterized by joint pain, acute attacks of abdominal pain, ulcerations of the lower extremities, sickle-shaped red blood cells. Shortened life expectancy.

Spina bifida: An anomaly, through multifactorial inheritance, characterized by defective closure of the bony encasement of the spinal cord, through which the cord and meninges may or may not protrude.

Stroke: A sudden damaging event within an artery of the brain (as a hemorrhage), causing sudden loss or diminution of consciousness, sensation, and voluntary motion; often called apoplexy, cerebral vascular accident. The site of the disease is in the cardiovascular system, with a secondary effect on the brain.

Thorazine: The trade name of the tranquilizer drug chlorpromazine hydrochloride.

---

*From the *Urdang Dictionary of Current Medical Terms* (New York: Wiley, 1981).

Ulcerative colitis: Chronic, recurrent ulceration in the colon of unknown cause. It is manifested clinically by cramping abdominal pain, rectal bleeding, and loose discharges of blood, pus, and mucus with scanty fecal particles. Complications include hemorrhoids, abscesses, fistulas, perforation of the colon, pseudopolyps and carcinoma.

References

Abram, Harry S. "Survival by Machine: The Psychological Stress of Chronic Hemodialysis," *Psychiatry in Medicine* 1 (1970): 37–51

Abram, Harry S.; Gordon L. Moore; and Frederick B. Westervelt. "Suicidal Behavior in Chronic Dialysis Patients, "*American Journal of Psychiatry* 127 (March 1971): 1199–2024.

Adler, Gerald, and Dan Buie, "The Misuses of Confrontation with Borderline Patients," *International Journal of Psychoanalytic Psychotherapy,* 1 (July 1972): 109–20.

Ahmed, Paul I.; Aliza Kolker; and George V. Coelho. "Toward a New Definition of Health: An Overview." In Paul I. Ahmed and George V. Coelho, editors, *Toward a New Definition of Health.* New York: Plenum, 1979, pp. 7–22.

Altman, Irwin. *The Environment and Social Behavior.* Monterey, Calif.: Brooks/ Cole, 1975.

Anderson, James E., and Ralph A. Brown. "Life History Grid for Adolescents," *Social Work* 25 (July 1980): 321–23

Aponte, Harry J. "Diagnosis in Family Therapy." In Carel B. Germain, editor, *Social Work Practice: People and Environments.* New York: Columbia University Press, 1979, pp. 107–49.

Barnett, Clifford R. "An Anthropologist's Perspective." In Jan Howard and Anselm Strauss, editors, *Humanizing Health Care.* New York: Wiley, 1975, pp. 269–75.

Bartlett, Harriett M. "Ida M. Cannon: Pioneer in Medical Social Work," *Social Service Review* 49 (June 1975): 208–29.

Beard, Bruce H. "Hope and Fear with Hemodialysis." In E. Mansell Pattison, editor, *The Experience of Dying.* Englewood Cliffs, N.J.: Prentice-Hall, 1977, pp. 268–79.

Berger, Raymond, and James J. Kelly. "Do Social Work Agencies Discriminate Against Homosexual Job Applicants?" *Social Work* 26 (May 1981): 193–98.

Berkman, Barbara G. "Innovations for Social Services in Health Care." In Francine Sobey, editor, *Changing Roles in Social Work Practice.* Philadelphia: Temple University Press, 1977, pp. 92–126.

Berkman, Barbara G., and Helen Rehr. "The Sick-role Cycle and the Timing of Social Work Intervention," *Social Service Review,* 46 (December 1972): 567–80.

269

Biagi, Ettore. "The Social Work Stake in Problem-oriented Recording," *Social Work in Health Care* 3 (Winter 1977): 211–21.

Bikales, Gerda. "The Dog as Significant Other," *Social Work* 20 (March 1975): 150–52.

Black, Rita Beck. "The Future of Social Work in Health in the 1980s." Keynote address, *Conference on Social Work Issues in Health Care,* University of Connecticut Medical Center, May 19, 1983. Mimeo, Columbia University School of Social Work.

Blanchard, Evelyn L. Response to Melvin A. Glasser, "Health as a Right." In *Social Welfare Forum, 1975.* New York: Columbia University Press, 1976, pp. 23–26.

Bloom, Martin, and Stephen R. Block. "Evaluating One's Own Effectiveness and Efficiency," *Social Work* 22 (March 1977): 130–36.

Blum, Henrik. "Utilization of the Health Delivery System." In *Social Welfare Forum, 1975.* New York: Columbia University Press, 1976, pp. 96–114.

Brager, George, and Stephen Holloway. *Changing Human Service Organizations: Politics and Practice.* New York: Free Press, 1978.

Brawley, Edward A., and Emilia E. Martinez-Brawley. "Teaching Social Work Students to Use the News Media for Public Education Purposes," *Journal of Education for Social Work* 18 (Spring 1982): 76–83.

Breslin, Ruth (Chief Social Worker, Yale–New Haven Hospital) Personal communication, 1982, 1983.

Brossart, Jeanne. "The Gay Patient: What You Should Be Doing," *RN* April 1979, pp. 46–52.

Bruner, Jerome. *Toward a Theory of Instruction.* Cambridge: Harvard University Press, 1966.

Bureau of Community Health Services and Programs 1978. DHEW Publication No. (HSA) 78–5002, 1978.

Burnham, John C. "American Medicine's Golden Age: What Happened to It?" *Science* 215 (March 19, 1982): 1474–79.

Burns, Joan. "A Social Worker's Role in the Identification and Counseling of Families at Risk for Genetic Disorders." In Robert C. Jackson and Jean Morton, editors, *Family Health Care: Health Promotion and Illness Care.* Berkeley: University of California, Public Health Social Work Program, 1976, pp. 81–98.

Cassel, John. "Psychiatric Processes and 'Stress': Theoretical Formulation," *International Journal of Health Services,* Vol. 4, 1974: 471–482. Reprinted in Robert L. Kane, editor, *The Behavioral Sciences and Preventive Medicine.* DHEW Publication No. (NIH) 76–878, 1976, pp. 53–62.

Cobb, Sidney. "Social Support as a Moderator of Life Stress," *Psychosomatic Medicine* 38 (September–October 1976): 300–314.

Cochrane, Edward. "Discharge Planning: The Central Role of Social Work," *NASW News* 26 (February 1981): 14.

Cochrane, Edward, et al. "Reference Article: Discharge Planning." Chicago: American Hospital Association, September 1980.

Coe, Rodney. *Sociology of Medicine.* New York: McGraw-Hill, 1970.

Coleman, Jules V.; Marcia L. Lebowitz; and Frederick P. Anderson. "Social Work in a Pediatric Primary Health Care Team in a Group Practice Program," *Social Work in Health Care* 1 (Summer 1976): 489–98.

Collins, Alice, and Diane Pancoast. *Natural Helping Networks*. New York: National Association of Social Workers, 1976.

Collins, Alice; Diane Pancoast; and June Dunn, editors. *Consultation Work Book*. Portland, Ore.: Portland State University, 1977, pp. 58–64.

Connecticut Hospice Newsletter 7 (Winter/Spring 1981): 5.

Cooper, Elaine J., and Margarita Hernandez Cento. "Group and the Hispanic Prenatal Patient," *American Journal of Orthopsychiatry* 47 (October 1977): 689–700.

Corea, Gena. *The Hidden Malpractice: How American Medicine Treats Women as Patients and Professionals*. New York: Morrow, 1977.

Coulton, Claudia J. "Developing an Instrument to Measure Person–Environment Fit," *Journal of Social Service Research* 3 (Winter 1979): 159–73.

———. "Research on Social Work in Health Care: Progress and Future Directions." In David Fanshel, editor, *The Future of Social Work Research*. New York: National Association of Social Workers, 1980.

Coulton, Claudia J., and Nathaniel Butler. "Measuring Social Work Productivity in Health Care, *Health and Social Work* 6 (August 1981): 4–12.

Court, Nancy J. "The 'Time Line': A Treatment Tool for Children," *Social Work* 25 (May 1980): 235–36.

Cox, Tom. *Stress*. Baltimore: University Park Press, 1978.

Coyne, James C., and Richard S. Lazarus. "Cognitive Style, Stress Perception, and Coping." In Irwin L. Kutash and Louis B. Schlesinger, editors, *Handbook on Stress and Anxiety*. San Francisco: Jossey-Bass, 1980, pp. 144–58.

Croog, Sydney H.; Alberta Lipson; and Sol Levine. "Helping Patterns in Severe Illness: The Roles of Kin Network, Non-Family Resources, and Institutions," *Journal of Marriage and the Family* (February 1972): 32–41.

Curtis, Patricia. "Animals Are Good for the Handicapped, Perhaps All of Us," *Smithsonian* 12 (July 1981): 49–57.

Dalton, Gene. "Introducing Change in Organizations." In Anent R. Negandhi, editor, *Modern Organizational Theory: Contextual, Environmental, and Socio-Cultural Variables*. Kent, Ohio: Kent State University Press, 1973, pp. 343–72.

Davidson, Kay Wallis. "Evolving Social Work Roles in Health Care: The Case of Discharge Planning," *Social Work in Health Care* 4 (Fall 1978): 43–54.

Davis, Karen. Quoted in the *New York Times*, July 12, 1981.

Delgado, Melvin. "Herbal Medicine in the Puerto Rican Community," *Health and Social Work* 4 (May 1979): 24–40.

Dohrenwend, Barbara S., and Bruce P. Dohrenwend, editors. *Stressful Life Events, Their Nature and Effects*. New York: Wiley, 1974.

Dubos, René. "Health and Creative Adaptation," *Human Nature* 1 (January 1978): 74–82.

———. *Man Adapting*. New Haven: Yale University Press, 1965.

———. *Mirage of Health*. New York: Harper & Row, 1959.

Edinberg, Mark A., and Dewitt C. Baldwin, Jr. "Levels of Interaction—Group, Team, Organization." In D. Baldwin, Beverley Davies Rowley, and Virginia Williams, editors, *Interdisciplinary Health Care Teams in Teaching and Practice*. Reno: New Health Perspectives, Inc., and The School of Medicine, University of Nevada, 1980, pp. 15–22.

Egbert, Lawrence D.; G. E. Battit; C. E. Welch; and M. K. Bartlett. "Reduction of

Postoperative Pain by Encouragement and Instruction of Patients," *The New England Journal of Medicine,* 270 (1964): 825–27.

Egbert, Lawrence D., and Ilene L. Rothman. "Relation Between the Race and Economic Status of Patients and Who Performs Their Surgery," *The New England Journal of Medicine,* 297 (July 4, 1977): 90–91.

Engel, George L. "The Need for a New Medical Model: A Challenge for Biomedicine," *Science* 196 (April 8, 1977): 129–36.

Ewalt, Patricia L., and Robert M. Honeyfield. "Needs of Persons in Long-term Care," *Social Work* 26 (May 1981): 223–32.

Fanning, John P. "Protection of Privacy and Fair Information Practices." In *Social Welfare Forum, 1975.* New York: Columbia University Press, 1976. pp. 115–20.

Farquharson, Andy. *Self-help Groups: A Health Resource,* University of Victoria School of Social Work, October 1978 (mimeo).

Finlayson, Angela. "Social Networks as Coping Resources: Lay Help and Consultation Patterns Used by Women in Husbands' Post-Infarction Career," *Social Science and Medicine* 10 (1976): 97–103.

Fisher, Dena. "The Hospitalized Terminally Ill Patient: An Ecological Perspective." In Carel B. Germain, editor, *Social Work Practice: People and Environments.* New York: Columbia University Press, 1979, pp. 25–45.

Foster, Zelda. "Standards for Hospice Care: Assumptions and Principles," *Health and Social Work* 4 (February 1979): 117–29.

Fox, Renée C. "The Medicalization and Demedicalization of American Society," *Daedalus* 106 (Winter 1977): 9–22.

Freidson, Eliot. "Dominant Professions, Bureaucracy, and Client Services." In W. Rosengren and M. Lefton, editors, *Organizations and Clients.* Springfield, Ill.: C. C. Thomas, 1970.

Friedman, Erica; Aaron Katcher; James J. Lynch; and Sue Ann Thomas. "Animal Companions and One-Year Survival of Patients After Discharge from a Coronary Care Unit," *Public Health Reports* 95 (July–August 1980): 307–12.

Friedman, S.; P. Chodoff; J. Mason; and D. Hamburg. "Behavioral Observations on Parents Anticipating the Death of a Child," *Pediatrics* 32 (1963): 610–25.

Garin, Louise. Personal communication, 1974; mimeographed materials. Long Island Jewish–Hillside Medical Center, New York City, Department of Social Work, A. Lurie, Director.

Garland, James; Ralph Kolodny; and Hubert Jones. "A Model for Stages of Development in Social Work Groups." In Saul Bernstein, editor, *Explorations in Social Group Work.* Boston: Boston University School of Social Work, 1965, pp. 21–30.

Germain, Carel B. "Work with the Community and the Organization in Child Welfare Practice." In Joan Laird and Ann Hartman, editors, *Handbook of Child Welfare.* New York: Free Press, forthcoming a.

———. "The Place of Community Work Within an Ecological Approach to Social Work Practice." In Robert W. Roberts and Samuel Taylor, editors, *Theories and Practice of Community Social Work.* New York: Columbia University Press, forthcoming b.

———. "Introduction: Ecology and Social Work." In C. Germain, editor, *Social Work Practice: People and Environments.* New York: Columbia University Press, 1979, pp. 1–22.

———. "Space, an Ecological Variable in Social Work Practice." *Social Casework* 59 (1978): 515–22.

———. "An Ecological Perspective on Social Work Practice in Health Care." *Social Work in Health Care* 3 (Fall 1977): 67–76.

———. "Time, an Ecological Variable in Social Work Practice," *Social Casework* 57 (July 1976), pp. 419–26.

Germain, Carel B., and Alex Gitterman. *The Life Model of Social Work Practice.* New York: Columbia University Press, 1980.

Ginzberg, Eli. *The Limits of Health Reform.* New York: Basic Books, 1977.

Gitterman, Alex. "Development of Group Services." In Hyman Weiner, editor, *Social Work with Groups in Maternal and Child Health.* Proceedings of a Conference cosponsored by Columbia University School of Social Work and Roosevelt Hospital Department of Social Work, June 14–15, 1979, New York, pp. 15–21.

Glaser, Barney, and Anselm Strauss. *Time for Dying.* Chicago: Aldine, 1968.

Glass, Lora, and Martha Hickerson. "Dialysis and Transplantation: A Mother's Group," *Social Work in Health Care* 1 (Spring 1976): 287–96.

Glover, Julia (Director of Social Work, The Door—A Center of Alternatives, New York City). Personal communication, 1979.

Golden, Janet M., and Joseph R. Steiner. "Unique Needs of People with Chronic Pain," *Health and Social Work* 6 (August 1981): 47–53.

Gonzales-Borrero, Maria (Executive Director, Hispanic Health Council of Hartford, Connecticut). Personal communication, March 9, 1982.

Goodluck, Charlotte Tsoi. "Strength of Caring," *Social Casework* 61 (October 1980): 519–21.

Graham, Cathey A.; Cynthia J. Howkins; and William H. Blau. "Innovative Social Work Practice in Health Care: Stress Management." In Miriam Dinerman, editor, *Social Work in a Turbulent World.* Silver Spring, Md.: National Association of Social Workers, 1983, pp. 167–79.

Greenberg, Daniel S. "The Author Meets the Health-Care System," *The New England Journal of Medicine* 296 (February 3, 1977): 291–92.

Groner, Edith. "Delivery of Clinical Social Work Services in the Emergency Room: A Description of an Existing Program," *Social Work in Health Care* 4 (Fall 1978): 19–29

Hage, Jerald, and Michael Aiken. *Social Change in Complex Organizations.* New York: Random House, 1970.

Hamburg, David A., and Sarah S. Brown. "The Scientific Base and Social Context of Health Maintenance: An Overview." In Philip H. Abelson, editor, *Health Care: Regulation, Economics, Ethics, Practice.* Washington, D.C.: American Association for the Advancement of Science, 1978, pp. 1–4.

Hamburg, David A.; John E. Adams; and H. Keith Brodie. "Coping Behavior in Stressful Circumstances: Some Implications for Social Psychiatry." In Berton H. Kaplan, Robert N. Wilson, and Alexander H. Leighton, editors, *Further Explorations in Social Psychiatry.* New York: Basic Books, 1976, pp. 158–75.

Hamburg, David A., and John E. Adams, "A Perspective on Coping Behavior," *Archives of General Psychiatry* 17 (September 1967): 277–84.

Hamburg, David; B. Hamburg; and S. DeGoza. "Adaptive Problems and Mechanisms in Severely Burned Patients," *Psychiatry* 16 (1953): 1–20.

Hammond, D. Corydon; Dean H. Hepworth; and Veon G. Smith. *Improving Therapeutic Communication.* San Francisco: Jossey-Bass, 1977.

Hartford, Margaret E. "Group Methods and Generic Practice." In Robert W. Roberts, and Helen Northen, editors, *Theories of Social Work with Groups.* New York: Columbia University Press, 1976, pp. 45–74.

Hartman, Ann. "The Extended Family as a Resource for Change: An Ecological Approach to Family-Centered Practice." In Carel B. Germain, editor, *Social Work Practice: People and Environments.* New York: Columbia University Press, 1979, pp. 239–66.

——. "Diagrammatic Assessment of Family Relationships," *Social Casework* 49 (October 1978): 465–76.

Hartman, Ann, and Joan Laird. *Family-Centered Social Work Practice.* New York: Free Press, 1983.

Harwood, Alan. "The Hot–Cold Theory of Disease," *The Journal of the American Medical Association* 216 (May 17, 1971): 1153–58.

Heald, Thomas. Plymouth State College, New Hampshire, Unpublished paper, 1982.

Health Resources Statistics: 1976–1977 Edition. National Center for Health Statistics.

Healthy People: The Surgeon General's Report on Health Promotion and Disease Prevention, 1979. DHEW Publication No. 79–55071, 1979.

HEW Secretary's Task Force on Hospice. Office of the Secretary, U.S. Department of Health, Education, and Welfare, December 1978.

Holland, Lin, and Lee Ellen Rogich. "Dealing with Grief in the Emergency Room," *Health and Social Work* 5 (May 1980): 12–17.

Holmes, Thomas H., and Minoru Masuda. "Life Change and Illness Susceptibility." In Barbara S. Dohrenwend and Bruce P. Dohrenwend, editors, *Stressful Life Events, Their Nature and Effects.* New York: Wiley, 1974, pp. 45–72.

Howard, Jan, and Anselm Strauss, editors, *Humanizing Medical Care.* San Francisco: Jossey-Bass, 1975.

Huntington, June. *Social Work and General Medical Practice: Collaboration or Conflict?* London: George Allen & Unwin, 1981.

Imbus, Sharon H., and Bruce Zawacki. "Autonomy for Burned Patients When Survival Is Unprecedented," *The New England Journal of Medicine* 297 (August 11, 1977): 308–11.

Janis, Irving. "Groupthink." *Psychology Today* 5 (1971): 43.

Jasanoff, Sheila, and Dorothy Nelkin. "Science, Technology, and the Limits of Judicial Competence," *Science* 214 (December 11, 1981): 1211–15.

Jayaratne, Srinika, and Rona L. Levy. *Empirical Clinical Practice.* New York: Columbia University Press, 1979.

Johnson, Jean, and Howard Leventhal. "Effects of Accurate Expectations and Behavioral Instructions on Reactions During a Noxious Medical Examination," *Journal of Personality and Social Psychology* 29 (May 1974): 710–18.

Johnson, Myles. Senior Staff Associate, National Association of Social Workers, personal communication, September 1983.

Kalish, Richard A. "Life and Death: Dividing the Indivisible," *Social Science and Medicine* 2 (1968): 249–59.

Kane, Rosalie. "Look to the Record," *Social Work* 19 (July 1974): 412–19.

Kane, Rosalie. "The Interprofessional Team as a Small Group," *Social Work in Health Care* 1 (Fall 1975): 19–32.

Karkalitz, Jane. "Interdisciplinary Effectiveness/Social Work Competence." In *Proceedings: Social Work in Maternal and Child Health*, a New England Regional Workshop for Professional Social Workers, May 1980, sponsored by the Office of Maternal and Child Health Services, Bureau of Community Health Services, DHEW and the University of Connecticut School of Social Work, pp. 28–35.

Kavanaugh, Robert E. "Humane Treatment of the Terminally Ill." In Rudolf H. Moos, editor, *Coping With Physical Illness*. New York: Plenum, 1977, pp. 413–20.

Kertesz, Joseph. "Permeability of Individual Boundaries: A Critical Factor for Effective Functioning of Interdisciplinary Health Care Teams." In DeWitt C. Baldwin, Jr., Beverley Davies Rowley, and Virginia Williams, editors, *Interdisciplinary Health Care Teams in Teaching and Practice*. Reno: New Health Perspectives, Inc., and The School of Medicine, University of Nevada, 1980, pp. 23–28.

Kiresuk, Thomas J., and Geoffrey Garwick. "Basic Goal Attainment Scaling Procedures." In Beulah Roberts Compton and Burt Galaway, editors, *Social Work Processes*. rev. ed. Homewood, Ill.: Dorsey, 1979, pp. 412–20.

Kirschner, Charlotte. "The Aging Family in Crisis: A Problem in Living," *Social Casework* 60 (April 1979): 209–16.

Kirschner, Charlotte, and Lucy Rosengarten. "The Skilled Social Work Role in Home Care," *Social Work* 27 (November 1982): 527–30.

Kleinman, Arthur. "Sickness as Cultural Semantics: Issues for an Anthropological Medicine and Psychiatry." In Paul I. Ahmed and George V. Coelho, editors, *Toward a New Definition of Health*. New York: Plenum, 1979, pp. 53–65.

Kleinman, Arthur; Leon Eisenberg; and Byron Good. "Culture, Illness and Care," *Annals of Internal Medicine* 88 (February 1978): 251–58.

Knowles, John H. "The Responsibility of the Individual," *Daedalus* 106 (Winter 1977) 57–80.

Kübler-Ross, Elisabeth. *On Death and Dying*. New York: Macmillan, 1969.

Kushida, Arlene Hori; Marilyn Montenegro; Paul Chikashisa; and Royal F. Morales. "A Training Program for Asian and Pacific Islander Americans," *Social Casework* 57 (March 1976): 185–94.

Laird, Joan. "Sorcerers, Shamans, and Social Workers: The Use of Ritual in Social Work Practice." Paper presented at the National Association of Social Workers Conference on Clinical Social Work, Washington, D.C., November 22, 1982. To be published in *Social Work*, forthcoming.

Lane, Helen J. "Working with Problems of Assault to Self-Image and Life-Style," *Social Work in Health Care* 1 (Winter 1975–76): 191–98.

Lazarus, Richard S., and Raymond Launier. "Stress-Related Transactions Between Person and Environment." In Lawrence A. Pervin and Michael Lewis, editors, *Perspectives in Interactional Psychology*. New York: Plenum, 1978, pp. 287–327.

Lazarus, Wendy; Lisbeth B. Schoor; and Judith Weitz. "Reaching Needy

Children with Health Care." In *Conditions for Change in the Health Care System.* DHEW Publication No. (HRA) 78–642, 1977, pp. 85–97.

Lebow, Grace. "Facilitating Adaptation in Anticipatory Mourning." *Social Casework* 57 (July 1976): 458–65.

Lee, Judith, A. B. "Human Relatedness and the Mentally Impaired Older Person," *Journal of Gerontological Social Work,* 4 (Winter 1981): 5–15.

Lee, Stacey. "Interdisciplinary Teaming in Primary Care: A Process of Evolution and Revolution," *Social Work in Health Care* 5 (Spring 1980): 237–44.

Lewis, Charles E.; Rashi Fein; and David Mechanic. *A Right to Health: The Problem of Access to Primary Medical Care.* New York: Wiley-Interscience, 1976.

Lifchez, Raymond. "The Environment as a Support System for Independent Living," *Architecture, Physical Medicine, and Rehabilitation* 60 (October 1979): 467–76.

Lipowski, Z. J. "Physical Illness, the Individual, and the Coping Processes," *Psychiatry in Medicine* 1 (1970): 91–102.

Lister, Lawrence. "Role Expectations of Social Workers and Other Health Professionals," *Health and Social Work* 5 (1980): 41–49.

Lorber, Judith. "Good Patients and Problem Patients: Conformity and Deviance in a General Hospital," *Journal of Health and Social Behavior* 16 (June 1975): 213–25.

Lowe, Jane Isaacs, and Marjotta Herranen. "Conflict in Teamwork: Understanding Roles and Relationships," *Social Work in Health Care* 3 (Spring 1978): 323–30.

Lowe, Jane Isaacs, and Virginia Walther. "Returning to Work: A Group Program for New Mothers." Paper presented to the 1981 National Association of Social Workers Professional Symposium, Philadelphia, Pennsylvania, November 1981 (unpublished).

Luft, Howard S., "How Do Health Maintenance Organizations Achieve Their 'Savings'? Rhetoric and Evidence," *New England Journal of Medicine* 308 (June 15, 1978): 1336–1342.

Mages, Norman L., and Gerald A. Mendelsohn. "Effects of Cancer on Patients' Lives: A Personological Approach." In George C. Stone, Frances Cohen, and Nancy Adler, editors, *Health Psychology: A Handbook.* San Francisco: Jossey-Bass, 1979, pp. 255–84.

Mahaffey, Maryann, and John W. Hanks, editors. *Practical Politics: Social Work and Political Responsibility.* Silver Spring, Md: National Association of Social Workers, 1982.

Mailick, Mildred D., and Pearl Jordan. "A Multimodel Approach to Collaborative Practice in Health Settings," *Social Work in Health Care* 2 (Summer 1977): 445–54.

Marion, Rodger. "Editor's Corner," *Prospective for Change* 5 (September–October 1980): 11.

Marion, Rodger, and Katie Angermeyer. "Defining the Qualities of the Collaborator," *Prospective for Change* 5 (September–October 1980): 5–7.

Marshall, Jo Taylor. "Criteria for Social Service Intervention." Unpublished, 1979a.

Marshall, Jo Taylor. "Results of Study of All Admissions on Weekend of June 4th and June 8th, 1979, Identifying Patients with Potential Discharge Planning Problems." Unpublished, 1979b.

Marshall, Thomas. "The Center and China," *Journal for Constructive Change* 1 . (Autumn 1979): 6–8.

Martens, Wilma M., and Elizabeth Holmstrup. "Problem-oriented Recording," *Social Casework* 55 (November 1974): 554–61.

Martinson, Ida M. *Home Care for the Dying Child.* New York: Appleton-Century-Crofts, 1977.

Mayer, John, and Aaron Rosenblatt. "The Client's Social Context," *Social Casework* 45 (November 1964): 511–18.

Mayeroff, Milton. *On Caring.* New York: Harper & Row, Perennial Library 1972.

McNerny, Walter J. "Control of Health-care Costs in the 1980's," *New England Journal of Medicine* 303 (November 6, 1980): 1088–95.

Mechanic, David. *Future Issues in Health Care: Social Policy and the Rationing of Medical Services.* New York: Free Press, 1979.

———. "Illness Behavior, Social Adaptation, and the Management of Illness: A Comparison of Educational and Medical Models," *Journal of Nervous and Mental Disease* 165 (August 1977): 79–87.

———. *The Growth of Bureaucratic Medicine.* New York: Wiley, 1976a.

———. "Stress, Illness, and Illness Behavior," *Journal of Human Stress* 2 (June 1976b): 2–6.

———. "Discussion of Research Programs on Relations Between Stressful Life Events and Episodes of Physical Illness." In B. S. Dohrenwend and B. P. Dohrenwend, editors, *Stressful Life Events: Their Nature and Effects.* New York: Wiley, 1974a, pp. 87–97.

———. "Social Structure and Personal Adaptation: Some Neglected Dimensions." In George V. Coelho, David A. Hamburg, and John E. Adams, editors, *Coping and Adaptation.* New York: Basic Books, 1974b, pp. 32–44.

———. "Social Psychological Factors Affecting the Presentation of Bodily Complaints," *The New England Journal of Medicine* 286 (May 1972): 1132–39.

———. *The Bureaucratization of Medicine.* New York: Wiley, 1970.

———. "Response Factors in Illness: The Study of Illness Behavior," *Social Psychiatry* 1 (1966): 11–20.

Mechanic, David, and E. H. Volkart. "Stress, Illness Behavior, and Medical Diagnoses," *American Sociological Review* 26 (1961): 51–58.

Menezes, Lucyamma. "Innovative Programs in a Health Care Setting." *Social Work in Health Care* 6 (Fall 1980): 101–5.

Mercer, Susan O., and J. Dianne Garner. "Social Work Consultation in Long-Term Care Facilities," *Health and Social Work* 6 (May 1981): 5–13.

Merton, Robert. *Social Theory and Social Structure.* Second Edition. New York: Free Press, 1957.

Miller, Arnold. "The Wages of Neglect: Death and Disease in the American Work Place." In *Social Welfare Forum, 1975.* New York: Columbia University Press, 1976, pp. 87–95.

Miller, Eunice. "The Social Work Component in Community-based Action on Behalf of Victims of Huntington's Disease," *Social Work in Health Care* 2 (Fall 1976): 25–32.

Millet, Nina. "Hospice: Challenging Society's Approach to Death." *Health and Social Work* 4 (February 1979): 130–51.

Mizio, Emelicia. "Impact of External Systems on the Puerto Rican Family," *Social Casework* 55 (February 1974): 76–83.

Moos, Rudolf H., and Vivien D. Tsu. "The Crisis of Physical Illness: An Overview." In Rudolf H. Moos, editor, *Coping With Physical Illness.* New York: Plenum, 1977, pp. 3–21.

Mullany, Joan Ward; Ruth Ann Fox; and Mary F. Liston. "Clinical Nurse Specialist and Social Worker: Clarifying the Roles," *Nursing Outlook* 22 (November 1974): 712–18.

Mullen, Edward J. "Improving Services in a Turbulent World: Evaluating Social Work's Effectiveness." In Miriam Dinerman, editor, *Social Work in a Turbulent World.* Silver Spring, Md.: National Association of Social Workers, 1983, pp. 63–75.

Munoz, Faye Untalan. "Pacific Islanders: A Perplexed, Neglected Minority," *Social Casework* 57 (March 1976): 179–84.

Nason, Frances, and Thomas L. Delbanco. "Soft Services: A Major Cost-effective Component of Primary Medical Care," *Social Work in Health Care* 1 (Spring 1976): 297–307.

"NASW Code of Ethics," *NASW News* 25 (January 1980): 24, 25.

NASW News. "Wyoming Chapter Helps Start Up a Child Nutrition Program" (November 1980): 9.

New York Times, "Medical Unit Issues Standards on Resuscitation of the Dying," September 19, 1982.

——. "Legal Action over Asbestos Widespread in Nation," September 5, 1982.

——. "Health Quality and Costs: A Delicate Balance," March 30, 1982.

——. "Costs of Health Care Increased in 1981," January 25, 1982.

——. "Health Care for Children Assailed as Chaotic," December 3, 1980.

Obier, Kathleen, and L. Julian Haywood. "Role of the Medical Social Worker in a Coronary Care Unit," *Social Casework* 53 (January 1972): 14–18.

O'Connell, Patricia. "Developmental Tasks of the Family," *Smith College Studies in Social Work* 42 (June 1972): 203–10.

Oktay, Julianne S., and Francine Sheppard. "Home Health Care for the Elderly," *Health and Social Work* 3 (August 1978): 35–47.

Pancoast, Diane, and N. J. Chapman. *Roles for Informal Helpers in the Delivery of Human Services.* (Report on DHHS Grant #18-P-00088.), Portland Ore: Portland State University, August 1980.

Parks, Ronda. "Parental Reactions to the Birth of a Handicapped Child," *Health and Social Work* 2 (August 1977): 52–66.

Parry, Joan K., and Nancy Kohn. "Group Work and Emphysema Patients," *Social Work in Health Care* 2 (Fall 1976): 55–64.

Parsons, Talcott, and Renée Fox. "Illness, Therapy, and the Modern Urban American Family," *Journal of Social Issues* 8 (1952): 31–44.

Patterson, Shirley. "Toward a Conceptualization of Natural Helping," *Arete* 4 (1977): 161–73.

Patterson, Shirley; J. Holzhuter; V. Struble; and J. Quadagno. *Utilization of Human Resources for Mental Health.* (PHS Grant No. MH 16618.) Lawrence: University of Kansas School of Social Welfare, 1972.

Patterson, Shirley; Eileen Brennan; and Jay Memmott. "How Effective Are Rural Natural Helpers?" University of Kansas, School of Social Welfare, 1983 (mimeo).

Patti, Rino J., and Herman Resnick. "Changing the Agency from Within," *Social Work* 17 (1972): 48–57.

Pattison, E. Mansell, "The Dying Experience." In E. M. Pattison, editor, *The Experience of Dying*. Englewood Cliffs, N.J.: Prentice-Hall, 1977a, pp. 303–16.

Pattison, E. Mansell. "Death Throughout the Life Cycle." In E. M. Pattison, editor, *The Experience of Dying*. Englewood Cliffs, N.J.: Prentice-Hall, 1977b, pp. 18–27.

Peak, Daniel T. "The Elderly Who Face Dying and Death." In David Barton, editor, *Dying and Death: A Clinical Guide for Caregivers*. Baltimore: Williams & Wilkens, 1977, pp. 210–19.

Pepper, Bert. "The Primary Group at Work." In Alfred Dean, Alan M. Kraft, and Bert Pepper, editors, *The Social Setting of Mental Health*. New York: Basic Books, 1976, pp. 174–84.

Phillips, William R. "Attitudes Toward Social Work in Family Medicine," *Social Work in Health Care* 3 (Fall 1977): 61–66.

Pilisuk, Marc, and Charles Froland. "Kinship, Social Networks, Social Support and Health," *Social Science and Medicine* 12B (1978): 273–80.

Practice Digest, Vol. 5, June 1982, full issue on resistance.

———. "'Foster Homes' for the Aged," *Practice Digest* 4 (December 1981): 10–12.

———. "Changing the Face of Health Services in Rural Colorado," *Practice Digest* 1 (March 1979): 20–22.

Rabkin, Judith G., and Elmer L. Struening. "Life Events, Stress, and Illness," *Science* 194 (December 3, 1976), 1013–20.

Rae-Grant, Quentin A. F., and Donald G. Marcuse. "The Hazards of Teamwork," *American Journal of Orthopsychiatry* 38 (January 1968): 4–8.

Rahe, Richard R. "The Pathway Between Subjects' Recent Life Changes and Their Near-future Illness Reports: Representative Results and Methodological Issues." In Barbara Dohrenwend and Bruce Dohrenwend, editors, *Stressful Life Events: Their Nature and Effects*. New York: Wiley, 1974, pp. 73–86.

Rehr, Helen; Barbara Berkman; and Gary Rosenberg. "Screening for High Social Risk: Principles and Problems," *Social Work* 25 (September 1980): 403–6.

Relman, Arnold. "The New Medical Industrial Complex," *New England Journal of Medicine* 303 (October 23, 1980): 963–70.

Resnick, Herman, and Rino J. Patti, editors. *Change from Within: Humanizing Social Welfare Organizations*. Philadelphia: Temple University Press, 1980.

Rhodes, Sonya L. "A Developmental Approach to the Life Cycle of the Family," *Social Casework* 58 (May 1977): 301–11.

Rosenberg, Gary, and Andrew Weissman. "Marketing Social Services in Health Care Facilities," *Health and Social Work* 6 (August 1981): 13–20.

Rosengren, William R., and Spencer DeVault. "The Sociology of Time and Space in an Obstetrical Hospital." In Harold M. Proshansky, William H. Ittelson, and Leanne G. Rivlin, editors. *Environmental Psychology: People and Their Physical Settings*. New York: Holt, Rinehart, & Winston, 1970, pp. 439–53.

Ross, Judith W. "Ethical Conflicts in Medical Social Work Pediatric Cancer Care as a Prototype," *Health and Social Work* 7 (May 1982): 95–102.

——. "Coping with Childhood Cancer: Group Intervention as an Aid to Parents in Crisis," *Social Work in Health Care* 4 (Summer 1979): 381–91.

——. "Social Work Intervention with Families of Children with Cancer: The Changing Critical Phases," *Social Work in Health Care* 3 (Spring 1978): 257–72.

Ross, Judith W., and Susan A. Scarvalone. "Facilitating the Pediatric Cancer Center Patient's Return to School," *Social Work* 27 (May 1982): 256–61.

Rotunno, Marie, and Monica McGoldrick. "Italian Families." In Monica McGoldrick, John K. Pearce, and Joseph Giordano, editors, *Ethnicity and Family Therapy*. New York: Guilford Press, 1982, pp. 340–63.

Roy, Ranjan. "Marital and Family Issues in Patients with Chronic Pain," *Psychotherapy and Psychosomatics* 37 (1982): 1–12.

Roy, Ranjan. "Social Work and Chronic Pain," *Health and Social Work* 6 (August 1981): 54–63.

Rubin, Irwin M., and Richard Beckhard. "Factors Influencing the Effectiveness of Health Teams," *Milbank Memorial Fund Quarterly* 50 (July 1972): 317–35.

Rubin, Irwin M.; Ronald Fry; and M. Plovnick. *Improving the Coordination of Care: A Program for Health Team Development*. Cambridge, Mass.: Ballinger, 1975.

Saegert, Susan. "Stress-inducing and -reducing Qualities of Environments," In Harold M. Proshansky, William H. Ittelson, and Leanne G. Rivlin, editors, *Environmental Psychology: People and Their Physical Settings*. Second Edition. New York: Holt, Rinehart & Winston, 1976, pp. 218–23.

Schild, Sylvia, and Rita Beck Black. *Social Work and Genetics: A Guide for Practice*. New York: Haworth Press, forthcoming.

Schoenberg, Bernard. "Interdisciplinary Education: Role Strain and Adaptations," *Seminar Reports*, No. 2, March 24, 1975. New York: Columbia University.

Schroeder, Christine M. "Communicating with Hard-to-reach Patients," *Health and Social Work* 5 (February 1980): 35–39.

Schuster, Eleanor. "Privacy, the Patient and Hospitalization," *Social Science and Medicine* 10 (1976): 245–48.

Schwartz, William. "Between Client and System." In Robert Roberts and Helen Northen, editors, *Theories of Social Work with Groups*. New York: Columbia University Press, 1976, pp. 171–97.

——. "The Social Worker in the Group." In *The Social Welfare Forum, 1961*. New York: Columbia University Press, 1961, pp. 146–77.

Schweiker, Richard S. (Secretary of Health and Human Services). Quoted in *The New York Times*, June 12, 1981.

Schweizer, Doreen, Unpublished manuscript, 1979.

Science. "Ethical Risks in Biomedicine," *Science* 212 (April 17, 1981): 307–9.

——. "Behavioral Medicine," *Science*, July 25, 1980, pp. 479–81.

——. "Withholding Medical Treatment," *Science* 205 (August 31, 1979): 882–85.

Selye, Hans. *The Stress of Life*. New York: McGraw-Hill, 1956.

——. "The General Adaptation Syndrome and the Diseases of Adaptation," *Journal of Clinical Endocrinology* 6 (1946): 117–230.

Shanker, Renee. "Occupational Disease, Workers' Compensation, and the Social Work Advocate," *Social Work* 28 (January–February 1983): 24–30.

Shapiro, Joan. *Communities of the Alone*. New York: Association Press, 1970.

Sherman, Etta. "Social Work with Groups in a Hospital Setting." In Hyman

Weiner, editor, *Social Work with Groups in Maternal and Child Health*. New York: Columbia University School of Social Work and Roosevelt Hospital Department of Social Work, 1979, pp. 22–33.

Shulman, Lawrence. *The Skills of Helping Individuals and Groups*. Itaska, Ill.: Peacock, 1979.

Silverman, Phyllis R. *Mutual Help Groups*. DHEW Publication No. (ADM) 78–646, 1978.

Silverman, Phyllis R., et al., editors. *Helping Each Other in Widowhood*. New York: Health Services, 1979.

Singer, Carolyn B., and Lillian M. Wells. "The Impact of Student Units on Services and Structural Change in Homes for the Aged," *Canadian Journal of Social Work Education* 7, No. 3 (1981): 11–27.

Sokol, Bernice. "The Clinical Social Worker as a Member of the Health Team in a Coronary Care Unit," *Clinical Social Work Journal* 4 (1976): 269–75.

Somers, Anne R. "Containment of Health Care Costs: A Diagnostic Approach," *Forum on Medicine*, February 1979, pp. 106–12.

Sommer, Robert. "Small Group Ecology in Institutions for the Elderly." In Leon A. Pastalan and David Carson, editors, *Spatial Behavior of Older People*. Ann Arbor: University of Michigan Press, 1970, pp. 25–39.

Spano, Robert M.; Thomas J. Kiresuk; and Sander H. Lund. "An Operational Model to Achieve Accountability for Social Work in Health Care," *Social Work in Health Care* 3 (Winter 1977): 123–42.

Stack, Carol B. *All Our Kin: Strategies for Survival in a Black Community*. New York: Harper Colophon Books, 1974.

Starr, Philip; Gary Ellis; and Oka Seishi. "A Social Worker's Use of a Patient Attitude Survey in the Administration of a Small Health Clinic," *Social Work in Health Care* 6 (Fall 1980): 45–50.

Stellman, Jeanne, and Susan Daum. *Work Is Dangerous for Your Health*. New York: Vintage Books, 1973.

Strauss, Anselm L., and Barney G. Glaser, editors. *Chronic Illness and the Quality of Life*. St. Louis: C. V. Mosby, 1975, pp. 13–67.

Strean, Herbert S. *Clinical Social Work*. New York: Free Press, 1978.

———. *Psychoanalytic Theory and Social Work Practice*. New York: Free Press, 1979.

Stubblefield, Kristine S. "A Preventive Program for Bereaved Families," *Social Work in Health Care* 2 (Summer 1977): 379–89.

Studt, Elliot. "Social Work Theory and Implications for the Practice of Methods," *Social Work Education Report* 16, No. 2 (1968): 22–24, 42–46

Suchman, Edward A. "Stages of Illness and Medical Care," *Journal of Health and Human Behavior* 6 (Fall 1965): 114–28.

Swenson, Carol. Unpublished research data, 1981.

———. "Social Networks, Mutual Aid, and the Life Model of Practice." In Carel B. Germain, editor, *Social Work Practice: People and Environments*. New York: Columbia University Press, 1979, pp. 213–38.

Tagliarozzo, Daisy L., and Hans O. Mauksch. "The Patient's View of the Patient's Role." In Gartley Jaco, editor, *Patients, Physicians, and Illness*. 2d rev. ed. New York: Free Press, 1972, pp. 172–85.

Tasto, Donald L.; Michael J. Collegan; Eric W. Skjei; and Susan J. Polly. *Health Consequences of Shift Work*. DHEW (NIOSH) Pub. No. 78–154, 1978.

Thomas, Edwin J. "Research and Service in Single-Case Experimentation: Conflicts and Choices," *Social Work Research and Abstracts* 14 (Winter 1978): 20–31.

Turner, Francis J. *Psychosocial Therapy: A Social Work Perspective.* New York: Free Press, 1978.

Valentine, Bettylou. *Hustling and Other Hard Work.* New York: Free Press, 1978.

Van den Noort, Stanley. "Life, Limbo, and Death with Multiple Sclerosis." In E. Mansell Pattison, editor, *The Experience of Dying.* Englewood Cliffs, N.J.: Prentice-Hall, 1977, pp. 205–12.

Visotsky, H.; D. Hamburg; M. Goss; and B. Lebovits. "Coping Behavior Under Extreme Stress," *Archives of General Psychiatry* 5 (1961): 423–48.

Wall Street Journal. "Detroit Syndrome," April 6, 1982.

———. "Treatment of Rare Illness Runs Up Huge Bill, Putting Hospital in a Bind," December 10, 1981.

———. "Beds and Boards," May 5, 1977.

Wax, John. "Power Theory and Institutional Change," *Social Service Review* 45 (September 1971): 274–88.

Weaver, Jerry L. "Toward a Definition of Health Risks for Ethnic Minorities: The Case of Hypertension and Heart Disease." In Paul Ahmed and George Coelho, editors, *Toward a New Definition of Health.* New York: Plenum, 1979, pp. 255–68.

Weissman, Harold. *Overcoming Mismanagement in the Human Services.* San Francisco: Jossey-Bass, 1973.

Weissman, Harold; Irwin Epstein; and Andrea Savage-Abramovitz. *Practicing Social Work in Agency Settings: Therapeutic Skills Are Not Enough.* Philadelphia: Temple University Press, 1984.

Wetzel, Janice Wood. "Interventions with the Depressed Elderly in Institutions," *Social Casework* 61 (April 1980): 234–39.

———. "Depression and Dependence upon Unsustaining Environments," *Clinical Social Work Journal* 6 (July 1978): 75–89.

White, Robert W. "Strategies of Adaptation: An Attempt at Systematic Description." In George V. Coelho, David A. Hamburg, and John E. Adams, editors, *Coping and Adaptation.* New York: Basic Books, 1974, pp. 47–68.

Wilkinson, Gerald Thomas. "On Assisting Indian People," *Social Casework* 61 (October 1980): 451–54.

Williams, Cindy Cook, and Donetta G. Rice. "The Intensive Care Unit: Social Work Intervention with the Families of Critically Ill Patients," *Social Work in Health Care* 2 (Summer 1977): 391–98.

Yarmolinsky, Adam. "What Future for the Professional in American Society?" *Daedalus* 107 (Winter 1978): 159–74.

Young, David W., and Richard B. Saltman. "Can Competition Really Lower Costs?" editorial, *Wall Street Journal,* December 22, 1981.

Zaltman, Gerald; Robert Duncan; and Jonny Holbek. *Innovations and Organizations.* New York: Wiley, 1973.

Zander, Alvin. "Resistance to Change: Its Analysis and Prevention." In Irwin M. Rubin, Ronald E. Fry, and Mark S. Plovnick, editors, *Managing Human Resources in Health Care Organizations.* Reston, Va.: Reston Publishing Co., 1978, pp. 312–17.

AUTHOR INDEX

Author Index

SUBJECT INDEX

Subject Index